Praise for *Confessions of an Eco Sinner*:

'This is a splendid book and will do much good to counteract the comfortable hypocrisy of urban and suburban greens who pretend to "save the earth" while carrying on business as usual. Fred Pearce goes out and sees the world as well as thinking and writing about it; he is one of the few that understand the Earth as it really is and we must listen to him.'
James Lovelock, author of *The Revenge of Gaia*

'Pearce shows us how our greed, and our wilful blindness, are ruining the world in faraway places . . . An excellent book.'
Guardian

'Sometimes frightening, always enlightening, it will teach you more about other people's lives than you ever thought possible.'
New Scientist

'Beguiling . . . honest and revealing . . . optimistic . . . A big book for big problems.'
Country Living

'Follow in his global footprints as you read this compelling, thoughtful, provocative and utterly fascinating book.'
Choice magazine

D0718522

www.edenprojectbooks.co.uk

Fred Pearce is an author and journalist. He is married with grown-up children and lives in Wandsworth in London. For much of the time he works from home. But reporting about environment and development has taken him all over the world for publications such as *New Scientist* (where he is environment consultant), the *Daily Telegraph* (for whom he writes a regular blog), the *Independent*, *Country Living*, *Geographical* and the *Ecologist*.

Fred's travels to find where his stuff comes from took him to more than twenty countries, from Alaska to Australia, Brazil to Bangladesh, China to Kenya, Siberia to South Africa and Mauritania to the market down his street.

CONFESSIONS OF AN ECO SINNER

Travels to Find Where My Stuff Comes From

FRED PEARCE

eden project books

TRANSWORLD PUBLISHERS
61–63 Uxbridge Road, London W5 5SA
A Random House Group Company
www.randomhouse.co.uk

First published in Great Britain in 2008 by Eden Project Books
an imprint of Transworld Publishers

This paperback edition published in 2009

A CIP catalogue record for this book is available from the British Library.

ISBN 9781905811120

Addresses for Random House Group Ltd companies outside the UK
can be found at: www.randomhouse.co.uk
The Random House Group Ltd Reg. No. 954009

Penguin Random House is committed to a sustainable future for
our business, our readers and our planet. This book is made from
Forest Stewardship Council® certified paper.

Printed and bound in Great Britain by Clays Ltd, Elcograf S.p.A.

Typeset in Sabon by Falcon Oast Graphic Art Ltd.

8 10 9 7

To Sarah

Contents

Part One: Introductions

1. Footprints: Me and My Stuff   3
2. Gold: A Lodestone for My Journey   14

Part Two: My Food

3. Coffee: Throwing a Hand Grenade into the Cosy World
   of Fair Trade   27
4. Going Local: My Ale, Cheese and Other Patriotic Delights   36
5. Wild Things: The Last Round-up on the High Seas
   and in the Hills   49
6. Curried Crustaceans: The Weird World of Mr Prawn   61

One in a Billion: *Agnes, the AIDS Granny*   71

7. Scorched Earth: A Sticky End with Palm Oil and Sugar   75
8. Unzipped: When the Banana Lost Its Seeds and Other
   Tales From the Orchards   84
9. Montezuma's Magic: How Joseph the Cocoa Farmer
   Became an Unlikely Green Warrior   93
10. Air Miles: Why Eating Kenyan Beans Is Good for the Planet   100

One in a Billion: *Severina, the Favela Queen*   114

Part Three: My Clothes

11. King Cotton: Drought, Diggers and Dirty Secrets 119
12. Behind the Label: Bless My Cotton Socks 128
13. Trouser Snakes: The Strange Truth of Dhaka's Sweatshops 138
14. White Gold: My T-shirt, Slave Labour and the Death of the Aral Sea 146

One in Billion: *Nellie, the Flower-stall Girl* 153

Part Four: The Chinese Dragon

15. Computing Power: Mice, Motherboards and the New Emperors of Suzhou 159
16. Zhangjiagang: The World Capital of Rainforest Destruction 169
17. The Great Mall: Toothpicks to Placentas, Everything Must Go 177

One in a Billion: *Ely, the (ex-) Slave Owner* 184

Part Five: Mines, Metals and Power

18. My Beer Can: Giant Footprints in Bloke Heaven 191
19. Shock and Ore: Where My Metal Comes From 202
20. Footprints in the Snow: Finding the Last Oil 214
21. My Electricity: Old King Coal Lives on at Drax 226
22. Wheels and Wings: Busting the Myths of Green Travel 232
23. London: My Part in the Metabolism of a Capital City 239

One in a Billion: *Greg, the Gold Man* 245

Part Six: Downstream

24. My Rubbish: Down the River and Across the World 251
25. Trade Not Aid: Joining the Great Global Jumble Sale 264
26. Beyond the Grave: A New Life for Joe's Old Phone 270
27. Unexpected Heroes: The Queen of Trash and Other Chinese Titans of Recycling 280

28. E-waste: What to Do with that Old Computer   287

Part Seven: The Footprint Doctors
29. Carbon Offsets: Green Fraud or Painless Panacea?   303
30. Too Few Planets: Scary Science in Siena   314

One in a Billion: *Paul, the African Laird*   319

Part Eight: My Species and Saving the Planet
31. Close Shave: Why We Are All the Children of Toba   325
32. Good News from Africa: Why We *Can* Feed the World   334
33. Beyond the Clockwork Orange: Why We *Can* Green
     Our Cities   344
34. Zero Carbon: Why We *Can* Halt Climate Change   354
35. Defusing the Bomb: Why We *Can* Halt Population
     Growth – and Save the World   360

Sources and Acknowledgements   373

Index   377

Part One

Introductions

1

Footprints: Me and My Stuff

We live in a charmed world. If we have money we can buy literally anything. And the majority of us live lifestyles undreamed of only a generation or two ago. One scientist I met recently told me he reckoned that the average household in Europe or North America has so many devices and such a variety of food and clothing that to produce the same lifestyle in Roman times would have required 6,000 slaves – cooks, maids, minstrels, ice-house keepers, wood-cutters, nubile women with fans, and many more.

I started thinking about that statistic. The scientist's point was that we now rely on machines and cheap energy to do the things that servants would once have done for an élite, while the rest of us went without. But of course it is not that simple. For one thing there are ecological consequences. We gouge out the Earth to find the materials to make those machines; and the cheap energy to run them is polluting our planet and warming our climate. And yet many of the servants are still there. Though now, rather than occupying the attics of grand houses, they are spread across the world, growing our food, making our machines and stitching our clothes.

People talk a lot about carbon footprints. But our personal footprints are much bigger than that. And they are social as well as ecological. The trouble is that, in our charmed world, we know little about what our footprints are. It all happens so far away. The people and the pollution that sustain us are invisible to us.

I want to change that. The purpose of this book is to discover the hidden world that keeps us in the state to which we have become accustomed. I have done that by exploring my own personal footprint. I have travelled the world to find out where the cotton in my shirt comes from, the coffee in my mug, the prawns in my curry, the computer on my desk, the phone in my hand, and much else. To discover who grows or mines or makes my stuff, and where that stuff goes after I have finished with it. And to find out whether I should be ashamed of my purchases and their impact on the planet, or whether I should be proud to have contributed to some local economy or given a leg-up to some hard-pressed community.

I have tried not to pick and choose my journeys too carefully. I simply took those that sounded potentially the most interesting. And certainly I made a point of not changing my way of living to avoid any embarrassments. These are true confessions. And I hope that in tracking down my footprints I will also have tracked down some of yours.

I estimate that I travelled some 180,000 kilometres on this journey, visiting more than twenty countries. It took me to the end of my street and the end of my planet, into the African rainforests and the Central Asian deserts, to Bangladeshi sweatshops and Chinese computer factories, to the brothels of Manila and the slums of Rio, to the summits of mountains, the Arctic tundra, the fishing grounds of the Atlantic and into the bowels of the Earth.

Along the way, I met an amazing cross-section of the more than 6 billion people with whom we share this planet. They included a handful of the richest and many of the poorest. It set me wondering as much about the past and future of our species as about the past and future of our planet. And, you may be surprised to learn, it left me with some optimism, about humanity and the huge potential we have to run our world better.

It is easy to be horrified by all the weirdness of humanity. The remote jungle tribes and urban sects, the horrible regimes in North Korea and Burma and elsewhere, the fanatics and the fantasists, the warlords and hoodlums, the obscene wealth of the super-rich and the abject state of the super-poor and those struck down by AIDS.

But in my travels I mostly found the commonplace – billions of ordinary people, mostly poor but not starving; mostly ill-educated but not uneducated. The resulting book is a kind of chronicle of humanity as represented by the people who grow and make and dispose of the things that I use and consume in my daily life.

So, before I continue with the story, I thought I would stop a moment and describe our strange species, *Homo sapiens*, which has so peremptorily taken over this planet. I drew up a list of things that describe more than a billion people, what we might regard as the mainstream of humanity. I was struck by both what we share and what divides us. So here we are. *Homo sapiens* circa 2008. In our pomp and our folly.

A billion of us drive, for instance. Another billion of us have mobile phones. A billion of us can speak English, and another billion eat rice every day. But a billion of us do not have flushing toilets. Some of us share a number of these attributes. But humanity is like a giant version of one of those Venn diagrams, with interlinking circles showing how we differ and how we are the same. A billion of us live in shanty towns, or have access to the internet, or are Indian, or support a football team, or live within a kilometre of where we were born, or drink coffee, or have a TV in our home, or cannot support our families. A billion of us have moved from a village to the city, or are Muslims, or have high blood pressure, or use contraceptives regularly, or depend on fish as our main source of protein, or wear trainers, or are illiterate. A billion of us too are agnostics, or cook with firewood, or have a bicycle, or have heard of Muhammad Ali, or keep chickens, or have a debt with a moneylender, or never consume dairy products, or own T-shirts, or have no mains electricity.

Collecting these statistics gave me a hugely kaleidoscopic image of *Homo sapiens*. The rainbow race. A billion of us have ridden a bus, or are malnourished, or go to school, or have no running water tap in our houses. A billion of us are under ten, or are circumcised, or wear jeans, or have a fridge, or smoke cigarettes, or carry the TB bacterium, or eat bananas, or possess some gold, or take annual holidays, or go to the cinema, or pay rent to a landlord, or live on less than a dollar a day. A billion of us drink Coke, or will get divorced, or have heard of David Beckham, or are Catholics, or will live beyond our sixtieth year, or are overweight, or are Chinese, or eat bread daily, or get less protein than a Western domestic cat.

I hope this common diversity comes through all the chapters in the book. But to underline it, I have interspersed the main chapters with brief portraits of six particular people that I met on my travels who seemed more than most to highlight how few of us fit into neat categories. Several of them I would never have believed existed until I met them. Six representatives of 6 billion. One in a billion.

But I promised this was going to be a personal journey. So let me introduce myself and, more importantly, my stuff. I am a journalist, in my mid-fifties, with a wife and grown-up children. I live in London and work from home. Most days, I commute to the back bedroom each morning and turn on my computer. But I report about the environment and development round the world. And to do my job, I also travel a lot. This is bad for my carbon footprint, but I really don't believe you can learn about and report on the world by sitting at home and logging on to a virtual reality. The world is much more bizarre and unexpected, and often much more joyful and positive, than you would imagine from reading about it and seeing it on the news. And I found that especially true while following my global footprint. I really did sometimes find that my footprint could be a virtuous one.

In drawing up a list of where I should travel to make this book, I went through my house one day to see where everything came from. It was a shock to find how much of a globalized consumer I have become. When out shopping, I am always the person holding back from a purchase, asking whether I really want it, whether I am being ripped off, or deciding I just can't be bothered to carry it home. And yet, over a lifetime and a couple of trips to Sainsbury's, it is amazing how much stuff I have, and from how many places.

The food cupboard was an obvious place to start. There were nuts from Brazil and bottles of sparkling water from Scotland; sardines canned in Portugal and anchovies put in a jar in Spain; Italian chopped tomatoes and French mayonnaise; oatmeal from Oldham and mustard from Dijon; coffee from Tanzania and Marmite from Sussex and soup from a farm in Peterborough. There was mango chutney from India and caster sugar from Mauritius and desiccated coconut from the Philippines.

In some jars at the back, I found dried basil from Egypt and sage from Turkey; arrowroot from Thailand and allspice from Jamaica; lemongrass from Malaysia and galangal from China; mace from Grenada and saffron from Spain. We still haven't got through the bag of white pepper I bought years ago in the market at Kuching in Borneo. Then there were walnuts from China and papadoms from Mumbai, cloves from Indonesia and oregano from Turkey and vanilla from Madagascar and cardamom and ginger from India. Not to mention Spanish olive oil and Italian pasta; Iranian dates and bay leaves from . . . well, an overgrown bush in our back garden, actually.

In the fruit bowl, I found grapefruit from Florida, mandarins from Argentina, bananas from Costa Rica, nectarines from Spain and apples from New Zealand. On the sideboard, I found bread made from Gloucestershire flour, honey made by Mexican bees and marmalade made by my wife from Seville oranges. There was beer brewed by monks in Belgium, by men in pullovers in Dorset, and by the country's oldest brewery, amid the hop fields of Kent. There were several bottles of my favourite peaty malt whiskies from the Hebrides, and some untasted spirit from The Netherlands that we have had for two decades. The fridge contained red peppers from Holland, Parmesan cheese from Italy, as well as 'the world's largest-selling cheese brand', manufactured on the edge of Bodmin Moor from Cornish milk, cucumbers from Essex and a lettuce from Cambridgeshire. The butter and margarine could have come from anywhere.

In the bathroom, I found clove massage oil from Zanzibar, citronella oil from China, tea tree oil grown in the Australian outback, plus a lot of bottles of various lotions and medicines from the Body Shop and Boots that don't declare where they came from. (Which talc mines exactly did that talcum powder come from, Mr Boot, because there are some very nasty mines out there?)

In my office, I have a rather nice leather briefcase my wife gave me for Christmas one year. It was made in Chennai, India, by Dilip Kapur, a child of a weird religious eco-city known as Auroville. My computer and printer and phone are all made by Taiwanese companies using cheap labour on mainland China; the printer paper came from Slovakia. A random check of the books on my shelves shows they were printed in England and India, Hong Kong and Denmark, the US and Italy.

Around the house, there are spoils from many of my previous reporting trips. I have a Panama hat from Ecuador, a Russian silk scarf, a Chinese paper dragon, an Alaskan plastic polar bear, a caiman made from a Brazilian substance rather like rubber, a tiny metal buddha from India, a job lot of Soviet Lenin badges, several Japanese fans and a hand-carved wooden platypus brought back from Queensland by my daughter.

In my wardrobe, I found shirts made in Mauritius and Indonesia, Morocco and Cambodia, the US and Hong Kong. Not to mention a couple of colourful numbers picked up on travels in China and Ghana that I have never worn. Then I found a rather holed pullover hand-knitted by a woman I met in the Falkland Islands, a Japanese kimono, Russian army fatigues – and a hat made out of plastic bags by an old woman in a shanty town in South Africa.

In the front room there was an Egyptian mat, an Ashanti stool from Ghana, and a wood spirit carved by a colony of artists in Nigeria. In the back room there was a mat from Jordan, and a mahogany bench we removed from a flat we once rented. A clay recorder and a tambourine are the only survivors of a batch of arty objects I bought for virtually nothing in Mexico in 1984. In the hall I have a cow bell from the Auvergne in France that I use as a dinner gong.

Frankly, our furniture is a bit rudimentary, picked up here and there. But we do have a kitchen table that came from a Victorian workhouse somewhere in Battersea, a gate-leg table, possibly even older, which was a wedding present from my father, and a solid beech desk in my office. We also have a piano. It was made in London in the 1890s by a company called Philips, Cambridge & Co., which is absent from contemporary lists of bona fide piano makers. Our piano-tuner said it was not worth tuning any more, but he tuned it anyway. There seems to be some disagreement about whether the wood is rosewood or mahogany. But there is no doubt that the keys are ivory, probably ripped from central Africa at the height of the greatest slaughter of the elephant ever seen. During the 1890s, Britain imported 500 tonnes of ivory a year, at a cost of some 15,000 animals.

There is other stuff whose legality and morality I wonder about. Somewhere in a cupboard I have two small bags made of sealskin, given to me on a trip to Siberia. We own Burmese teak salad bowls and apartheid-era South African salad servers. Some garden furniture is of dubious provenance, though the stone lion on the lawn is a guaranteed chunk of Cotswold limestone, as carved by my wife's cousin. And the veneer on our kitchen units looks terribly like an offcut of illegally logged timber from New Guinea, given to me by Greenpeace.

I also got to thinking about the stuff that leaves my house. What happens to the contents of my waste bin, for instance? Where do our drains empty? Do the things I take to the recycling bins in Sainsbury's car park really get recycled? The signs on the bins perplex me. 'Each tonne of paper recycled saves an average 15 trees,' says one. In what sense saves? Do they know what actually happens to the paper I put in there? Recycling one glass bottle or jar saves the energy 'to power a TV for 20 minutes'. How does it do that exactly? And twenty-five plastic bottles 'will produce one fleece jacket'. But I thought that waste plastic all went to China. How on earth do they know what happens to it there? Donate your laser cartridge and 'help save tiny lives' by providing cash for 'Tommy's, the baby charity . . .' Who?

I can't say I'm going to track down the source or destination of all these items. It would be a life's work and I have a life to lead. But I am going in search of some of the most critical to my life – and I hope some of the most interesting. And from the start I have been determined to make the journey about people as much as about ecology. Whatever the downsides of globalization, one of the upsides is that it connects us with more people from more places. Usually those connections are hidden. But I am off to find them.

RUSSIAN FEDERATION
(ASIATIC RUSSIA)

UZBEKISTAN

TURKEY

CHINA

INDIA BANGLADESH

PHILIPPINES

KENYA

TANZANIA

INDONESIA

SOUTH
AFRICA

AUSTRALIA

2

Gold: A Lodestone for My Journey

Helmet on. Belt weighed down with emergency oxygen pack. The steel doors shut, a bell sounds from far below and the cage descends. Very slowly at first. Then suddenly faster. Within fifteen seconds we are travelling at 60 kilometres an hour down a shaft into the Earth. The cage rocks slightly but keeps on descending, longer than you can believe. Somewhere in the dark beside us, another cage shoots past in the opposite direction, hurtling to the surface and full of rock.

Soon we have gone down deeper than the Grand Canyon. It gets warmer. Every 100 metres – every six seconds – the temperature rises by a degree. Down at the bottom of the shaft, almost 4 kilometres below the Earth's surface and deeper than the ocean floor, the rocks are at more than 50°C. The muggy air is at twice the pressure it is at the surface. And radioactive. Scientists have found microbes down there in the dark whose only source of energy is the radiation from the Earth's core.

Gradually the lift slows and halts with a reassuring clunk. The doors open and we step out into the Earth's crust. I switch on the lamp on my helmet and peer around at the rocks. Three billion years ago, they were the gravelly deposits of a river delta. All sorts of metals were washed down from surrounding mountains that have long since eroded away. And some of those metals settled in the gravel beds. One metal in particular accumulated here. And, as a result, this tunnel leads through the heart of what is by a huge margin the richest goldfield on Earth. The West Witwatersrand goldfield in South Africa is also the deepest workplace on the planet. Welcome, says my guide, to Driefontein mine, shaft 7.

I am here to find out where the gold in my wedding ring came from. It is the one thing I never take off; the one thing that came with me every step of the way on my journeys to find my global footprint. As I step out into the Driefontein tunnel, I look again at it. My wife and I bought our bands of gold back in the summer of 1979, in a jeweller's shop on The Strand in central London. We still have the receipts. They cost £50 each. Where did those rings come from? In theory, every piece of gold can be traced back to an individual mine. The gold has its own chemical fingerprint because of the impurities that come with it as it leaves the earth. But in practice, gold in jewellery is usually cast from a range of sources, and my ring defies fingerprinting.

Because most of the 140,000 tonnes of gold that humans have ever mined is still in circulation, the gold on my finger could have been mined in Persia 6,000 years ago, or worn by Cleopatra. But the odds are against it. Ever since gold was discovered in Johannesburg in 1886, and shiploads of Cornish mining engineers came south to exploit them, the mines of West Witwatersrand have produced more than a third of all the gold ever mined.

And on the Witwatersrand, Driefontein is king. The mine that I have entered, 50 kilometres south-west of Johannesburg, has been in operation for fifty-five years. During the 1970s, when my ring was cast, Driefontein was the number-one producer in the world's number-one goldfield, yielding up more than 80 tonnes of gold a year. In the whole of history, more gold has come out of Driefontein than from anywhere else on Earth. Sometime in the first quarter of 2008, it became the only mine ever to have produced more than 3,000 tonnes of gold. So, as the gates shut behind me, the lift glides on down and we are left on our own at level 6/41, I can be fairly certain that this hole in the ground is where much of the gold in my ring came from.

We follow some narrow railtracks away from the shaft and deeper into the mine: tracks that take the miners in each day, and carry out the rock they blast from the gold face. Ducking wooden pit-props and electric cables and pipes carrying water and fresh air, I head towards the distant sound of drilling.

The Earth's crust here is a maze of different tunnels threading out from each level of the lift shaft. There are fewer than a dozen people in this tunnel today. But at any one time, 8,000 men are working underground in Driefontein alone. On the whole West Witwatersrand goldfield, there are some 60,000 miners underground. A vast infrastructure is needed just to keep the miners alive. Huge amounts of water naturally course through the mine. Sometimes that water bursts from the dolomite rocks above and into the tunnels. Past floods have threatened to drown the mine for ever. To keep the tunnels dry, some 40 million litres are pumped out of the mine every day. And as the water is removed, air is sent down to keep the tunnels cool enough to work in. Driefontein has a refrigerator the size of a hangar dedicated to this task.

We continue walking down the tunnel, past a sign warning about a recent death in a neighbouring mine. These are dangerous places. There is a constant risk of rockfalls. All along the tunnels wooden pit-props, metal jacks and miles of wire mesh hold up the roof and prevent the walls from falling in. But there are other hazards. Four years ago, here in shaft 7, four miners died after fire caught among the old pit-props of some distant abandoned tunnel. Smoke filled the tunnels and more than 100 miners survived only because they took refuge in air-sealed 'refuge chambers'.

Down here is like a separate country. The miners and supervisors, black and white, have their own language, called Fanakalo. It contains about 1,000 words, mostly commands and exhortations and warnings, culled from the numerous African languages spoken by the miners, along with bits of English and Afrikaans. This is the common language of survival. 'It's dangerous down there,' a geologist told me before we took to the lift. 'At four or five kilometres down, we really don't know how the rocks behave. People die when things go wrong.'

This is an underworld in every sense. Groups of illegal miners smuggle themselves down in the freight lifts. They stay below ground for months at a time, armed with pistols and home-made grenades, chiselling out ore and then grinding it and extracting the gold using mercury, just as poor gold miners do at the surface. Rob Chaplin, the operations manager for the western half of Driefontein, says his supervisors often find, stashed away underground, the balls of mercury used in the crude processing. Syndicates are reckoned to smuggle up to 40 tonnes of gold out of Witwatersrand every year. This is around a tenth of the total gold taken from the mines. The tunnels are simply impossible to police, Rob says. The hills around are so riddled with old mine shafts and tunnels that you could walk to Johannesburg – a distance of some 50 kilometres – without once going to the surface.

Since the end of the apartheid era, conditions have improved somewhat for the official miners. At Goldfields, the company that runs Driefontein, the all-male dormitories remain, but there are also houses for conjugal visits. And many miners live in local communities or squatter settlements. Some can make it a modest way up the management chain. There are even a few women working underground, though the white supervisors complain that they strip off to their waists, which is distracting.

Most of the miners have come a long way to take these jobs. They are recruited by agents in their villages in Mozambique or Lesotho or distant parts of rural South Africa – just as they were during the apartheid era. The money they send home is often the mainstay of their communities. Miners' remittances make up 60 per cent of Lesotho's GDP.

Every day, the Driefontein miners leave their company hostels and squatter settlements at 4 a.m. to throng the lifts that hurtle into the Earth down one of the mine's eight operational shafts. They fan out along the numerous tunnels at more than twenty different levels. Once at the face, they spend hours with drills the size of gun emplacements, making holes in the hard rock. Then they insert dynamite into the holes. At 5 p.m. every day, the dynamite is exploded all across the mine. The seismic forces sometimes cause high-pressure cave-ins. Then, after the smoke has cleared and any rockfalls have been checked, the night shift goes in to drag out the rubble. Some 20,000 tonnes of rock come out of Driefontein every day – 2.5 tonnes for every miner. In it, invisible to the naked eye, are about 100 kilograms of gold – 5 grams of gold for every tonne of rock brought to the surface.

At the surface, the rock is milled and mixed with cyanide to dissolve the gold, which can then be released from the cyanide by adding one of a range of other chemicals, such as zinc. Across the Witwatersrand bush, reservoirs holding the resulting waste ooze cover 400 square kilometres. Eventually, the rock is transformed into recognizable bars of 85 per cent pure gold – before going off to the national Rand Refinery in Johannesburg, where it is refined to 99 per cent purity.

So it took 2 tonnes of rock, blasted from the Earth's crust, hauled 2 kilometres and more to the surface, ground up and treated, to provide enough of the metal for my 10-gram ring. On top of that, making my ring required 5 tonnes of water, 30 tonnes of air pumped underground to keep the mine cool, enough electricity to run a large house for several days – and about 10 man-hours of labour. The endeavour behind a simple £50 ring is hard to fathom until you have been down a mine.

The miners, needless to say, see little of the wealth that comes out of these mines. In 2006, while his drillers took home £140 a month, the Goldfields' CEO Ian Cockerill was paid almost £50,000 a month. And many of the miners will not live long. The men are far from home and have sex with a lot of different women in the nearby squatter settlements. HIV is widespread in South Africa, and in the mining areas prevalence rates among the men and the female sex workers are as high as 35 per cent. Goldfields offers voluntary HIV testing and hands out drugs to its workers, though not to the prostitutes. I meet Stella Ntimbane, head of the company's AIDS operation, as she emerges from a testing tent in the compound of one of Driefontein's residential areas. She takes gruesome but genuine pride at having uncovered 600 HIV-positive men in the previous two months, and nine more that morning. 'They are getting treatment, and hopefully soon they will be back at the rock face,' she says. But ultimately many of them will go back to their villages to die.

For several years from the late 1990s, world gold prices slumped. High-cost mines like Driefontein seemed destined to close. But gold prices have soared again since 2005. The credit crunch created a whole new gold rush, and the push is on to extract more and more of the precious metal while prices stay high. Billions of dollars are being bet on that eventuality. Goldfields plans to excavate yet deeper at Driefontein. Shaft 9 is set to go down a further half-kilometre or so, to give the mine another twenty years' life.

It is a miracle these shafts are open at all. Shaft 7, the shaft I have descended, has already been mined once. With me below ground is the mine's chief geologist, Melville Haupt. He has masterminded a return to take out the pillars that were left behind last time to hold up the roof, and to penetrate the areas of difficult geology and fractured rocks previously deemed unsafe. 'By rights this place should have shut seven years ago, but Mel just keeps finding more gold,' says Chaplin. But Mel is betting his skills as a mine geologist against potential disaster.

Crouching, I follow a narrow passage up to see some old

workings. I slip and grab a piece of wood above me. An old pit-prop comes away in my hand. Guiltily, I remember an instruction given when we were coming down in the shaft: 'Don't grab anything above you. If you slip, just fall.' I feel lucky to have survived my indiscretion. They claim to have got through a million man-shifts here since the last fatality. So it would have been a shame to damage the record.

Gold is incorruptible. Since the earliest records, humans have worn gold and hidden gold, bought and sold gold, worshipped gold, fought for gold and displayed it as a symbol of power. It pervades our language. Some of us are gold-diggers, while others have hearts of gold. We have the Midas touch, strike gold, make a pile and find the golden goose. We pay with gold cards, travel the Yellow Brick Road – or simply watch how things pan out. We look back to a golden age.

Gold is soft and malleable, yet totally indestructible. Nothing in nature attacks it. It is ideal for filling teeth, and for plating critical connections on computer circuit boards. But these are side-shows. Most of the gold ever mined has had no functional purpose other than its beauty and as a source of value. Gold mainly excites passion. Humans panned for gold before they worked iron or made bronze – perhaps even before they tilled the soil. Gold-diggers were certainly among the first people not to have to hunt or grow their own food. Others would do these jobs for them, in return for gold. Gold thus became both the symbol and the substance of wealth.

From the first Egyptian pharaohs and ancient Celtic kings of England, it has been the ultimate form of saving. The first known European gold jewellery dates from 7,000 years ago. For 1,000 years, the Ancient Egyptians, for whom gold represented the sun god, maintained a mining colony far away in modern-day southern Sudan to secure their gold. Tutankhamun was found buried in a gold coffin weighing more than 100 kilos. Ancient Britons were mining gold 4,000 years ago. The Romans crossed the Sahara for gold. Macedonian gold mines funded Alexander the Great's conquest of the world.

Alchemy was the great science of the Middle Ages; Isaac Newton spent more time trying to turn base metal into gold than he did researching gravity and the laws of nature. Later, Europeans colonized the New World for gold, and spent decades searching for Eldorado. The gold rushes of California and Australia and South Africa and the Klondike globalized the world's economy in the nineteenth century. Gold smuggling, more than oil, made the fabulous wealth behind the modern mega-city of Dubai.

The Gold Standard was for a long time the guarantor of the world's currencies; and every national treasury still keeps a store. A third of all the world's gold is locked up in the vaults of various banks and private investment houses. There is Fort Knox, of course. And vaults beneath the Bank of England in the City of London store the bullion reserves of more than seventy countries – hundreds of times more gold than is contained in the Crown Jewels, on display close by in the Tower of London.

Gold is still a refuge in times of trouble. When currencies crash, gold gains in value. The political uncertainty post-9/11 is regarded as the main reason why gold prices have soared since. Wars are good for gold miners. Dictators from Hitler and Stalin to Ferdinand Marcos and his wife lusted after and obsessively hoarded gold. Gold made apartheid. And the biggest ever stock market scam. In the 1990s, there was feverish trade in a company that claimed to have found the world's largest gold mine, in the heart of the Borneo rainforest. Billions of dollars went down the drain when the find was exposed as a fraud.

But gold is also loved by the poor. More than half of all the gold ever mined is in the form of jewellery worn by hundreds of millions of people across the planet. Every Indian bride takes gold for her dowry. There is more gold stored in simple chests in tens of millions of Indian homes than in Fort Knox and the vaults of

London put together. African peasants fleeing from wars carry gold as their only possession of value. The world's population agrees on very few things. The value of gold is one of them.

And I have my wedding ring. I can remove it from my finger, if I try very hard and apply a little Vaseline. But it feels like a betrayal even to do it, and I hastily put it back on – such is the power of gold.

At last, we approach the gold face. The roar of three drills pounding into solid rock becomes so loud that even shouting into the ear of the person next to me is useless for communication. I look for signs of gold. Amazingly, here in the heart of the world's most productive mine, there is no sign. Not the slightest glimmer. Mel shows me the rock containing the gold. It is a dull grey quartz, with large pebbles embedded in it. These were the pebbles in a river delta 3 billion years ago, before anything more sophisticated than microbes lived on the Earth. Before there was oxygen in the atmosphere, there was gold in these hills. Back then, the gold brought down by rivers from the mountains concentrated round the pebbles. Occasionally, if you look carefully, you can see a sparkle round the edge of the pebbles, he says. But miners can go years here, drilling in these black holes, without once seeing any indication at all of what they are devoting their lives to winning from the Earth.

Down shaft 7 in Driefontein, I feel as if I am penetrating not just into the Earth's crust, but into the psyche of humanity. A lust for gold may have been one of the first things that distinguished *Homo sapiens* from our fellow hominids. My footprints down this tunnel feel like the footprints of my species. A search for something so elusive but so desired; something obsessional but sacramental; something venal but pure.

This journey into Driefontein is the start of my journey to find my footprint. This is in part a geographical journey to discover where my stuff comes from. But it is more. It is a journey of the psyche too. And gold sums it up. The pursuit of gold is in one sense the most absurd human endeavour. Environmentally and in humanitarian terms, it makes little sense. You might say it encapsulates the folly of mankind, and how we abuse each other and the planet. Like King Midas, we are cursed by it. And yet who would forgo our love of beauty, and of a metal that seems to touch us to our core? Of all the metals mined by man, none has survived so well, been recycled so often, or been cosseted as carefully as gold. It symbolizes some of the best in us too.

This is not a book about gold. But gold is a lodestone for my journey. And I wore my ring every inch of the way.

Part Two

My Food

3

Coffee: Throwing a Hand Grenade into the Cosy World of Fair Trade

I think we were a bit pleased with ourselves, John and I, as we sat in a shed on the slopes of Mount Kilimanjaro. A sudden rainstorm had erupted outside, and water was crashing on to the corrugated-iron roof. But we were warm and dry, self-satisfied missionaries for the fairtrade cause. John Weaver – tall, diffident, but with a slight military bearing – is the chief buyer of coffee beans sold in supermarkets by the fast-growing British fairtrade company Cafédirect. He was on his annual tour to check the quality of the new coffee harvest in Tanzania, and to agree whose beans would go into the next year's packets of the company's top-selling Kilimanjaro brand.

We were visiting the Mwikamsae Kenyamvou Cooperative Society, whose beans were the biggest component of the previous year's batch. And he wanted to congratulate them on their beans. I too had a story to tell. I bought Kilimanjaro coffee in my local Sainsbury's, I told the twenty or so farmers assembled on benches in the shed. I had drunk their beans for years, because I liked them best. Now I had come to find out for myself who grew them. The farmers had come to puncture our complacency.

The meeting began formally. There was a brief prayer and

discussion of the society's minutes. When John spoke, the farmers applauded as he announced that last season Cafédirect had bought 222 sacks of coffee, weighing about 13 tonnes, from their 900 smallholder farmers. They listened intently as he described how the international price of coffee was determined each day in New York, and how this was relayed to the Tanzanian auction in Moshi, the town at the bottom of the mountain where all their coffee was sold.

There were rumbles of agreement when he acknowledged that low prices caused problems for farmers. And nods all round as he explained how the purpose of Cafédirect was 'to ensure you always have a reasonable return for your work. We guarantee you a minimum price, whatever the international market price might be. For your high grade of gourmet Arabica coffee that is one dollar forty-six cents a pound – twenty cents higher than the world market price at the moment.'

John finished. I thought it had gone down well. Then Jacob Rumisha Mgase, an old farmer with a weathered face, got to his feet. 'I speak for the farmers,' he said. There was a hush. 'We'd like to know how much our coffee costs in the shops in England.' It was a hand grenade thrown into the cosy world of ethical trade.

John picked up one of his packets: 'This pack of Kilimanjaro coffee weighs half a pound and sells for about three pounds. So a pound costs just over six pounds, or about twelve dollars.'

His audience may have been peasant farmers, but they knew how to add up. Jacob turned his hat slowly in his hand. 'So you buy our coffee for one dollar forty-six. And sell it for twelve dollars. Is that fair trade?' His family, he said, could live for a week on the price of a pound of coffee in London.

John did his best. He explained that, after the coffee beans leave the farmers, they have to be cured and graded and packed and shipped to Europe, where they are roasted, ground, packaged, distributed to retailers, advertised and finally sold to the public. And even in fair trade everyone had to make a profit. To general bemusement, he pointed out the importance to supermarket sales of the smart metallized polymer packet, made in Spain. Jacob responded that his farmers had to fertilize the soil, plant the coffee, grow it, pick it, de-pulp it, dry it, carry it to the co-op, weigh it and put it into sacks. 'All our costs are going up, but the coffee price keeps going down. We farmers are totally exhausted by what we do. I request on behalf of the farmers, try to think of us. Please pay more.'

At the back of the room, as Jacob talked, a man wet from the rain came into the shed with a small sack and put it on the scales. It contained just 7 pounds of beans – the output of his smallholding for a month. His income for that sack was about £5. Not for low-grade beans destined for a jar of instant, but for acknowledged high-quality 'gourmet' Arabica coffee, labelled as fairtrade and destined for sale at a premium price to some of the most discerning coffee-drinkers in the world. And me.

No wonder that these farmers, though educated themselves, struggle to send their own children to school. No wonder their roofs leak. No wonder that no farmer I met had even a motorbike to take his beans to the shed. No wonder that they have not been able to afford to replant bushes that were put in the soil by their grandfathers and are losing productivity.

Mount Kilimanjaro is prime coffee-growing land. The climate here, over 2,000 metres up the slopes of Africa's highest mountain and away from the heat of the equatorial plains, is perfect. The sandy soils are fertile, and the vegetation lush. Except during droughts, there is sufficient water. And the farmers are up to the job. In among the coffee, they keep a cow or two. They grow maize for their bread, finger millet to make a potent banana-beer called *mbege*, and bananas for sale in the local market and to shade their coffee bushes.

After the meeting broke up, Jackson Kombe, one of the co-op's leading lights, showed me his house and 2-hectare farm. He had 1,400 coffee trees that produced 300 kilograms of beans in an average year. That was an income of about £500. His coffee was organic, because he didn't have the cash for expensive pesticides. His four cows provided organic fertilizer. He showed me a weed by the path: 'I mix its leaves with water; it makes a bio-insecticide.' Ecologists say this mixed, largely organic, farming system is ideal for conserving water, soils and wildlife. The farmers were doing everything right, and producing a superb product. Their problem was that their plots were tiny. And with coffee prices so low for so long, it has been hard for them to make a living.

Back at the shed, a truck had arrived from the Kilimanjaro Native Cooperative Union (KNCU), the 'mother co-op' to which all the local co-ops round the mountain are affiliated. The driver was loading up with sacks of beans. Only about a fifth of them would end up sold to Cafédirect at its premium price. The rest would be sold on the open market. They might end up in a high-price cappuccino in Rome, a fierce black brew in Riga, or a Starbucks almost anywhere on the planet.

Starbucks. Now that word set off a hubbub in the co-op shed. Much as Cafédirect courts these farmers (their photos appear on Kilimanjaro packets), many barely recognized its name. But they knew about Starbucks. As the rain set in again, Jacob almost spat its name across the shed. They knew all about its 13,000 branches purchasing one in every fifty coffee beans round the world. They knew the price of a latte better than I did – $5 in some places, someone said. They knew that you could get more than sixty cups out of a pound of coffee. And they were quite capable of working out that that meant Starbucks charged $300 for coffee for which the farmers received less than $1.50.

That's a bit unfair on Starbucks. The company has branches to run and ambience to create. But everyone likes an ogre. And after thinking about Starbucks, the farmers liked John and Cafédirect rather more. One thing still rankled, however. Cafédirect was selling their coffee as fairly traded, and they just did not regard even its premium prices as fair. I was beginning to agree with them.

John and I travelled back down the mountain, catching glimpses of its melting ice cap. This is the road taken by Kilimanjaro coffee from some 60,000 smallholders in almost a hundred local co-ops to Moshi, where KNCU collects, cures and ships beans. KNCU is the oldest cooperative in Africa, about to celebrate its seventy-fifth anniversary. It was set up in the 1930s, when the British colonial authorities were introducing coffee on the mountain and the local farmers felt they were being cheated on price. Its members produce about 5,000 tonnes of beans a year. In 2006, about 80 tonnes went to Cafédirect, in five shipping containers.

Moshi is Kenya's coffee capital. Every bean of Tanzanian coffee is sold at the auction here. KNCU coffee is auctioned beside lots from smallholders' co-ops and large private coffee estates from across the country. The auction itself – held at 10 a.m. every Thursday morning – was a bit of a disappointment. There were no loud men shouting bids. Instead, every buyer sat at a desk and each lot was displayed on computer screens in front of them. They pressed buttons to bid. Even the sound of the auctioneer's hammer was made by pressing a button. As ersatz as any instant blend.

Lots were sold, at around $1.25 a pound, to young traders who had flown in from Nairobi for the day. Their nametags bore the logos of local-sounding organizations like Mwanze and Mazao and Kilimanjaro Planting. But in reality, they were mostly the employees of global trading conglomerates. They included Volcafe Holdings, Ecom and Edmund Schluter, all based in Switzerland; Neumann Kaffee from Hamburg; and the US-based Louis Dreyfus Group. These traders of the most valuable commodity in world trade after oil sell to five big coffee manufacturers: Nestlé (the world's largest coffee titans), Kraft (makers of Maxwell House and Kenco), Sara Lee (makers of Douwe Egberts), Procter & Gamble, and the German giant Tchibo.

But I was most interested in Lot 198, the KNCU coffee chosen by John and destined for Cafédirect. Legally, it had to go through the auction, the same as any other coffee. But because Cafédirect pays premium prices, it normally gets what it wants. Sure enough, Lot 198, one containerload of prime KNCU Arabica coffee, was sold to Twin Trading, Cafédirect's buying partner, for $1.46 a pound. It was the highest-priced sale of the day, and meant extra money in the pockets of the KNCU's farmers. Fair trade in action. Except that down on the farm, things look far from fair. Why so?

I don't think the answer lies with the motives of the fairtraders. Their hearts are in the right place. In Britain, the fairtrade movement began as an initiative of the old Greater London Council under Ken Livingstone. The idea was to link cooperative stores in London to producer groups in the developing world, and cut out the middlemen. Nicaraguan cigar makers and Cuban textile workers were among the first beneficiaries. From the beginning, it was about more than the prices paid to individual farmers. It was also about promoting co-ops and helping communities. So under the rules of the London-based Fairtrade Foundation, an extra premium is also paid to community projects. On Kilimanjaro, Cafédirect hands back more than £20,000 in this way each year. The farmers I met were spending their dividend to set up a tree nursery and on scholarships so their children could go to secondary school. Money from other fairtrade buyers was going into tourism, roads and other local infrastructure.

That near-socialist philosophy persists as Ken's baby grows into a fully fledged capitalist enterprise, embracing fruit, herbs, spices, rice, yoghurt, honey, flowers and wine; and as the logo has moved from Oxfam shops and hippie bean co-ops to the big stores. Cafédirect alone fills a billion British coffee mugs a year. Marks & Spencer sells nothing but fairtrade coffee, bought through its own-brand network. Nestlé too has one fairtrade brand.

But fairtrade coffee is far from taking over the world. If Nestlé were a true convert, it would be paying a premium price for all its coffee rather than, at last count, just 0.2 per cent. And therein lies the problem. Fair trade pays a premium, but on a global coffee price that remains catastrophically unfair to the coffee farmers.

After the collapse in 1989 of the International Coffee Agreement – a cartel that had managed production, kept prices fairly high and stable, and ensured that small coffee farmers had markets for their products – prices crashed, reaching rock bottom in 2001. By 2007, coffee prices were starting to creep back up, but they remained well below their level in the mid-1990s. And small farmers like the members of the KNCU have lost out most dramatically. While Cafédirect's sales of KNCU coffee may be booming, KNCU's overall output is only a quarter what it was a generation ago.

I saw the decline most obviously on the last morning of my trip, when I visited KNCU's curing plant in Moshi. Curing is a fairly simple process of cleaning and hulling and sorting the beans into different grades for dispatch to roasters. I expected a fairly modest factory, but instead I found a huge building twice the length of a football pitch and six storeys high. In the 1920s, when it was built, more than 700 people worked there. Now the place was largely empty, with a part-time roster of fewer than seventy staff. 'We have the capacity to handle a million sacks of beans in a year in here, but we only had eighty thousand sacks last year,' said my guide. Beneath piles of dust, I made out the chipped and discoloured remains of beautiful floor tiles. The place must once have been magnificent. But now it is a mausoleum commemorating the old state-run industry.

From Moshi, my Kilimanjaro coffee takes the pot-holed road to Dar port, from where it is loaded on to a container ship for the journey up the east coast of Africa, through the Red Sea and the Suez Canal to Tilbury dock on the Thames estuary and to a bonded warehouse close by. About once a fortnight, 3-tonne batches leave the warehouse for a Dutch-owned coffee roaster called Gala in Dartford in Kent.

Gala is Europe's largest roaster of own-brand coffee. It has helped nurture Cafédirect's growth to becoming the UK's sixth-biggest coffee brand, selling more than 1,200 tonnes a year, including Kilimanjaro, Palenque from Mexico and Machu Picchu from Peru. In the tasting room, Gala's technical manager Nick Boxall said he'd seen all the coffee fads come and go, but admitted that fair trade has given a new buzz to the industry. Was this more than just a new way for traders to make more money out of coffee? He smiled rather enigmatically.

Some see fairtrade coffee as cynical marketing of a 'premium' product, an ethical veneer for an industry built on exploitation. That would have been grossly unfair back in 2001, when for a while Cafédirect was paying three times the market price. But today, the virtue is perhaps less clear-cut. Yes, the Kilimanjaro farmers get a small premium – an extra 5p from the price of every half-pound bag I buy. But most of the extra I currently pay in the supermarket is taken up by the extra costs involved in grading and inspecting and trading in the smaller volumes of coffee. Probably this is inevitable, but it does leave a bad taste.

The Chagga people, who make up most of the coffee farmers on Kilimanjaro, are not surprised by this. They have a long and fairly shrewd acquaintanceship with global markets. This began in earnest more than a century ago, in the 1890s, when a Chagga king called Rindi established Moshi as a world centre for the ivory trade. Where today the town's warehouses are full of sacks of coffee, back then they were lined with elephant tusks culled from animals killed on the plains west of the mountain. Most of the buyers were German settlers, who shipped the ivory out via Zanzibar to make billiard balls and ivory statuettes and piano keys for the drawing rooms of Europe. Quite possibly, the ivory keys on my piano back home were traded through Moshi. Doubtless the Chagga were complaining about the price then, too.

Eventually the elephant population collapsed, and when the British took over in 1922, they introduced coffee. But the Germans are still around in Moshi. One set up the Salzburg bar, where I ate. And a VW dealership still dominates the local motor trade. I was driven back to the airport in an old VW van. As we drove, I felt I wanted to shake the fairtraders and demand that they charge me more. Jacob's accusing words came back to me: 'Is that fair trade?' Why, I thought, should feeling virtuous come so cheap when it still leaves farmers so poor?

I did not fall out of love with the idea of fair trade. Far from it. Companies like Cafédirect are on the side of the angels, fighting the global giants who constantly attempt to drive down prices. I drink fairtrade coffee, and would encourage you to do the same. But I do think it is a misnomer. Fairtrade coffee is not fairly traded. The price is still dictated by market conditions in Britain, rather than living conditions in Tanzania. I read an academic study on the fairtrade business by Verena Bitzer from the Copernicus Institute for Sustainable Development in Utrecht, which concluded rightly that the ethical coffee business is as 'buyer-driven' as the regular business. But beyond that, she made some interesting discoveries. For instance, that the old, established labelling systems like the Fairtrade Foundation and its adherents like Cafédirect had far tougher standards than some newer ones set up to allow big brands left behind by the ethical rush to muscle their way into the market – Fairtrade lite, you might say. And she warned that fair trade only works at the margins. Once it grows, it will start to depress the regular market price of coffee. In effect, the premium price will become the new market price. And all the farmers will be left with is the price of certification.

But let's be clear. If there is a problem with fair trade, it lies with us and not the people at Cafédirect. The critical question is how much extra are we consumers prepared to pay, as we peruse the coffee packets on display in the supermarket, in order to feel good about our coffee? So far, we are not prepared to pay very much. We want our ethics on the cheap. If we convince ourselves on a Saturday morning in Sainsbury's or Tesco that we are paying a truly fair price, giving the coffee farmers a proper return, then we are deluding ourselves.

4

Going Local: My Ale, Cheese and Other Patriotic Delights

This book is more about people and places than about any arid analysis of my ecological footprint. And it is about my idiosyncrasies. After meeting the Chagga coffee growers on Mount Kilimanjaro, I came home to explore the less exotic pleasures of good local produce: of cheese and bread, of Scotch and strawberries. But first I went in search of that most distinctive of local products: beer.

I have always loved breweries. For a while, I was paid to go from one to another, supping free ale and trying to remain sober enough to write about the experience afterwards. I was chief reporter for the Campaign for Real Ale (CAMRA). It was a nice job that fitted my lifestyle. And I got out before my liver packed up.

There are a lot more global beer brands than there used to be. Bland brews, mostly. And, under pressure from the big combines, local breweries have been shutting down for as long as I have been drinking. But even today, a lot of beer is local. Every part of Britain has its own taste in ale: maltier or hoppier or yeastier, with full head or flat. Wherever I go, I try to drink the local ale. It gives me a sense of being somewhere in particular. Adnams of Suffolk or

Wadworth of Wiltshire, Holt's of Manchester or Fuller's of London, Shepherd Neame of Kent or Timothy Taylor of West Yorkshire, Hook Norton of Oxfordshire or . . . I can taste them as I write.

Local brews tend to have local ingredients. Barley from Scotland rather than the US; hops from Kent rather than New Zealand. The total 'beer miles' for an English regional ale could be as little as 1,000 kilometres, against 40,000 kilometres for an international lager brand. But the list of local brews is shortening. While I was writing this book, two of the beers I drank most, because they are brewed near places in which I live, disappeared: Gale's of Horndean in Hampshire, and Young's of Wandsworth in London.

Non-beer-drinkers cannot know the tragedy of losing a favourite brew. Even those who shut the breweries suffer. It broke the heart of old John Young, proprietor of Young's brewery, when he offered his prime industrial site in the heart of Wandsworth for sale at £100 million. He died literally as the last brew was being produced. I know that something masquerading as Gale's now comes from Fuller's Chiswick brewery, and barrels of ersatz Young's roll out of the otherwise estimable Charlie Wells brewery in Bedford. These are decent ales, but not the same. Proper beers are complex living things, as much a product of their place as their recipe.

Mourning these losses, I began my tour of the British places that supply my food and drink at the Badger brewery on the water meadows of the River Stour in Dorset. There I tracked down the secret behind an un-real ale, a bottled brew that I drink with my Saturday-night curry. Golden Champion Ale is light, hoppy and laced with a strange fruity flavour that has enough bite to cut through a tandoori. I had come to Blandford St Mary to find its mastermind: head brewer Tim Morris.

Not long ago, Tim was dodging the cocaine cartels of Bogotá to set up and run a brewery in Colombia. Coming home, he chose well. The Badger brewery – more properly the 'independent family brewer' of Hall and Woodhouse – is a classic Victorian pile. It has a Dickensian feel. A chilly place even in summer, with men in pullovers sitting in panelled offices running a process unchanged since Queen Victoria was on the throne. Half the brewing kit is more than a century old, much of it cast-offs from other breweries that have shut down. I didn't see a computer screen the entire time I was there.

The five-storey building is designed vertically so the precious fluid can work its way downwards, taking advantage of gravity. The malted barley is loaded in the roof, and milled to crack the grain. Then it is boiled up with water in 100-year-old vessels called 'mash tuns'. Down one level, the liquid is strained and hops are added in a 'copper', also 100 years old and so thin it may not have long to go. After reboiling, the malty, hoppy brew ferments with yeast, during which the sugars from the malt are converted to alcohol. And, now at ground level, it is put into casks or bottles. Happily they were brewing a batch of Golden Champion during my visit.

Besides their beer, one thing I like about local breweries is that they usually have clear family ownership. My pension fund hasn't got its mitts on them yet. Hall and Woodhouse was founded 250 years ago by Charles Hall, a farmer. And while the Halls have fallen by the wayside, the Woodhouses still own the brewery. A member of the fifth brewing generation, David Woodhouse, is the current managing director.

Tim sat me down to some tasting. Every ingredient was critical, he said. The water comes from a well sunk 40 metres into the chalk beneath the brewery. Hard, chalky water makes better beer. The barley was more variable. A lot depended on the harvest. 'The most nervous part of my brewing year is around Christmas, when we have to choose the new barley malt for a new year,' Tim said. Making a mistake can mess up the taste of the beer, and bring a summer of complaints from regulars at the company's 200 pubs. When we talked, he was unsure whether to stick with Fanfare, a winter variety hit by pre-harvest rains in 2006, or switch to a spring variety called Optic. But it would be British.

So far, so pragmatic. Brewers are industrial chemists. But the dark arts take over when the conversation turns to yeasts. These are living things, cultivated continuously on the premises. If brewers have to go out and buy more, you know they are in trouble. Successive head brewers at Blandford have been cultivating the same strain since 1934. They have a back-up supply in the freezer, but have never had to use it. Yeast, says Tim, 'is the primary reason for the unique character of our ales. It is the house flavour, the background flavour you find in all our beers.' His is citrussy and melony. I supped some more.

But there was something else distinctive in Golden Champion. Tim's eye lit up when I asked about it. Here was the artist at work. He developed the brew to win a competition for a new bottled summer ale. The competition was run by Tesco, but I won't hold that against him. 'We wanted a distinctive taste,' he said. His answer was elderflower. I had heard of elderflower champagne and cordial, but not beer. Putting elderflower in a beer sounded sacrilegious to me.

But it is not so new. 'English brewers were putting herbs like thyme and marjoram and elderflower into their beers four hundred years ago, before the Dutch introduced them to hops. So I was going back to an earlier tradition of brewing,' said Tim. The taste is quite like some hops. When Tesco brought in its big-league judges – like my old CAMRA editor Roger Protz – they were persuaded that the strange taste was in fact an unusual hop. Only later did they twig that Tim had hoodwinked them. The brew won and has never looked back. Badger brews five of the twenty top-selling bottled beers in Britain today, including Golden Champion, Tanglefoot and Stinger – another summery ale, which is made with nettles. Another first for Tim.

The hills of the West Country are still rich in English produce. The free-range organic chickens that I buy from my local butcher come from Springfield Farm outside Leominster in Herefordshire, courtesy of Rodney Mee, who lets his chickens grow for twelve weeks, twice the battery norm, before slaughter. But my journey took a turn for the worse when I sought out my regular Cheddar cheese, called Cathedral City. It transpires that it comes neither from the Somerset town of Cheddar nor from a cathedral city. The self-styled 'world's largest-selling cheese brand' is confected at a new 'super-dairy' at Davidstow on the edge of Bodmin Moor in Cornwall. The dairy produces 55,000 tonnes of cheese a year. And, according to *Farming News*, the new plant has rewarded its 500 dairy farmers for the success of the brand by lowering the prices it pays them for their milk.

The Davidstow dairy is owned by Dairy Crest, one of the privatized successors of the old Milk Marketing Board. I consume more of their products than I knew. Pat, my milkman, loads his milk float early in the morning from the Unigate Dairy in Hanworth, west London, which Dairy Crest bought in 2000. The company has almost a fifth of the British milk market. It buys from around 1,600 dairy farmers. It sells milk, butter, spreads like Country Life – and cheese like Cathedral City. The power of the big dairies and supermarkets has reduced milk prices so much that bottled spring water costs more. Half of the country's dairy farmers have left the business in the past decade.

It was thoroughly depressing. But I cheered myself up by checking out my two all-time favourite cheeses: the ones I queue for hours outside Neal's Yard Dairy in Covent Garden to buy every Christmas. For once, marketing accords with reality. Mrs Kirkham's handcrafted Lancashire cheese is indeed handcrafted by a Mrs Kirkham – in Lancashire. Her name is Ruth, and she is the third-generation Mrs Kirkham producing cheese from a small dairy at Beesley Farm, just north of Preston. They have their own herd of Friesian-Holstein cows and use the milk unpasteurized. Her cheese matures for up to a year before I buy it. Crumbly and creamy.

There was even better news about my Stilton from Colston Bassett. The blue-veined 'king of cheeses' can only be made in a small area of the East Midlands, on the border between Nottinghamshire and Leicestershire. It is one of the few English foods to have the same legal protection afforded to Europe's prestige local foodstuffs like Bordeaux wine and Parma ham. The Colston Bassett dairy has been making Stilton since 1913. It is a farmers' cooperative and the milk comes from cows grazing the same handful of village fields that their predecessors munched on the first day of production. There are no compromises here. The dairy uses proper animal rennet – the stuff that makes the milk coagulate into curds and whey – rather than cheap vegetable substitutes. Four tonnes of curd are hand-ladled each day. They say it improves texture. I know of few better tastes. For me, my Stilton is the taste of Christmas.

Colston Bassett dairy has only ever had three managers. The first, Tom Coy, lasted almost half a century, and handed over in 1960 to Ernie Wagstaff, who in 1969 passed the chains of office to Richard Rowlett. Cussed old sod, Richard. I wrote him a fan letter asking if I could see his dairy and write about it. He turned me down flat. He gets 'all too many' visitors, he told me. 'It's an imposition at the best of times.' It was the run-up to Christmas, when he makes 40 per cent of his sales, but after Christmas he wasn't even answering my emails. I suppose that when your product is as good as his – sorry, you'll just have to go and taste it – who needs journalists? Maybe I'll try again when he hands over to his no. 2, Billy Kevan.

It's funny how things come back to basics. Beer, cheese and bread: the ploughman's lunch. I think I could live for ever on those three. So what about my bread? Most Saturday mornings I go to a street market in Clapham Junction. There, besides buying fruit and veg, I usually visit Dove's, the butcher's (where I buy my Springfield chickens from the lugubrious Bob, the third generation of Doves to run the place), and then until its recent closure, I crossed the road to the Lighthouse Bakery.

We'd been going here for years, because they baked on the premises. The Lighthouse was one of London's few surviving 'artisan' bakeries. It used to be run by a West Indian and his Swedish wife. Then it was run by Rachel, a former senior executive in the arts world, and her partner, an American called Elizabeth. I usually saw Rachel out front in the shop on a busy Saturday morning. I fixed up a tour (if three small rooms counts as a tour) on a 'quiet' day. But quiet just meant that Rachel was in the back, up to her armpits in flour, fulfilling an order for 300 mince pies. It was the run-up to Christmas. The place was full of Post-it notes about special orders for tarts.

I knew their stuff tasted better, but I wanted to know why. The answer is that all the big bakeries use a process of industrialized baking called, after the lab where it was invented, the Chorleywood process. And there is, said Rachel, all the difference in the world between Chorleywood baking and the real thing. 'The Chorleywood process in particular speeds things up,' she said. 'In a big bread factory, they make a loaf in ninety minutes. They add huge amounts of yeast to cut fermentation from fourteen hours to forty minutes. It is cheap and quick, but it produces an air-filled, tasteless stodge. Good bread needs time. We leave ours to rise overnight, just as I do when I bake at home.' The extra time in particular allows the gluten – the key protein in the flour that reacts with the yeast to make bread rise – to do its work naturally.

So what about the ingredients? Well, mainly it is flour and yeast. Rachel's yeast came from Mauri, a global brand made on an industrial estate in Hull. So no mystique there. But the flour. That was the footprint I wanted to follow.

The Lighthouse Bakery used a couple of tonnes of flour a month. The flour for my regular stoneground wholemeal loaf was milled at Shipton Mill, in the Cotswolds in Gloucestershire. There's been a mill on a tributary of the River Avon at Shipton Moyne since the

Domesday Book more than 900 years ago. Back then it was part of the Estcourt estate, given to the Estcourt family from Normandy by William the Conqueror. The mill worked till 1910, then lay derelict at the end of an abandoned track in the woods until it was discovered by John Lister, an anthropologist from London who decided to change career and become a miller. He bought the place from the Norman conquerors – shortly before they sold the rest of the estate to a Saudi prince. Now the estate trains horses and the mill turns out 100 tonnes of grain a week.

The mill tour was like a rummage through a specialist car-boot sale. 'Nothing here cost more than a fiver,' said John, a lanky man who continues to convey a boyish enthusiasm for his new career. His grain elevators are made of 110-year-old pitch pine, liberated from a mill in the local port of Avonmouth. His floorboards are old packing cases from Avonmouth docks. And the rest of his kit mostly came second-hand from other mills. The centrifugal sieve that grades the flour is 1930s vintage. The millstones that allow John to sell 'stoneground' flour came, via an old Wiltshire mill, from a quarry in the Marne Valley in France's champagne country. The entire works fills the old watermill and a timber-framed barn that he moved piece by piece from a Herefordshire farm.

This is both a delightful and, as is evident from the huge grain trucks going up and down the lane by the hour, a roaring business. Milling wholemeal flour with stones is slow, but produces the flour best able to impart its taste when baked the proper way. Most of John's competitors go for high-speed pulverizing of the grains. This allows the flour to absorb moisture more quickly at the bakery, adding bulk and allowing quick and cheap processing. Taste? Who cares about that when you can have volume?

Making good flour also requires good wheat. John's small lab measures enzymes and moisture and starchiness, the gluten and nitrogen content, and much else. 'But looks and smell are the best guide,' he said. 'If it looks bright and smells fresh and grassy it will have good flavour. If it was harvested wet and has started to sprout, that is bad and it will have a fusty smell and make poor bread.' I had the idea that English wheat wasn't hard enough to make good bread. Not so, said both John and Rachel. The problem is persuading farmers and the people who supply their seeds to grow the right kind.

Plant breeders and farmers spend all their time trying to produce varieties that deliver high-volume and low-quality flour, he said. The industrial bakers reckon they can make up the missing ingredients through additives. But Rachel and Elizabeth need flour with plenty of gluten for an elastic dough which catches the gases given off by the fermentation, making a tastier loaf that can be made without the additives. The number of people willing to supply such grain is declining. Mother's shame.

Most of John's grain is grown within 60 kilometres of Shipton, by farmers he knows. Every few days, a truck pulls up from Prince Charles's organic estate close by at Highgrove. It contains an old and specialized wheat called Maris Widgeon. It is good for traditional baking, but John doesn't get enough to sell to commercial bakers like Lighthouse. Home bakers can buy it, though.

After beer, cheese and bread, I'll take a Scotch, please. To be precise, a glass of the peaty, and extremely smoky, single malt that comes from the Hebridean island of Islay. No taste in the world – not even fine French wine – is quite as tied to location as a good Scotch. My three favourites come from distilleries within 3 kilometres of each other, on the southern shore of the island, beneath the summit of Beinn Sholum. In reverse order they are: Ardbeg, Laphroaig and Lagavulin. This, I admit, is very personal. Lagavulin, pronounced Lagga-voolin, meaning the hollow where the mill is, sits beside the ruins of the 1,200-year-old Dunyveg Castle, once a stronghold of the Donald clan.

Why the special taste? Here we are into black arts again. The distillery points to the larch wood in its vessels, and the unusual onion-shaped stills with swan-necked pipes, which convey vapour from the distillation process. Others say it is the chemistry of the water, which absorbs peat as it cascades in a hundred waterfalls down the mountainside. Whatever the truth, change to the process would be disastrous.

The Lagavulin distillery has been in business for 190 years. It is now owned by United Distilleries, which is in turn part of Diageo, the world's biggest Scotch-whisky maker and one of the world's biggest drinks combines, also incorporating Gordon's gin and Guinness beer, Smirnoff vodka and that abomination called Baileys Cream. But they don't seem to have destroyed the product yet. And maybe they will leave well alone since the distinctive flavour forms part of best-selling company blends like White Horse and Bell's and Johnnie Walker. Though why you would want to blend this nectar with anything else is beyond me.

I like local. Not exclusively, but occasionally. Once during the preparation of this book we ate an entirely local meal. While on holiday in Chichester we sat down at our own table to Selsey crab landed just 10 kilometres away, accompanied by potatoes, lettuce and tomatoes bought in the town market three minutes' walk away and grown at a farm visible from the back garden. For dessert we ate charmingly named knobby russet apples, windfalls bought that day at the nearby West Dean estate, and cake made by someone from the local Women's Institute. In preparation for the feast, we had drunk a pint of Gale's, but this was before they shut the brewery.

I am not a 'food patriot', in David Cameron's helpful phrase. But I tried to keep a check through one year on where my fresh produce came from. And mostly, I noticed how farming had become big business, and buying local had rather lost its bucolic image. Lots of my salad tomatoes came from Wight Salads, which has half a square kilometre of greenhouses in the Arreton Valley on the Isle of Wight. The company grows about 200 million tomatoes a year. Many of my lettuces came from a company called Bedgro based at

Biggleswade in Bedfordshire, which cultivates 10 square kilometres of onions, Brussels sprouts, potatoes, marrows, pumpkins, parsnips, beetroot, tomatoes and courgettes – all stored in a 2,000-tonne freezer on the farm before delivery to supermarkets across the land.

And checking online one day to find out more about the growers of my strawberries, I discovered that S & A Produce, which calls itself 'the largest independent strawberry grower in Europe', had been engaged in a series of unedifying, summer-long battles. A decade ago, outside Wimbledon fortnight, most of our strawberries were trucked from Spain or air-freighted from California. Then British farmers discovered polytunnels, succeeded in lengthening their growing season and the fight-back began. Now we have British strawberries all summer. It may sound local, but much of the backbreaking work of picking them is done – judging from the languages used on S & A's website advertising for workers – by Poles, Russians and Lithuanians.

I say 'advertising' jobs. I was struck by the tone of the website's pages (www.sagroup.co.uk) for prospective workers. It began in large capitals: 'DO NOT TRAVEL TO S & A UNLESS YOU HAVE BEEN INVITED'. Most employees are recruited by agents in their home countries, it said. 'Strawberry picking is hard work: you will be expected to pick a set number of kilograms of berries each day ... the number will be displayed each day in the field where you are working ... We are unable to give you any assurance about the continuity of work, you will only be offered work when it is available, you will be employed as a casual worker ... work may start as early as 4.30am.'

Oh, and those who do make it to the farms in Hereford or Kent will find themselves living on a caravan site. So they must, the website said, bring sleeping bags, waterproofs and a torch. In case they are injured, they must bring insurance that will pay to get them home. You might say the pickers have been warned what to expect, but the Transport and General Workers' Union complained that many of the 3,500 seasonal workers at the S & A farms in 2006 were being made to work fourteen-hour days in the fields in searing heat, with breaks of only thirty minutes and no days off, in order to pick the 180 tonnes a day required by S & A at the height of the season. S & A denied the allegations, saying they were made by disgruntled workers who had subsequently been sacked. 'We don't work people that long and they all have breaks longer than half an hour.'

Strawberry picking has always been a backbreaking job in the sun. But once you could work as hard as you felt able. No more. In 2006, the company installed a new computerized tracking system to provide 'full traceability on each and every punnet as it moves from the field through processing to a retailer's shelf.' That meant full traceability for the workers as well. 'Live data', the press release from the computer company noted, allowed S & A to 'measure the performance of the pickers.' As each worker put their pickings on the field scales, the machine read their personal barcode, and the information flagged up in the company's data centre in Hereford.

All through the summer of 2006, there was strife on S & A's farms. The Transport and General Workers' Union, which helped organize it, claimed 'the largest agricultural demonstration in one hundred years'. *Socialist Worker* was on the case. Comparisons were made with the Tolpuddle Martyrs, farm labourers from Dorset whose travails with a landowner in the 1830s started the trades union movement in Britain.

A third of the strawberries on British supermarket shelves come from S & A farms, and through the long, hot summer the union set up pickets outside stores. At one point, Sainsbury's banned fruit from the company's Kent farm, after hearing of some workers ending up with the equivalent of £13 for a twelve-hour shift. As a consumer, it is hard to be certain who is right on the details in such disputes. And I make no claims about right and wrong. But it is clear that employee relations had gone badly wrong and my strawberries didn't taste quite so sweet. Thankfully, after the season was over, the T & G, the supermarkets and S & A brokered a deal for 'improved rights'.

S & A has also been in dispute with neighbours and local authorities in Hereford over its campsites. As the 2005 season opened, the county council applied to the high court to have proprietor John Davies locked up for contempt of court, for carrying out 'unauthorized work' on his farm in breach of a previous court injunction. Actually, it seems he was attempting to improve conditions for his workers by turning an old farm building into a 'village complex' with an internet café and a swimming pool (S & A's website advised workers to bring swimsuits). Later, Davies had an application to install another 300 caravans turned down, and the 2007 picking season opened with the Secretary of State for Communities and Local Government, Ruth Kelly, ordering the dismantling of a sewage works at the caravan site, which won't have been popular with his workers.

The English countryside is not what it was when I was a youngster in Kent, joining in with the strawberry harvest more or less when I wanted. Back then, there were no computer chips to monitor our work, but no trades unions or swimming pools either. Like most of us, I guess, I am caught between a romanticism about the countryside and local produce and a realization that the world has moved on – for good as well as ill.

Anyone for cream?

5

Wild Things: The Last Round-up on the High Seas and in the Hills

I love fish. More than meat, really. Kippers from a Whitby smokery, haddock from the North Sea, mackerel from Cornwall, Dover sole from Hastings, crabs from Selsey, oysters from Whitstable, salmon from Ireland and sardines from Spain. But the terrifying disappearance of marine stocks suggests that ours could be the last generation to enjoy this pleasure.

Everybody knows that the North Sea cod is on its last fins. Grimsby remains the world's biggest fresh-fish auction, but only 1 per cent of the sales are from domestic boats. As symbolic as anything was the closure in 2007 of the factory in nearby Hull where the food combine Unilever, masquerading as Captain Birds Eye, has been making cod fish fingers since I was a child. But this is a global crisis. Scientists say that most of the world's commercial fisheries will be gone by mid-century. Soon there will only be farmed fish.

Where should I go to see this crisis at first hand? I have been appalled at the squalor of Asian fish factories in Kisumu, the Kenyan port on the shores of Lake Victoria. And at seeing Filipinos using squeegee bottles full of cyanide to stun reef fish so they can be caught live and sold days later in the restaurants of Hong Kong. I have watched mussels being harvested from the lagoons of Venice and eaten Atlantic tuna in Tenerife; sat cross-legged to consume delicious smoked cod in Kyoto, and picked at unnamed fresh fish straight from the waters of the River Taz in Siberia, the Ganges in Bangladesh, the Amu Darya in Uzbekistan and an ice-hole near Yellowknife in Canada. But I remember most a journey to find out why Europeans like me can eat fresh fish from a strange desert state called Mauritania.

As the sun set over the Atlantic, Italie de Silva worked fast: gutting the sharks, rays and guitar fish, cutting off their fins and laying out the flesh to be salted by the incoming tide. It was a good catch, he said. Good for recent times, anyway. Two days at sea had yielded maybe 100 fish, worth £1,500. As he slit the bellies of the female sharks, I watched in amazement as foetuses spilled out. He threw them aside to be eaten by birds. He didn't seem too concerned. But those foetuses should have been next year's catch. The fishermen were, in effect, killing many fish for the meat and fins of just one.

This scene took place on a beach by the tiny village of Iwik in the Banc d'Arguin, a giant national park in the isolated West African state of Mauritania. The country is virtually all desert, but the park's coastal fringe contains one of the world's richest fishing grounds. For now. Because the fate of the shark foetuses sums up an escalating crisis here. A crisis for which hundreds of European trawlers that bring shark and squid, lobster and bream, hake and grouper, mullet and much else to the restaurant tables of Europe are responsible – hook, line and sinker.

Fish from the Banc d'Arguin feature regularly in British fish markets. You can dine out on Mauritania's finest natural resource in the restaurants of south London. But soon our plates will be empty. Already some species are gone. 'In the old days, we could see the mullet coming,' remembered Mohammed ould Swidi, Iwik's village chief. 'We just walked into the water with our nets to catch them.' But that was before the rest of the world got wise to the riches here.

The Banc d'Arguin is a large submerged sandbank extending from the Sahara out into the Atlantic. Cold waters well up from the ocean depths near here, bringing to the surface a rich reservoir of nutrients. As the nutrients flush across the Banc, they feed plankton and sea grass. These rich marine meadows are the prime breeding and nursery area for a fishery that stretches more than 2,000 kilometres along the West African coast from Morocco to Guinea-Bissau. But as fishing grows more intense, the fishermen are drawn ever closer to the source of this marine fecundity, the Banc itself. And that threatens the survival of the entire ecosystem.

Thirty years ago, European conservationists, led by the Swiss industrialist and co-founder of the World Wildlife Fund (WWF) Luc Hoffman, went to the Banc and persuaded the Mauritanian government to declare it a national park. The conservationists were mainly interested in the vast birdlife that feeds on the fish there. In winter, the Banc has the largest collection of wading birds in the world. But protecting the birds protected the fish too.

The only fishers allowed in the park's waters are the Imraguen, the poor black desert inhabitants alternately ostracized and enslaved by their Arab and Berber masters. And under the park's rules, they have to use traditional sailing boats. That system would have worked well to protect the fish, except for events outside the park. For on the fringes of the Banc, a fishing free-for-all has taken hold in recent years.

First, thousands of African fishermen, in motorized versions of their traditional boats called *pirogues*, started to make the journey north from Senegal, The Gambia and even further afield. They cruised the waters outside the park, taking rich pickings but leaving the nursery intact. Then came the European trawlers, sold licences by the Mauritanian government to fish the same waters on the edge of the park as the *pirogues*. It was after the trawlers came, say the Imraguen, that the mullet stocks collapsed. Since then, the octopus catch has halved, and sawfish have disappeared completely, along with hammerhead and tiger sharks.

Theoretically, the trawlers and *pirogues* can share the waters outside the park's boundary 12 kilometres off shore. But in practice, it is far too dangerous for the small *pirogues* to jostle with factory ships up to 140 metres long. Collisions are frequent, as are deaths. So *pirogue* captains head inshore, into the park, where rangers regularly impound their boats for illegal incursions.

While visiting a tiny fishing village on the site of an old Portuguese fort on Agadir island, I met Lamin, a nineteen-year-old poacher. He had no money, little food and the only bed he could call his own was 1,000 kilometres away at his mother's house in The Gambia. His boat had been impounded here for two weeks. His lodging, until the owner of the boat showed up to pay the fine, was a tiny asbestos-roofed hut on the beach, which he shared with twenty other captured poachers.

Lamin told me that he and his fellow crewmen – two Senegalese and a Mauritanian – went to sea for a week at a time in the open 8-metre boat. Its owner paid them about £40 per trip. 'I need the money for my mother, who is ill,' he said. Dozens of *pirogue* like his lay their nets in the park at night when the patrol boats have little chance of catching them, and scarper before dawn. He got caught because his navigation went wrong.

As the world's other great fish stocks are decimated, more and more fishermen like Lamin come to the Banc, and more and more people come to rely on their catches. Farmers from the arid lands of the Sahel are turning to fishing to provide protein for their families. Hann beach on the edge of the Senegalese capital Dakar has seen a huge boom in recent years. Bira Gueye told me that when he first came, in the late 1960s, 'there were just five boats here'. It was hard to believe as we walked down the beach past the Yamaha outboard-motor showroom and the large freezer warehouses. There are now more than 1,000 boats regularly pulled up on the sand.

But here too, the fish are disappearing. We watched several crews head out to sea. In the old days, said Bira, he could sail for twenty minutes and fill his nets. 'We were so close as we drew nets that we could see people having lunch on the beach. Now it takes four hours and three hundred litres of petrol just to get to the fish.' Many crews go out for a fortnight at a time. They take ice boxes with them to stop the fish rotting before they get them to shore. Most of them go to the Banc.

On shore, they sell to traders on the beach. I met Victoria from Ghana, who buys from beach traders and regularly ships home 12-metre containers full of salted shark meat. She makes enough, she told me, to have one child training to be an airline pilot and another at an American university. Her grandson was beside her, learning the trade. But she wondered if there would be any fish left by the time he was grown up. Also meeting the boats as they came ashore was Dimas Santos, a Portuguese fish exporter. He bought fish such as grouper, bream and hake from the *pirogues* for sale at high prices to European restaurants. As we toured his packing plant, he told me he used to buy 30 tonnes of fish a day from local fishermen, but now it was down to 10 tonnes. 'There just aren't the fish in the sea any more,' he said. 'We are paying the price for years of over-fishing.'

The *pirogues* are routinely blamed for the collapse of the Banc fisheries, mainly because it is only their activities that fall foul of the law. But here it is the law that is at fault. For the *pirogues*, though huge in number, take only about a twentieth as much fish as the trawlers out on the horizon.

The European Union has for a decade now bought the rights to take most of the fish from these waters. In 2006, it signed a new deal with Mauritania worth 86 million euros a year, allowing access for 200 boats to catch some 50,000 tonnes. The EU's fisheries policy states that all fishing by European trawlers should be 'sustainable'. But that brings a hollow laugh on the beaches, as well as from industry observers. 'Foreign trawlers are strip-mining African waters. It is a scandal,' says Callum Roberts, a marine biologist from York University. 'They are wrecking the future of African fisheries.'

The trawlers mostly unload either in the Canary Islands or back in Europe, so the nearest I got to them was watching forty slow-moving white blobs on the radar screen at the Mauritanian navy's coastal tracking station; each blob was a trawler from Spain or the Netherlands, China or Portugal. 'It's like a town out there,' said Antonio Araujo, the Portuguese park manager. 'They are taking everything,' he said.

It is not just Mauritania. Foreign trawlers take almost as many fish from neighbouring Senegalese waters. According to a report from the UN Environment Programme, the catch has had 'a serious impact on local food supplies'. But the West African governments feel powerless. Fish make up two-thirds of Senegal's export revenues. 'These countries have large debts. They cannot refuse the EU,' said Pierre Campredon, a French marine biologist and long-time adviser to the Mauritanian government.

What should be done? WWF, which is one of the sponsors of the park, says the trawlers should retreat and be replaced by a small, élite trade of line-fishing boats, selling to high-price traders like Dimas, and by high-rolling tourists. Such a strategy might mean the Mauritanian government could continue to harvest cash from its waters, and it might be environmentally sustainable. But why should the upmarket sellers to European restaurants have priority over the crews of the *pirogues*? Surely, they have first rights to the fish. The way the locals see it, Europeans have taken over their waters. One group keeps them out of the park to protect the birds; the other group keeps them out of the ocean so the fish can fill bellies in Europe.

I never met the European trawlermen. But I did meet the 'conservationists'. On my last night in the park, a group of over-weight European businessmen turned up. They had come to watch birds. It was their perk for helping fund the park. But they seemed like a hunting party from another age, lounging in luxury tents erected by local labourers. They had no interest at all in the people living in or dependent on the park. They just came to see birds. I don't like that kind of environmentalism.

Meanwhile, as the fish disappear, the *pirogue* owners have stumbled on a new business. Smuggling destitute Africans, many of them fishermen no longer able to make a living, to the Canary Islands which, as part of Spain, give them access to the European Union. The bigger boats can cram 100 people in. If the tides are wrong, the boats deliver emaciated and sometimes dead would-be migrants on to the beaches of Tenerife and Fuerteventura. But the number of people coming to the beaches and willing to pay for a ride into the unknown continues to grow. Granting their wish, the boat owners say, is more lucrative now than fishing. If Europe wants the fish, some might say, it has a duty to take the impoverished migrants too.

We still hunt for fish. But otherwise, there are not so many foods that we gather from nature. Outside hunting estates, the chase is a distant memory. Our meat is domesticated – and frequently industrialized. But we do still consume food from the wild. I was surprised to discover that one wild delicacy in many kitchens is oregano, my favourite herb. I have a small jar of oregano in the kitchen, and when I am cooking I add it more often than any other herb. A lot of the world agrees with me. Its slightly bitter, vaguely minty flavour is the signature of Italian pizzas and pasta dishes. The word oregano comes from the Greek *oros ganos*, or joy of the mountain, and most of it still comes direct from a mountainside.

There are lots of local varieties of oregano growing wild round the Mediterranean. In Waitrose you can buy fresh oregano from Israel (and sometimes next to it are packs labelled from the West Bank, though it turns out that it is the same stuff labelled for customers of different political persuasions). But most is from Turkey, which exports about 7,000 tonnes of dried oregano leaves a year – a figure that has doubled in less than a decade. Someone worked out that was enough for 7 billion slices of pizza, so everyone on the planet could get a piece.

Every Turkish hillside is said to produce oregano with a different taste, but the best is hand-cut by peasants with serrated knives in the spectacular limestone hills of the Sütçüler district in Isparta in the west of the country. Each summer, whole villages leave their homes to scour the gorges and hilltops, taking branches of the dwarf shrub back to their villages, where they dry the leaves and pack them for sale to international buyers. For a few weeks, the world comes to Sütçüler.

In theory, oregano should be easy enough to cultivate in fields, but it is not done much because the resulting plants are inferior. There are different stories about whether all the harvesting is endangering the plant in the wild. Stefano Padulosi of Bioversity International (formerly the International Plant Genetic Resources Institute) in Rome, an oracle on obscure food crops, says: 'Some of the varieties are disappearing before we know much about them. One indigenous variety in Crete has almost gone.' He fears for the Turkish varieties, too. But interestingly, in the Sütçüler district, villages like Candir, Sarmemetler, Gumu and Buydilli have responded to the soaring popularity of their ancient herb by establishing their own cooperatives, with strict conservation rules. So perhaps there is hope.

The Mediterranean harbours many wild herbs. In Spain, some 80 million thyme plants are uprooted every year for their leaves and oils. Wild chicory is picked in the Lebanon, and wild capers in Syria. Until the recent explosion of interest encouraged cultivation, the salad vegetable rocket was little more than a southern Italian weed with a half-forgotten culinary pedigree.

This set me thinking about what else I eat that comes direct from the wild. With the exception of fish, the options are limited. I have eaten wild rabbits and pheasant occasionally, and supposedly wild boar. I once nibbled at whale and seal meat on canapés in northern Norway, and caribou in Alaska and turned down wild rat at a roadside chop-house in Ghana. I am told you can buy shrinkwrapped wild elephant meat in some African supermarkets. (Probably the biggest market is in Chinese medicinal food, and I will come back to that in a later chapter. The Chinese eat everything.)

I have never personally hunted. But I have frequently gathered blackberries from the hedgerows of England, and also sloes – the fruit of the blackthorn tree. Our household uses sloes to flavour gin, which I thoroughly recommend. I have picked dandelion leaves for a salad. Once, in the northern Siberian town of Krasnoselkup, I had a whole meal of wild mushrooms and berries. And in bars in El Paso I have drunk a spirit, rather like tequila, made from a wild cactus picked over the border in the Chihuahua desert.

On a visit to Turkey a few years ago, I bought a packet of salep, a flour made from the boiled tubers of a local orchid. When heated with milk, the flour made a good evening drink, a bit like Ovaltine. Salep was popular in England before tea and coffee. The word is Arabic for fox's testicles – a description of the shape of the tuber, apparently. I discovered only after bringing the packet home that the orchid is mostly harvested from the wild and is now highly endangered. A kilogram of flour requires 1,000 orchids, so my small brown box bought at a supermarket in Istanbul had uprooted at least 200 of them. I then found that the export of salep from Turkey is banned. Probably I could have been clapped in a Turkish jail for smuggling it out. I kept thinking of the film *Midnight Express* whenever I looked at the packet, and eventually threw it out.

The sage in my kitchen might be harvested from the wild. The jar just says it is a product of Turkey. But herb-world insiders like Al Goetze, who buys for the American company McCormick, say 'Turkish' sage is not usually Turkish at all. It is picked from the wild in the mountains around Albanian towns like Tepelene, Berat and Shkoder, and shipped out via Montenegro and Istanbul. According to Goetze, 'Albanian is the best sage in the world.' Sage harvesting and export, he says, was about the only part of the trading economy that worked under the bizarre Communist regime of Enver Hoxha, in the days when Albania was a Cold War equivalent of North Korea today – so isolated it made enemies even of its ideological friends.

Albania continues to export half of all the world's dried sage and medicinal sage oils. But now the 2,500-tonne business is in private hands, allowing people like Mehmet Guga from Tepelene, who spent half a lifetime running the business for Hoxha, to grow rich in their old age. Almost all the sage is harvested from the wild, by hand using a sickle. The leaves are dried in the sun in the villages, rather like Turkish oregano. Certainly, when I stuff a free-range chicken with sage and onion, the stuffing is much wilder than the chicken.

Most herbs and spices have long since moved from wild harvesting to cultivation. But the hint of the exotic often lingers. The forested slopes of the Moluccas 'spice islands', between the Philippines and New Guinea, were once the only home of the trees on which cloves and nutmeg grow. These spices have always been in huge demand in Europe. Cloves cure bad breath, and nutmeg preserved meat in the days before refrigeration. The casing surrounding the nutmeg seed provides mace.

When the Portuguese explorer Ferdinand Magellan embarked on the first round-the-world cruise in the 1520s, the bill was paid by trading Moluccan cloves. And, after the Dutch captured the islands, their spices were worth more than gold on the wharfs of Amsterdam. The Dutch prospered for centuries on their monopoly over these spices, till a French diplomat stole samples and established plantations in the Indian Ocean. The descendants of the pilfered cloves eventually turned Zanzibar into the world's largest producer of cloves, a position the small island holds to this day. If you are ever there, I recommend buying the clove massage oil, too.

Similar stories are told about the taming of cinnamon (from Sri Lanka), ginger (from southern China) and cardamom (from India), though the crocus that produces saffron, which was once the most expensive of all spices, is a sterile mutant unknown in the wild.

I enjoy all these herbs and spices. But most of all I love vanilla. When everyone else is buying exotic-flavoured ice creams, I often stick to its familiar and subtle taste. Vanilla is a bean from Latin America that grows in long pods on a climbing orchid. But today, two-thirds of the world's crop is cultivated on small mountain farms beneath the rainforest canopies of Madagascar and the nearby Indian Ocean islands of Réunion and Comoros. There it is called Bourbon Vanilla after the French kings who transplanted the orchid 200 years ago. Cultivating the bean in Africa is not easy. In its American heartlands, vanilla is pollinated by a small bee. But without the bee, African farmers tour their fields each morning looking for newly opened flowers, which they must pollinate by hand that day, before the flower wilts and drops off.

After picking, the ripened pods are boiled, and cured by alternately leaving them to sweat in wooden boxes and exposing them to the sun – a laborious process that lasts for several months. The end result, as Goetze puts it, is 'a rich, dark brown, moist and pliable bean that is loaded with aroma and flavour.' Then villagers sell the pods to agents of the world's biggest vanilla trader, AGK, who take the beans to the coast for export round the world.

Vanilla has gone from boom to bust in recent years. Cyclones in the Indian Ocean destroyed much of the crop early this decade. Prices soared; farmers replanted to cash in. Uganda and Kerala, the spices capital of India, tried to join in the bonanza. But when the new crops matured in 2005, there was a glut. Production far exceeded the world demand for 1,000 tonnes a year. Prices crashed again, and a year on, in late 2006, they were still only at 5 per cent of their 2003 level. The crash has been a disaster in particular for Comoros, where vanilla is the main employer and export crop.

Many herbs, spices and natural medicines have a long history. But some have risen from total obscurity to become global brands only in recent years. One of my favourite stories is the rise of tea tree oil, a natural antiseptic frequently used in our house. Until the 1970s, the tea tree was known only to a handful of traditional bush pharmacists in the Australian outback. Then a young Australian hippie called Christopher Dean got a nasty infection under his toenail while travelling in Africa. It would not heal until, in despair after he got home, he tried a bush 'healing oil' made from the leaves of the tea tree. It worked. Within minutes.

The tea tree had become rare as the bush of northern New South Wales fell under cultivation. And most trees produced only poor-quality oil. So Chris and his friends began a search for surviving stands that could produce quality oil. They hit pay-dirt with a single grove in the remote Bungawalbyn basin. Many old hippies have turned into astute capitalists (from Steve Jobs to Ben and Jerry). And soon a motley, long-haired crew had set up camp to distil the oil. Local authorities repeatedly tried to evict them as undesirables, but they eventually established a small plantation and began selling the oil. Old hippies bought it first. Gradually, word spread about its ability to cure everything from pimples to stings and burns to vaginal infections. Today tens of millions of trees have been planted to meet soaring demand, reversing a 200-year decline for the 'healing tree'. Take it from an old hippie: it works.

I have a no doubt romantic liking for things from the wild. But we have to be realistic. Where demand for products is high, the chances are that the resource, whether animal or vegetable, will be hunted to extinction. In general we have to accept that domestication is essential to feed a world of approaching 7 billion people. And especially if we want some nature to survive. But what Jack London described as 'the call of the wild' is in us all. And sometimes, even if it is just going blackberrying on a sun-soaked autumn afternoon, I hope we can still respond to it.

6

Curried Crustaceans: The Weird World of Mr Prawn

The curry houses of Britain are coy. I have often wondered where the prawns in my Saturday-night curry come from, but I have never got a straight answer. While supermarkets are keen on 'traceability', and refuse to sell prawns if they don't know where they are grown and how, curry houses don't go beyond the rhetoric of their own menus. I have always assumed that, because most British 'Indian' restaurants are run by Bangladeshis, Bangladesh is where their warm-water king prawns come from. My hunch proved right.

And there is, it turns out, a clear leader in the business. His name is Iqbal Ahmed, or 'Mr Prawn' as he is known in the trade, after one of his brands. He is a big fish in the British Bangladeshi community, and a hero among restaurant owners. I went to see him at his headquarters in Droylsden, right by Manchester City football stadium. In the boardroom, surrounded by photographs of him shaking hands with royals and political leaders, and collecting his Order of the British Empire from Prince Charles, he fed me plates of breaded prawns and the story of his success.

Iqbal is the son of Bangladeshi parents who fell on hard times and moved to Britain. 'Our family were landlords, but we lost our land,' he said. In Britain, his father ran a small grocery shop in nearby Oldham, 'open all hours'. Iqbal has restored family fortunes by creating a £200-million prawn business, called Seamark, which has two processing plants, one in Chittagong, the main port in Bangladesh, and the other in Manchester. His big coup came in the 1980s, when he introduced Britain to black tiger prawns, usually known here as king prawns. They spread fast, making him today one of the twenty richest Britons of Asian origin.

Mr Prawn is now diversifying. His cash-and-carry operation sells vegetables, meat and anything else a curry house could want. The day I visited there was a container of frozen chicken from Brazil sitting outside. But prawns remain the main business. He shifts a million of the beasts a day. Half of all the king prawns sold in British restaurants – Chinese and Thai as well as Indian – are bought from Seamark. Exports are now 70 per cent of sales, making Manchester – home of the chip butty – the unlikely prawn capital of Europe.

As I worked through a second plate of prawns, their proud purveyor told me that my Saturday-night curry most likely came from Chittagong in freezer containers through the Suez Canal to Felixstowe or Southampton docks, before taking a truck to Manchester. But when we got down to the nitty gritty of how the raw prawns got to his processing plant in Chittagong, Mr Prawn told me that he buys from brokers and never goes near the farming end of things. So I figured I would have go to and find out for myself.

On my journey across Bangladesh, I found the prawns that go into my curry, the farmers who grow them, and the men who supply them to the world market. It is a major business. It ships out 50,000 tonnes of prawns a year, mostly to Britain and the US, and is the country's second biggest export earner. But its ecological footprint is huge. In pursuit of prawn pounds and dollars and euros, landowners have flooded some 2,000 square kilometres of the delta lands in the south of the country. And, far from spreading wealth, the trade is miring millions in misery, poverty and corruption. I stumbled on mafia bosses and their 'musclemen', and cycles of debt and dependency that made me wonder whether I should boycott my Saturday tandoori.

I went to south-western Bangladesh, which has 80 per cent of the country's prawn farms, including most of those growing black tiger prawns. I headed for Khulna, a city of 2 million people, but with virtually no cars, only a few motorbikes and tens of thousands of cycle rickshaws. It must be one of the few cities of its size where human muscle-power has yet to be replaced by fossil-fuel energy in transportation. What wealth there was on display was under the control of the new prawn oligarchs. Apart from flop houses, there were only three hotels in town – all owned by the princes of prawn.

Prawn farms stretch from Khulna to the Bay of Bengal. In the past three decades, they have largely replaced the old landscape of mangrove swamps interspersed with small farms. The swamps once protected large amounts of wildlife, including the famous Bengal tiger, and acted as a nursery for fisheries. Now the tigers are giving way to tiger prawns, which are not the same thing at all.

As the landscape has been transformed, a whole social system has disappeared, explained Ashraf-ul-Alam Tutu, head of the Khulna-based non-governmental organization (NGO) the Coastal Development Partnership, when we met in his offices round the corner from one of the prawn hotels. Once there were rice paddies and mangroves, with creeks full of fish, ducks in the yard, and cattle and birdlife and grazing pastures – much of it on commonly owned land available to the poorest as well as the richest. Now there is only private land and prawn ponds. The pastures are gone and the rivers are almost empty of fish.

Outside Khulna is a small administrative district called Dumuria. There are more than 500 prawn farms here. I went to see Amal (not his real name), a strapping Bengali of about thirty whose father grew rice here and had chickens and a couple of cows. But now prawns are the only business. It was the start of the tiger-prawn season, and Amal was throwing nets into his pond. I recognized the crustacean instantly from many a tandoori. He carefully picked it out of the net and threw it back to grow a little more.

Amal and his wife, a feisty woman whom he insisted was his 'business partner' too, looked like a model for hard-pressed but determined business activity. Independent producers using local resources to create a product destined for a global market. Heroes, you might have said, of grassroots globalization. But it wasn't quite like that.

Amal's farming methods, like most out here on the delta, were simple. The only fertilizer for the ponds was dung from his two cows. Farming was organic by default. His half-hectare pond produced just over 100 kilograms of prawns in a year. This sounded a pitiful quantity, only a tenth of typical yields in rival exporting countries like Thailand. But I learned later that it was actually slightly above the average for the Dumuria area. Amal said it brought him an annual profit of 33,000 taka, or £250.

The scene was poor but tranquil, deceptively so. After we had been talking a while, Amal mentioned that he had problems with a big local landowner. About ten 'musclemen' worked for the owner of the ponds between Amal and the river. They were threatening to stop the water reaching Amal's pond unless he paid a hefty bribe. I tried to track down the culprit. Close by was a giant pond covering 30 hectares. It was wider than the river that supplied it with water. As soon as we arrived there, we were besieged by a gang of workers. They told me the name of the owner. 'He is a big political leader and a big muscleman,' someone said. The pond was surrounded by huts where his workers lived, keeping watch on the pond day and night in case of prawn thieves, they said. Was their boss the man threatening Amal? Could I meet him? There seemed to be a wall of silence, and I was left to guess about that. 'He doesn't live here,' is all they said.

Amal was lucky still to have his land. Millions of rice farmers have been bundled off theirs, often illegally, by big landowners anxious to maximize their prawn profits. A quiet terror has spread across the delta, with musclemen responsible for dozens of murders and rapes and hundreds of injuries. The killings are well documented. But the local police, who are clearly often in cahoots with the gangs and their bosses, rarely act.

On local advice, I did not always admit to being a journalist. Round here investigative reporting is a dangerous profession. Seven months before my visit, a local reporter for a national paper was beaten up by thugs and then arrested, tortured and held overnight by the Dumuria police, apparently for writing about land-grabs. But he got off lightly. During the previous decade, fourteen local newsmen had been murdered in the area, including successive presidents of the Khulna Press Club. The NGO Transparency International calls Bangladesh the second most corrupt nation on Earth. I began to see why.

That evening, I met a group of landless women, a small delegation from the 5,000 or so landless people living round Dumuria alone. They had waited for hours to see me. One by one they stood up to tell their stories as we sat in the dark, with mosquitoes from the ponds besieging us. One woman told me simply, 'We are poor. We have no shelter and no proper work. The musclemen have taken our land.' They said the government had a policy of settling homeless people on unused state-owned land. But corruption was rife, and usually the big landowners grabbed what was going.

Until recently, many of these women earned money by collecting prawn fry from the rivers. Fry are the basic raw material for any prawn pond. In the early days of the industry, there were enough in the rivers to seed the ponds naturally. But as the mangroves declined, so did the supply of natural fry, and a huge informal industry developed to collect them. Up to half a million of the country's poorest people in the remote delta regions spent their days up to their waists in water, netting fry from tidal creeks and rivers.

Inevitably, most of what they caught was the fry of other species, including fish. Most were simply dumped on the bank. Now the fish are disappearing too and the government has banned the harvesting of fry. Instead, farmers must buy from new commercial hatcheries owned by the industry's big players. The hatcheries turn out billions of fry a year and air-freight them across the country. This is clearly an environmental improvement. But few outsiders seem to have thought about the social impact of the ban. Hundreds of thousands of collectors have lost their livelihoods. There are, so far as I could gather, no statistics on what is happening to them. And few efforts to help them. Hence the women in front of me in the Dumuria night.

The new commercial fry hatcheries are mainly in the south-east of the country, adjacent to the coastal waters, where the brood stock – the 'mother prawns' – are trawled from the open ocean. One mother prawn can provide millions of fry. But already the mother prawns are disappearing.

The impression I gained was of a delta ecosystem in meltdown, thanks to prawns. And yet the economic gains for all this destruction seemed so tiny. Amal's prawns might end up on my plate in London at almost £10 a portion. But his profits from that were a few pence. Why? Somewhere between south London and Dumuria most of my money disappeared. So I began to follow the trail of his prawns to find out where.

Amal packed his black tiger prawns in ice and sold them at the door to middlemen. The middlemen provided him with credit to buy his fry and maintain his business, so he had little choice, he said. Anyway, if he tried to bypass them, the musclemen would be round. The middlemen in turn sold Amal's prawns to gentlemen at a depot a couple of kilometres away in the centre of Dumuria. When I dropped by the depot, the main activity seemed to be collecting the boxes brought in by the middlemen, adding more ice and then selling them on to a new set of middlemen, equipped with vans to take the prawns 10 kilometres to the wholesale market in Khulna.

So, back to Khulna. The wholesale market there was a long line of workshops down a street close to the ferry port. I watched one worker sorting a large pile of prawns by size, and putting them into different boxes. That, he said, was all they did. Oh, and add more ice. His boss said this one workshop dispatched about 300 tonnes of prawns a year to one of the city's numerous processing plants. He had a mark-up of about £100,000. There were about 300 registered wholesalers here, with a throughput of about 300,000 tonnes of prawns. I began to see why Amal made so little income.

Huddled close to the wholesale market were the processing plants. I visited three. They were spick and span, all stainless steel and tiled walls, refrigeration and running water. Lines of uniformed workers removed the heads and shells, sometimes cooked and always froze and packed the prawns ready for dispatch. In general, the hygiene rules seemed to be observed, though in one plant there was a brief panic when I lifted my camera in a packing area where none of the young women workers were wearing the required plastic gloves.

The biggest processor in Khulna was M. M. A. Salam, the moustached owner of two large plants and vice-chairman of the Bangladesh Frozen Food Exporters Association. His main brand was Castle Salam – also the name of his hotel. Iqbal in Manchester is his biggest customer. 'He came here for our opening ceremony in 2001. We sell up to thirty containers a year to Seamark.' That is more than 300 tonnes. With his own large processing plant in Chittagong and as a big buyer of prawns in Khulna, Iqbal seemed as big an exporter in Bangladesh as he was a seller in Manchester.

After visiting some traders selling prawn fry, I thought that at last I had seen the full extent of a ludicrously over-elaborate supply chain, with far too many hands taking a share of my curry-house bill. I counted six sets of middlemen taking their cut. There were fry wholesalers and fry retailers; the guys who purchased prawns from the farmers; those who traded at the local depots; and those who sold to the Khulna wholesalers and the processors. But I felt there was a missing link. Then I met Dadu, who explained it all.

Dadu lived in a grand house in the centre of Khulna. He was one of the pioneers of the prawn business here, a well-travelled man and a proud 'freedom fighter'. As a military mariner, he said he had sent sailors on suicide missions to destroy Pakistani ships during Bangladesh's war for independence thirty-six years before. He clearly despaired about where his industry, indeed his country, had ended up. As his servant brought tea, he mentioned that I had missed a link in the chain, and it was the most important link. It turned out that, even on the 100-metre journey between the warehouses and the doors of the processors, more middlemen intervened. Dadu called them 'the unseen', the moneylenders. 'They operate behind the scenes at the Khulna warehouses. They are the real problem in this industry,' he said.

In the absence of an efficient banking system in Bangladesh, 'the unseen' effectively run the entire industry. They control the flow of prawns to the processors. And they provide the loans that trickle, at extortionate interest rates, all the way down the line to the farmers. The cash allows business to be transacted before Iqbal and the other processors and purchasers in Europe and North America pay up. Without them, Iqbal would have no prawns, and nor would my local curry house. Nobody would introduce me to 'the unseen'. And I found no academic who had ever done a study of their activities. They were just that: unseen.

Back in Manchester, I wondered again why Iqbal would not use the market power of his company, Seamark, to cut out the middlemen, raise standards and improve the lot of farmers like Amal. He had an interest in doing so, I thought. Bangladeshi prawns still have a poor reputation for quality and reliability. Western retailers say they pay 10 per cent less for them than for others. It is self-evident that in Bangladesh this is a business mired in inefficiency, exploitation and corruption.

Iqbal agreed about that. He had told me before my visit: 'Things have not been done properly. There are few auctions and I can't deal with a thousand farmers all delivering a kilo of prawns in baskets. So I have to deal with the middlemen. I'd like to see a proper auction house in Khulna, but the local processors don't agree. They think I just want to buy everything.'

What was needed, surely, was some kind of certification scheme, where prawns with a clear supply chain, ethical standards of production and good quality could command higher prices. The 'sustainable shrimp' in other words. And the Aquaculture Certification Council, a US-based organization, had tried to set up just such a system in Bangladesh, with the backing of NGOs and aid agencies. It failed, according to Bill More of the Council, for want of interest among prawn processors. 'Seamark, one of the largest exporters, has not shown any interest,' More told me. 'It could have made all the difference.' Tutu, the social reformer in Khulna, was of a similar mind. 'We want to use efforts by the corporate sector to set up a certification system to introduce rules about social responsibility. But it is hard to get the processors interested.'

When I raised this with Iqbal, he was unapologetic. He knew about the certification schemes being mooted, but wanted nothing to do with them. They were, he told me, designed to extract money from him. 'I'd have to pay for certification, but what would I get in return?' Then he launched an attack on the NGOs, whom he accused of trying to shut down the industry. 'If the shrimp industry gets closed down, the entrepreneurs will be OK, they will go and do something else with their money. But the farmers will die of starvation if that happens,' he said. 'You'll punish them.' Ouch. Why that sudden switch from 'they' to 'you'? I had the feeling his growing hostility to my line of questioning was now addressed at me.

I took his point that boycotts can be dangerous things, and that Bangladesh is a far from easy place to do business. Things will always be messy. However, there did seem to be an inconsistency between what he was saying to me and his presence just a couple of weeks before on the British government's 'champions' group' of industrialists. Set up to promote 'sustainable sourcing' in the food industry, its declared aim was to double the amount of food goods in supermarkets covered by ethical trading schemes. But in his own industry, Iqbal seemed, at best, indifferent to the scheme on offer.

So should I carry on buying Bangladeshi prawns? In Khulna, Tutu said he had campaigned to keep out the prawn barons when they first came. But he now accepted they were there to stay. So he was working to improve conditions for the 4 million small prawn farmers and landless workers in the industry. 'We want to improve the industry, not destroy it.'

But in Dhaka, on my way home, I dropped in on Bangladesh's most outspoken campaigner for the poor: Khushi Kabir from an NGO called Nijera Kori. 'I'm against the industry. Period,' she said. 'If I could, I would shut it down.' She doesn't buy the reformist argument. 'Sustainable shrimps are a myth. I'm not against all prawn farming; it was part of the old ways. But then they were a luxury for local consumption. Mass production for export is disastrous. It is the scale that is the problem, and the damage it has done to the indigenous, centuries-old farming system. It was a system of survival, but it has been destroyed. We need to bring it back. The poor farmers need to take the land back and return it to paddy and mangroves.' That would provide more jobs, more security – and fewer musclemen.

So I had found the alternative solution. I could see why Iqbal would have no interest in encouraging it. But after seeing the state of the industry that is supplying his customers, and me, it was hard not to agree with her. I've stopped eating prawns from Bangladesh.

One in a Billion:
Agnes, the AIDS Granny

Agnes held her two-year-old granddaughter close. The child was crying. She seems disconnected and permanently unhappy, Agnes said. The child was HIV-positive, and without drugs she was likely to die soon. This was South Africa, where drugs against the AIDS virus are still not getting through to millions who need them. So the chances of Agnes getting her hands on any were small, she admitted with a shrug as we sat in her two-room house in Mamelodi, a predominantly black township on the outskirts of Pretoria. The baby girl was called Keletso. She was almost certainly infected at the moment of her birth. Isabel – Keletso's mother and Agnes's daughter – had died recently at the age of twenty-seven. Agnes, who was fifty-nine, had nursed Isabel in her final weeks. And now she attended to Keletso.

Around 5 million South Africans are HIV-positive. In the urban heartlands and among workers in the gold mines, more than a quarter of all adults under fifty carry the virus. The funerals of young parents in the prime of their lives are becoming ever more frequent. The country has more than a million AIDS orphans already. This is a calamity for the families caught up in it. It is also creating a frightening demographic change. In the traditional demographic 'pyramid', the number of citizens in each age band declines with age. But here the pyramid is being turned into an hour-glass, with the young adults ripped out of the population. And increasingly it is the elderly who become the care-takers and the heads of households, particularly grandmothers like Agnes. In places like Mamelodi, where there are a million people and next to no state social services, it is the elderly women who can be seen minding the children, going shopping and cleaning the yard.

I was visiting the township with HelpAge International, which has offices in Johannesburg. The organization was set up to help the elderly and infirm through their final years. But it finds that it is now sustaining them as they take on new responsibilities as the heads of large, often traumatized, households of young AIDS orphans. In many cases, orphans like Keletso are themselves infected. Doctors estimate that there are more than a million HIV-infected young children across South Africa. Up to a fifth of new HIV patients are babies. A third of babies born to HIV-positive mothers pick up the virus in the womb or during childbirth.

Hanging on to Agnes's legs as she nursed Keletso were the twin baby sons of her other daughter, Adolphine. Adolphine was a distressed, distracted woman of twenty who came and went through the house as we discussed the family, but seemed unwilling to talk herself. Was she sick, too? I asked when she was out of the room. Perhaps, Agnes said.

And where were the men? 'They went long ago, I don't know where,' Agnes said of her own lovers as well as those of her daughters. Many men in South Africa have given up all pretence of being heads of households. No father turned up to provide for Keletso when Isabel died. As far as Agnes was aware, no man ever knew he was the father of Keletso. In any event, HIV being what it is, the father was likely to be dead too. Nor was there a man to provide for Adolphine and her sons. 'They father the children and then go,' said Agnes.

The elders have always been the pillars of African societies. In the past, while many children died young, those who made it to adulthood could expect a long life. But AIDS has given this phenomenon a new twist. The old of today largely escaped the AIDS epidemic. Their peak of sexual activity came before the virus was widespread. So, as the young adults die in ever-increasing numbers across Africa, the elderly find that they make up a fast-growing proportion of the adult population.

While nobody has precise statistics, it is clear that tens of thousands of grandmothers across South Africa, and probably millions across Africa, have been left holding the babies, after the trauma of seeing their own children cut down by the virus. They are the hidden victims – and heroes – of the continent's AIDS disaster, and more or less the only glue left holding together many fractured households and communities.

Veronica Khosa is trying to deal with this crisis daily. She retired from a nursing job in Mamelodi to speak out about AIDS and provide help for those caring for AIDS patients at home. 'People were dying in locked houses with nobody touching them,' she told me. 'Many people wanted them killed or put into camps. Even in hospitals, the nurses wouldn't go near. Black HIV patients in particular were turned away by the hospitals. But the families were not equipped to care, and did not know how to do so safely.'

The caretakers, including many aging parents and grandparents, were at grave risk of contracting the disease themselves. They still are. 'I know of grandmothers who eventually died HIV-positive after nursing infected babies,' said Veronica. 'I am sure that nursing their own grandchildren was the route of infection.' Many carers, she discovered, remove mucus from the nasal passages of children dying of AIDS by sucking it out. It is a traditional practice, and might have been fine for babies with a cold. But not for those with a lethal disease spread through bodily fluids.

Pauline, aged eighty-seven, was another of Veronica's clients. She lost three of her children to AIDS. Then, after losing her own brood, she took on the task of bringing up three young grandchildren. All three sat obediently on the sofa to talk to me. Nine-year-old Jabulane said, 'We love Grandma because she is so patient telling us right from wrong. I'd love to play football with her, but she says she can't.' He seemed amazed that there were limits to her skill and stamina. Pauline said, 'If the parents leave the children, you just carry on with it. You have no choice.'

In Elim, a remote township north of Pretoria on the road to Zimbabwe, I met seventy-two-year-old Georgina. At night, she was attending to a bedridden ninety-seven-year-old neighbour. By day, she looked after the children of her son, whose wife had left him after discovering he was HIV-positive. 'She told him to take the children back to his mother. So he brought them to me. He is here, too, but he has no work and he suffers from TB because of the AIDS.' So she looked after him as well.

Undefeated, she insisted, 'I want to put the children into university, so they can get a job.' Another child appeared as we talked. 'This is my adopted daughter,' Georgina announced with pride. Not legally, of course. But she had lived with Georgina ever since her mother 'disappeared' – a frequent euphemism in South Africa for dying of AIDS. So Georgina took over again.

A couple of streets away, sixty-three-year-old Molly was looking after two of her own adult children, one of whom was clearly mentally ill, as well as her wraith-like seventy-two-year-old husband and eight grandchildren. They were the offspring of two other daughters who died of AIDS within a month of each other.

South Africa is not the country worst hit by AIDS. And in many ways its old people are lucky. Unlike their counterparts in much of the rest of Africa, they get a small pension. But that only increases the pressure on them. In many large and fractured families they are the only members with any kind of regular income. They have little choice but to assume charge. And as Molly put it, 'You can't throw the children out. It's what God gives you.'

7

Scorched Earth: A Sticky End with Palm Oil and Sugar

Once, our margarine was made from whale oil. This was always controversial. In the 1930s, Norwegian ports blockaded 'blubber-boiling' ships owned by the Anglo-Dutch foods giant Unilever, demanding that they cut the cull in order to save the whale. In the 1950s, the Greek shipping mogul and socialite Aristotle Onassis was employing Hitler's old whaling captains to run the world's largest whaling fleet – and, far from being bashful about the business, he boasted to the guests on his yacht that the bar stools were covered in white skin from whale scrotums. All this so the processed blubber could be spread on our sandwiches. The slaughter was indiscriminate and all but wiped out blue whales, the largest mammal on the planet.

Thank heavens, that's over. Most whaling is now banned, and our taste in margarine has moved on, too. Concern about coronaries has encouraged us to replace animal fats with vegetable oils. But now some of those vegetable oils are in trouble, blamed for rainforest destruction. More than logging, more than slash-and-burn farming, the global push to grow ever more soya in the

Amazon and palm oil in South-east Asia is wrecking the rainforests. We saved the whales, but we are losing the jungles.

I eat palm oil several times every day without knowing it. So do you. Palm oil is in an estimated one-third of all the products we pick up off the supermarket shelves. When I buy margarine or biscuits, chocolate or crisps, ice cream or commercial pastry, instant soup or noodles, I am buying palm oil. And we don't just eat it; we wash in it and adorn ourselves with it. Palm oil has replaced whale oil in my soap, and as the base lathering material in my detergents, toothpaste and shampoo. It is in waxes and polishes, and in my daughter's lipstick. Environmental warpaint. Britain alone consumes over a million tonnes of palm oil a year. Put personally, that works out at about 20 kilograms each – or forty tubs.

The oil palm – not to be confused with the coconut palm – is super-fecund. The plum-sized fruit grows in bunches of up to 3,000, weighing down the squat trees. It is a native of West Africa, and was the original source of the wealth of Lever Brothers, the British wing of Unilever. Even before it was making margarine from whale oil, it was establishing huge palm-oil plantations on former forest land in West Africa to turn into soaps like Lifebuoy, one of the first global brands. In the 1960s, Nigeria was still the world's dominant supplier. But back then the world produced less than 2 million tonnes of palm oil a year. Today the figure is approaching 30 million.

The boom has spread palm-oil plantations across the tropics, from Mexico to New Guinea. But two rainforest nations have oiled the wheels of this new agribusiness best. Malaysia and Indonesia between them have planted an area the size of England, and account for 80 per cent of global production. The Malaysian Palm Oil Council promotes palm oil as a fruit of the forests with 'the scent of violets, the taste of olive oil and a colour which tinges food like saffron.' But the truth is that, as in West Africa, forests in South-east Asia are often cleared to make way for palm oil. That became dramatically clear in 1997, when rainforests and peat bogs burned across the Indonesian islands of Borneo and Sumatra, creating smogs that engulfed the region. Subsequent studies showed that three-quarters of the fires had been lit by people clearing land for palm oil.

When I nibble at a biscuit or open a packet of crisps or brush my teeth or whiten my coffee or tuck into an ice cream, I am helping wipe out the rainforest and reduce the most diverse ecosystem on the planet to a botanical desert. And I am helping release hundreds of millions of tonnes of carbon dioxide into the atmosphere as peat bogs drained to grow palm oil oxidize.

Now a new threat looms. Not content with filling our kitchens and bathrooms, the purveyors of palm oil now want to top up our fuel tanks. Technically speaking, palm oil is an ideal source of biofuel. European Union laws will shortly require filling stations to mix vegetable oils with regular diesel. Domestic rapeseed oil will not meet the demand. So Malaysia and Indonesia want to fill the gap. In mid-2006, the two countries announced joint plans to set aside 40 per cent of their palm-oil output for biodiesel. By that they meant they will increase production that much.

Malaysia's leading supplier, Loders Croklaan, recently doubled its global refining capacity. And Indonesia intends to expand its plantations from 6 to 9 million hectares. Where will the world's fourth most populous nation find all that land? You guessed. Some 2 million hectares will come from converting an area of rainforest in central Borneo the size of Wales into the world's largest palm-oil plantation. Most of the rest will come from peat bogs. Friends of the Earth concluded that the farms could 'sound the death knell for the orang-utan and hamper the fight against climate change, the very problem biofuels are supposed to help overcome.' But green business is green business.

Right now, I can't imagine a diet that would allow me to boycott palm oil. But there are many other edible oils that could be used instead by food manufacturers without returning to slaughtering the world's whales. Palm oil is used in large part because it is cheap and readily available, while there are few effective controls on the destruction of rainforests. I would, at the very least, like to be able to choose a brand that doesn't trash the jungles and fill the atmosphere with oxidized peat. But good manufacturers and retailers who promote 'sustainability' in the abstract seem remarkably reluctant to reveal where their fats come from. Campaigners who have asked have met a blank wall. Manufacturers simply say that they 'buy palm oil on the world market' and so do not know where their stuff comes from. See no evil, hear no evil. They could find out if they wanted. But, revealingly, at the time of writing the industry's new Roundtable on Sustainable Palm Oil has failed to find a single plantation worth certifying.

The ethical cut-out, incidentally, is provided by the same band of big commodity brokers who turn up in other agribusinesses. The palm oil that oozes through my diet comes mainly from three sources. There is Cargill, which has its own palm-oil plantations in the jungle regions of Indonesia and neighbouring Papua New Guinea, as well as refineries in Malaysia, the Netherlands, Britain, Germany and the US. There is US-based commodities giant Archer Daniels Midland (ADM), which part-owns the Singapore-based Wilmar Group, the largest exporter of Indonesian palm oil. ADM supplies a third of the edible food oils reaching Britain, through its London subsidiary Puma Foods. And finally there is ever-present Unilever, which currently buys about 7 per cent of global palm-oil production for its margarines like Flora, its Walls ice cream and its soaps like Dove and Lifebuoy, still the world's number-one soap.

This is an industry that appears to be out of control, where the growing corporate claims of sustainability have yet to get much beyond greenwash. The commodity is still often produced in an ethical vacuum. And we consumers are given little choice but to be part of it. Personally, I will only believe in the greening of the palm-oil companies when they announce that they will not buy the oil from Indonesia's new super-plantation. Perhaps the big service stations would like to join in too.

*

I don't eat a great deal of meat. And my home-cooked lamb and chickens (and Christmas turkeys) come from organic British sources. Not too many worries there. But my take-away chicken tikka has a different provenance. There is a good chance my tikka comes from Sun Valley Foods, based just outside Hereford. It rears about a million chickens a week, and supplies caterers across Europe – including half of all McDonald's Chicken McNuggets, though I can't say I have ever eaten one of them.

Sun Valley's 'vision' is to be 'the market leader in the global chicken value chain'. It is owned by the commodities giant Cargill. Cargill is better known for selling bulk agricultural commodities like vegetable oils and grain and cotton. So why chickens? One reason seems to be that it can feed them on one of its commodities – soya beans. Until early 2007, Cargill was exporting 200,000 tonnes of Brazilian soya beans through a purpose-built terminal at the port of Santarém near the mouth of the Amazon. The beans were destined for Cargill's dock in Liverpool, and from there were driven to Hereford and Sun Valley Foods.

This chicken run attracted Greenpeace's attention. Wittingly or not, it said, Cargill was accelerating rainforest destruction by providing a ready market for soya grown on former Amazon rainforest. And it produced plenty of evidence of soya grown on recently lost forest around Santarém. Greenpeace mounted a sustained campaign against both McDonald's and Cargill, until the burger chain announced a two-year moratorium on taking meat fed on soya from 'recently deforested' areas of the Amazon, and Cargill shut down its terminal at Santarém. Sun Valley remains open for business, of course, its vision intact. Only the source of the feed has changed. It's an environmental gain, but how big is far from clear.

I have a sweet tooth. Most of us do. So I wanted to go to the heart of the sugar industry. The world's largest sugar refinery is run by Tate & Lyle at Silvertown in east London. It processes more than a million tonnes of raw cane sugar a year on the site where Henry Tate set up his sugar-refining business 150 years ago, before later merging with Abram Lyle.

Tate & Lyle today seems a hangover from the days when Britain ruled the world and the world's commodities all ended up in the docks of London. The refinery is just downstream from Canary Wharf, which occupies the site of the old West India Docks where most of Britain's sugar was landed. The company still sells what is often called the world's oldest brand, Lyle's Golden Syrup. I have a tin in my larder. The design of its label has been unchanged for 150 years, they say.

But the story behind that tin, and the packet of granulated that sits beside it, is not sweet at all. Over a couple of centuries, some 4 million Africans were kidnapped by slave traders and shipped to the Caribbean to work on the sugar plantations of Barbados and Jamaica, Haiti and Cuba. All to satisfy Europe's sugar craving. Though the involvement of Mr Tate and Mr Lyle started after slavery ended, their company is the inheritor of that trade, and still gets most of its sugar from the Caribbean and other former British colonies such as Swaziland, Mauritius and Fiji.

Tate & Lyle sold off its plantations in the 1960s and 1970s, as the British Empire itself dissolved. And we have other sources of sugar now, such as home-grown European sugar beet, sold under the brand name Silver Spoon by a subsidiary of the food giant Associated British Foods. But Tate & Lyle is still the dominant buyer from a string of countries that remain hugely dependent on growing sugar cane. And that makes those countries hugely dependent on Tate & Lyle.

Take Swaziland. A small landlocked kingdom in southern Africa, Swaziland doesn't make the headlines much. But soon it might. Maybe even before this book reaches the shops. Swaziland is the last absolute monarchy in Africa, a place where national wealth appears to be indistinguishable from royal wealth. It also has the highest rate of HIV infection in the world, at more than

40 per cent of the adult population. Life expectancy is down to thirty-two years.

Swaziland has two main sources of income: cash returned by its young men working in the gold mines of South Africa – and sugar. In the streets of its capital, Mbabane, they call sugar 'Swazi gold'. It makes up a quarter of the country's GDP, more than half its agricultural output, and directly or indirectly employs most of its workforce. Currently more than 160,000 tonnes of sugar are shipped annually from Swaziland, via Maputo port in Mozambique, to the European Union. That is 160 kilograms per head of the country's population. Most of it ends up on a conveyor belt into Tate & Lyle's Silvertown refinery.

Tate & Lyle buys from the Royal Swaziland Sugar Corporation, the country's largest employer. The corporation's dominant share-holder is UK-educated King Mswati III, through his private company, Tibiyo Taka Ngwane. The company coyly calls itself 'a unique business entity'. Besides sugar, it controls most of the rest of the Swazi economy, including mining, manufacturing, property and finance. The king, by the way, has ten wives and by tradition chooses a new one each year. (His father collected seventy before he died.) The wives all have BMWs. The king also appoints all ministers and can overrule parliament and the judiciary.

Besides the king's sugar plantations, thousands of the country's farmers have stopped growing staples like maize in order to feed Europe with sugar. For much of the country, the king's corporation is not just the dominant employer, it is also the dominant purchaser of farm produce and acts as a surrogate government, providing clinics, housing, schools, police and care programmes for AIDS orphans, as well as building roads and power lines. The entire country thus depends on a house of cards comprising the king, his corporation, sugar – and Tate & Lyle.

But I left out one other player: the European Union. And it is the European Union that is now about to bring this house tumbling down. The European Union is awash with sugar. For a long time, it has operated a sugar-trading system designed to protect both its domestic beet farmers – the world's highest-cost sugar producers – and a select group of around twenty ex-colonial sugar-producing countries. It guarantees these privileged suppliers both a certain market and prices well above the global rate. Featherbedding meets philanthropy. But such rigged markets are out of fashion. The World Trade Organization abhors them. And the EU ends up buying so much sugar that shiploads of the stuff en route to Europe from Africa or the Caribbean are frequently diverted at sea, and their contents dumped on to the world market. That angers big American sugar traders and plantation owners in Brazil.

Anyhow, in the name of a free market, the EU is now dismantling this system. By the end of the decade, prices paid to formerly favoured suppliers will fall by almost 40 per cent. Having been encouraged into sugar dependency, some of the poorest countries in the world now face ruin. All could be destabilized in the process, with some unable to export at all at the new low prices.

What alternatives does Swaziland have? Most other commodity crops are already over-produced round the world, resulting in falling prices. Nobody wants to invest in more production. One way out of the crisis, the king's courtiers suggest, is to compensate for lower sugar prices by increasing production. There might be a growing market, they argue, for sugar as a feedstock for biofuels. But here the major constraint is water, Swaziland's most precious commodity. Droughts are already hitting production. It takes 700 tonnes of water to produce every tonne of cane. And because sugar has deep roots, it can dry out the soil to a greater depth than most crops, so shrivelling other crops in neighbouring fields. The country is building new dams, but they will serve little purpose if there is no water in the rivers.

With its income set to be slashed, the Royal Swaziland Sugar Corporation is already cutting back on social services – though the king has yet to cut back on his acquisition of new wives or their BMWs. And the Swazi government, which will in theory have to take over the services once provided by the king's corporation, is itself losing tax revenues. The compact between king and country in Swaziland looks on the verge of breakdown. My guess is that we will hear a lot more about Swaziland in future. And sugar will be at the heart of it.

Sugar is the ultimate monoculture crop, and it is grown on a prodigiously large scale. In seven countries, including Mauritius and Barbados, it covers more than half of the entire land area. In many more, including Swaziland, sugar occupies most of the cultivated land. Rainforests and wetlands and rich pastures have all been cleared for the crop. Elsewhere, from India to Queensland and Barbados to Fiji, sugar is one of the major causes of the emptying of rivers and aquifers. In the Indian state of Maharashtra sugar covers just 3 per cent of the land, yet takes 60 per cent of the state's irrigation water.

Sugar is the main cause of the rampant soil degradation in Cuba and the almost complete deforestation of Haiti. A study by the environment group WWF concluded that 'the production of sugar cane has probably caused a greater loss of biodiversity on the planet than any other single crop.' Sugar is a menace, an imperial crop that countries should simply stop growing. Their addiction to it is as great as that of the consumers in Europe, and rather more damaging.

8

Unzipped: When the Banana Lost Its Seeds and Other Tales From the Orchards

Pity the banana. Despite its unmistakably phallic appearance, it hasn't had sex for thousands of years. The world's most erotic fruit is a sterile, seedless mutant – and therein lies a problem. The banana is genetically old and decrepit. It has been at an evolutionary standstill ever since humans first propagated it in the jungles of South-east Asia at the end of the last ice age. And that is why some scientists believe that the banana could be doomed. It lacks the genes to fight off the pests and diseases that are invading the banana plantations of Central America and the smallholdings of Africa and Asia.

The banana needs a pick-me-up, fast. But science has so far let it down. For decades, plant breeders have all but ignored it, because developing new plant varieties without the help of sexual reproduction is expensive and time-consuming. As a result, most people in the developed world eat just one variety, the Cavendish. And the world's favourite fruit – the one I eat most regularly – could be on the cusp of extinction, says Emile Frison, an old banana hand and head of Biodiversity, formerly the International Plant Genetic Resources Institute, in Rome.

In some ways, the banana today resembles the potato before blight brought famine to Ireland a century and a half ago. But it holds a lesson for other crops, too, says Emile, about how the increasing standardization of food crops is threatening their ability to adapt and survive. Popular fruits are at risk more than most. Your favourite could be on the verge of extinction.

The banana is among the world's oldest crops. The first edible banana was unzipped around 10,000 years ago in South-east Asia. Its very survival is a testament to the wisdom and inventiveness of our Stone Age ancestors. The wild banana is a giant jungle herb with a fruit that normally contains a mass of hard seeds that make it inedible. But now and then, hunter-gatherers discovered plants that produced seedless, soft fruit. And it was very tasty. Plant scientists now know that these mutations resulted from an occasional genetic accident that prevented seeds and pollen from developing normally inside the fruit. The dark lines within the flesh of an edible banana are all that remains of the vestigial seeds. So the mutant plants were sterile, but their fruits were edible.

The early farmers cultivated these sterile freaks by replanting cuttings. And so began mankind's love affair with the banana. The first banana boats took the giant herb to Africa several thousand years ago. Anthropologists believe it became the nutritional mainstay that allowed the Bantu people to colonize most of the continent. And when Europeans first went to the Americas, the banana was among the first old-world fruits that they planted in the new world.

But on this long journey the sterile, constantly cloned banana has barely changed. Today we eat the descendants of the original cuttings taken by the Stone Age cultivators, probably from somewhere in the Malaysian jungle. Normally, cultivated plants develop genetic variety through random mutations during sexual reproduction, just as humans do. This process means that different varieties develop resistance to various pests and diseases, and adaptability to stresses like droughts. Plant breeders tap into this genetic variety all the time. But without sexual reproduction to throw the genetic dice every generation, each variety of modern banana – yellow, red and green, from big starchy ones to small sweet ones – has come down almost unchanged from a separate sterile forest mutant. Each is a virtual clone, almost devoid of genetic diversity. And that uniformity makes the banana ripe for disease like almost no other crop on Earth.

Until the 1950s, one variety, the Gros Michel, dominated the world's commercial banana business. Found by French botanists in Asia in the 1820s, the Gros Michel was by all accounts a fine banana, richer and sweeter than today's standard Cavendish, and without the latter's bitter aftertaste when green. I don't remember, but I must have eaten it when I was young. However, the Gros Michel was vulnerable to a soil fungus that produced a wilt known as Panama disease. 'Once the fungus got into the soil, there was nothing farmers could do. Even chemical spraying wouldn't get rid of it,' says Rodomiro Ortiz, top banana in charge of research at the International Institute for Tropical Agriculture in Ibadan, Nigeria. So plantation owners played a running game, abandoning infested fields and moving to 'clean' land – until in the 1950s they ran out of clean land and had to abandon the ill-fated Gros Michel. The king of the plantations – a fruit that ruled nations and toppled governments, that brought us the phrase 'banana republic' – is now just a laboratory curiosity.

Its successor, and the reigning commercial king, is the Cavendish. This is a variety from southern China 'discovered' by British colonial botanists and brought home in 1828, where it was named after the English lord who provided house room for the first samples. Being less tasty than the Gros Michel, the Cavendish languished until the latter's demise. But in the 1960s, tastiness mattered less than resistance to Panama disease. The Cavendish resisted the fungus and almost overnight replaced the Gros Michel in plantations and on supermarket shelves. If you buy a banana today, it is almost certainly a Cavendish.

But, less than half a century on, the day of reckoning may be coming for the Cavendish. The plan-B commercial banana is already being stalked by another fungal disease. Black Sigatoka has become a global epidemic since its first appearance in Fiji in 1963. Commercial growers keep it at bay by a constant chemical assault. Forty sprayings of fungicide a year is typical, making the Cavendish the most heavily sprayed food crop in the world. This is not good news for the employees of the big Latin American banana-plantation owners. In Costa Rica, the second-largest banana exporter after Ecuador and the place where my bananas usually come from, women in banana-packing plants suffer double the average rates of leukaemia and birth defects. Meanwhile, a fifth of male banana workers are sterile, allegedly as a result of exposure to dibromochloropropane, which is now banned, and other fungicides that are not.

Organic farmers, who use natural pesticides, are much healthier, but they face the same problems of infestation. However the banana is farmed, black Sigatoka is getting more and more difficult to control. And now comes what could be the *coup de grâce*. Panama disease is making a comeback in a new form – known as tropical race 4 – that attacks the Cavendish with particular virulence. So far, tropical race 4 has reached South Africa, Australia and much of Asia. Millions of banana plants have died in southern China, the Cavendish's original home. Chemical fungicides cannot control it. So, it is only a matter of time before what they are calling the banana cancer makes it to the commercial plantations of Ecuador, Costa Rica, Honduras and Colombia.

One footprint could do it, says Richard Markham, director of the International Network for the Improvement of Banana and Plantain. 'A dirty boot with a few grams of soil from an infested site in Asia planted inadvertently in a Latin American plantation is all it would take. It's just a matter of time.' And when it arrives, it will do to Cavendish what its predecessor did to Gros Michel. Game over.

With most crops, such a threat would unleash an army of breeders, scouring the world for resistant relatives whose traits they could breed into commercial varieties. Not so with the banana. Because all edible varieties of banana are sterile, introducing new genetic traits to help cope with pests and diseases is nearly impossible. Nearly, but not totally. Very rarely, a sterile banana will itself experience a genetic accident that allows an almost normal seed to develop. This gives breeders a tiny window for improvement. Honduran breeders tried to exploit this to create a disease-resistant Cavendish variety.

Every day for a year, workers laboriously hand-pollinated 30,000 banana plants with pollen from wild fertile Asian bananas. The resulting fruit, some 400 tonnes, had to be peeled and sieved in search of any seeds. 'I'll let you guess how many seeds they collected,' says Emile. 'About fifteen. And of those, only four or five germinated.' Further backcrossing with wild bananas nonetheless yielded a new seedless banana resistant to both black Sigatoka and Panama disease. Bingo! Well, no. Western consumers didn't like the new hybrid. Some accused it of tasting more like an apple than a banana. The only buyers today are Cubans, where black Sigatoka wiped out normal Cavendish plantations and there is nothing else on the shelves.

Not surprisingly, given the difficulties, the majority of plant breeders have till now turned their backs on the banana and got to work on easier plants. Even the commercial banana companies fight shy. 'We supported a breeding programme for forty years, but it wasn't able to develop an alternative to Cavendish. It was very expensive and we got nothing back,' says Ronald Romero, head of research at Chiquita, which, along with Fyffes and the Dole Corporation, dominates the international banana trade.

Could genetic modification come to the banana's rescue? Maybe. A global consortium of scientists is trying to produce a genetic map of wild banana varieties. If they can pinpoint the genes that help them resist diseases like black Sigatoka and tropical race 4, those genes could be spliced into edible varieties in the lab. Whether we will want to eat GM bananas is another matter, but Emile sees it as the only hope for the Cavendish. Without it, the most popular single product on the world's supermarket shelves could be heading for a sterile grave.

All over the world there are fruits, nuts and other foodstuffs vulnerable to genetic fortune. The story is usually the same. Commercial growers have concentrated on a handful of varieties, discarding the others. They have bred the chosen few to maximize yield or for some specific trait that they value most. In the process, the plant's natural ability to withstand pests and disease has been undermined. Meanwhile, the genetic stores of old varieties and wild relatives alike have often been lost. Most of the time, commercial planters spray their way out of trouble. But sometimes, as when Gros Michel stumbled, the sprays prove useless and the crop is doomed.

It could happen to some of our favourites. There are six major types of pineapple, for instance. But we eat only one, the Smooth Cayenne. By neglecting the others, and ignoring the fruit's genetic base in the wild, we risk losing the genes they contain and undermining the future of the fruit. The mango is suffering similar genetic erosion. A thousand or more varieties of sweet potatoes in New Guinea are undocumented and uncollected. In the Himalayan foothills of northern India, cultivated varieties of garlic and its wild ancestors are dying out.

The farms and hedgerows of dozens of tiny Italian islands in the Mediterranean are the last refuges for many rare and ancient plants. Watermelons are holed up in Vulcano, tomatoes in Elba and cabbages in Linosa. But as holiday villas and desertification encroach, how long will they survive?

Or take the world's most widely eaten nut. The peanut began in the jungles of South America. The Portuguese took it to Africa, from where it reached North America and first gained wide popularity. Today, it is not just the world's favourite nibble, but also the most important source of vegetable protein for half a billion of the world's poorest people, mostly in Africa. But cultivated peanuts have lost much of their natural resistance to disease. In an echo of the banana story, a fungus is chasing the nut across the world, and it has few genetic defences. The peanut's wild ancestors are believed to live only in a tiny area of remote rainforest in eastern Bolivia. Researchers believe that if they can find them, they can extract genes that can counteract the fungus. But the forest has been declared out of bounds to scientists because of local unrest caused by opposition to an oil pipeline through the forest. Can the peanut survive? It would make a great movie.

A few botanical Indiana Joneses are out there trying to track down the wild ancestors of many modern crops. One of them is Emile's colleague Stefano Padulosi, the world's foremost authority on rare, unusual and plain exotic fruits and vegetables. Without him, the chic salad vegetable called rocket would still be a forgotten weed in the ruins of his home town, Pompeii. His main stomping ground is Central Asia, the genetic heartland of many of our most familiar crops, where he tracks down both wild ancestors and the collectors of traditional varieties. Soviet scientists were masters at the business of collecting obscure Central Asian crop varieties. But many of their collections have languished since the Russians went home after 1989. And, like your grandfather's stamp collection, the fate of the plant collections is in doubt because nobody realizes their value. The loss of these plants could prove another casualty of the fall of the Berlin Wall.

The future of the apple, for instance, may now hang in the balance. Britain, famously, has more than 2,000 apple varieties, but few are now grown commercially and most of the rest survive only on one site, in the national fruit collection at Brogdale in Kent. But the greatest genetic resource of the apple is far away in the Tien Shen mountains of Kazakhstan, where wild apple woods still grow. Ninety per cent of the world's apples are believed to come from parent trees taken long ago from these woods. Many apple trees with potentially invaluable genetic traits are still in these hills. Or were, when Stefano last looked. They could have been chopped down for firewood by now.

Stefano is also concerned about what has happened to the watermelons and pistachios that once grew wild across Uzbekistan, and the native walnuts of Kyrgyzstan, not to mention the equally prized forerunners of modern apricots, peaches and almonds in their homeland of Afghanistan – a country where protecting wild genes does not have the highest priority right now.

Quixotically perhaps, I am most interested in the fate of another native of Central Asia, the pomegranate, one of the world's juiciest fruits and prized for its exceptional nutritional qualities. Some say it fights prostate cancer. I enjoy its taste but, to be truthful, what interests me most is the prospect of one day going to find its genetic homeland in one of the world's oddest and most inaccessible countries.

Turkmenistan was, until his recent death, the fiefdom of Turkmenbashi, an eccentric leader of the former Soviet socialist republic. Once off the Moscow leash, he became an increasingly paranoid and megalomaniac leader of the independent state. Such was his omnipotence that he renamed the days of the week after members of his family and on a whim banned men from growing beards and anyone at all from sporting gold teeth. He prevented all access to the world wide web, shut down most of the country's universities, uprooted the state botanical gardens and cut off funding for the country's other plant collections. Which left the pomegranate in the lurch.

People have been growing pomegranates in the remote valleys of the Kopet Dam mountains of southern Turkmenistan for 6,000 years. While other countries grow pomegranates, the assemblage of ancient varieties is found only in Turkmenistan. In recent decades most of the old varieties have been lost from the country's orchards. Only around fifty are still grown. But on the edge of the mountains, starting in the 1930s, Soviet scientists assembled a unique collection of more than 1,000 varieties of pomegranate trees at the Garigala experimental station. It is the holy grail of pomegranate biodiversity.

How is the collection doing? Few people really know. Most of the varieties have never even been catalogued, says Stefano. Garigala has been all but impossible to get to for some years. The last curator was Russian-born botanist Grigory Levin, who spent much of his life nurturing the collection, but eventually fled to Israel. He keeps in touch with the demoralized and frequently unpaid staff. 'Many of the trees are being ploughed under to make way for vegetables,' he says.

The world's pomegranate collection is expiring. I want to go and see it before it is too late. But the fruit could still survive. For Grigory says that the Kopet Dam mountains have one last treasure. Somewhere up there is the world's one and only wild pomegranate forest. Still flourishing, it is said. I want to walk through that forest, pick some fruit. Just for the hell of it. And now Turkmenbashi is gone, I may get my chance.

9

Montezuma's Magic: How Joseph the Cocoa Farmer Became an Unlikely Green Warrior

Before ransacking the Aztec court of Montezuma in Mexico, the Spanish conquistador Hernando Cortez noted that the king 'took no other beverage' except a drink made with a mysterious bean, the cocoa bean. He noted too that the king's subjects rarely got a look-in. Because a humble mug of drinking chocolate – albeit spiced up with vanilla, spices and honey, and sometimes a local hallucinogenic mushroom – was seen as the food of the gods. Chocolate in sixteenth-century Central America was a great delicacy. And it is a shame it didn't stay that way.

We probably have a Brit, Sir Hans Sloane, to blame for turning Montezuma's bean into the most popular confection on the planet. In the late seventeenth century, having seen Jamaicans preparing a chocolate drink similar to Montezuma's, the explorer came up with the idea of mixing it with milk and marketing it as 'Sir Hans Sloane's Milk Chocolate . . . for its lightness on the stomach and its great use in all consumptive cases.' Sloane, who later gave his name to a famous square in London and created a treasure trove of foreign delights that formed the basis for the British Museum collection, also brought opium and cannabis and

Chinese rhubarb to Britain. But none took so well to the British palate as milk chocolate.

From Sir Hans Sloane's milk chocolate, it was a small step to Mr Cadbury's Dairy Milk and Mr Fry's Chocolate Cream. And the British Empire did the rest. The cocoa bean from the forests of Central America became one of the world's most profitable and addictive commodities, loved by hundreds of millions of chocoholics round the world. The human race consumes around 3 million tonnes of cocoa beans a year – half a kilo for everyone on the planet. The business of meeting our predilection employs 14 million people, 10 million of them in Africa. But it has also done untold ecological damage, especially to the tropical rainforests. Cocoa, above all other crops, destroyed the jungles of West Africa, from Ghana to the Ivory Coast and Cameroon.

I went to meet one of the destroyers. Not one of the big cocoa growers, but a smallholder with an acre or so of cocoa trees that he planted sixty years ago outside Yaoundé, the capital of Cameroon. Joseph Essissima and millions like him have for years been branded as environmental pariahs, pioneers of deforestation. And yet something has changed in the jungle. Now ecologists are coming to Cameroon not to pillory Joseph, but to praise him. Joseph has not changed. But the ecologists' view of the world certainly has. Now they want to help him make more money out of his trees, so that he can plant more. They say that planting cocoa could be the best way to save Africa's surviving forests. So how exactly did environmental bandits became environmental heroes, and is there any truth in the new story that farmers like Joseph could be the rainforest's salvation?

Cameroon harvests some 120,000 tonnes of cocoa a year. That is not as much as the market leader, the Ivory Coast, but enough to give the country a place among the world's top six cocoa growers. In the Ivory Coast, most of the cocoa is grown on big plantations, but in Cameroon a typical cocoa farm is a smallholding close to the forests – in fact a smallholding that looks rather like a forest itself.

Joseph's farm is dark, dank and full of life. There are cocoa trees, but also many others, some natural and some planted. He led me in. When he originally cleared the forest, he kept plenty of the natural trees to provide him with timber, fruit and bark for local medicines, and to give shade to his growing cocoa trees. Most of his neighbours did the same. As we walked through his cocoa forest, Joseph pointed out each tree. Dotted around, I spotted oranges and mangoes, avocados and cherries. One I couldn't make out. 'We keep this because it attracts caterpillars that we eat,' he said. 'They are very tasty.'

With us was Jim Gockowski of the International Institute for Tropical Agriculture (IITA) in Yaoundé. 'By maintaining a shaded canopy of diverse forest species, these farmers manage one of the most biologically diverse land-use systems in Africa,' he said. 'The cocoa plantations have more than half the species you would find in a natural forest. It may not be virgin forest, but if the farmers didn't plant cocoa here, they would be doing slash-and-burn agriculture, planting maize or palm oil or turning the land over to cattle pasture.'

Across southern Cameroon, large areas of former rainforest land now lie fallow after the slash-and-burners exhausted the soils. Yet in their midst are the cocoa forests. Once dismissed as a scar on the natural landscape, they are now green oases. 'The environmental benefits of a closed natural forest are now being provided by cultivated forests of cocoa and fruit trees,' said Stephan Weise, the IITA station chief. He is trying to persuade landowners to convert their abandoned farmland into cocoa forest. And some large chocolate makers like Mars are funding his work.

On a small scale, Stephan is making headway. Near Joseph's cocoa forest I met Abomo, a widow who was growing cocoa trees and bananas in abandoned maize fields. Barefoot, in a vest, leggings and a skirt, she took me round. The cocoa was for cash; the bananas were for food, but also to provide shade. She said she was one of a group of local women farmers who were taking up cocoa growing.

They are brave women. Out here on the edge of the forest, it is a long way to my local corner shop, where I may buy a chocolate bar while picking up the morning paper. And the tragedy is that at the very time when cocoa has emerged in Cameroon as an ecological crop, its profitability has slumped. The price paid for the cocoa that goes into my chocolate bar has collapsed.

I was invited to a meeting of farmers among the cocoa forests. There was a big sign chalked up in the clearing, advertising my appearance. About twenty cocoa farmers assembled in a circle. They described their business. After harvesting the beans, they broke the pods and fermented them in the fields, often under piles of banana leaves. About a week later, they carried the fermented beans from the forest to the village, where they laid them out in the sun, on tables or at the roadside. Then travelling middlemen showed up to buy the beans.

And that was where voices started to rise. Until a decade ago, the farmers explained, the middlemen had worked for a state marketing system. It bought at agreed prices and sold to international traders, under a negotiated price regime. But that system has collapsed, much as the coffee price regime has also collapsed. In its place is a free-for-all, in which the middlemen have a take-it-or-leave-it attitude to negotiating prices. With a perishable product and no storage, the farmers have no choice but to take whatever price they are offered.

The middlemen, the farmers said, sell on to even more shadowy figures in the coastal town of Douala. Frequently Lebanese, these men also act as moneylenders to both the farmers and middlemen. The beans eventually find their way in trucks to the port of Bonaberi, where 90 per cent of the harvest is bought by representatives of the trading companies Cargill, ADM or Barry Callebaut. These three, plus Nestlé, control around half the total global market, and sell on to the chocolate manufacturers like Mars and Cadbury.

'The government used to be like a father to us,' complained a tall skinny man at the meeting whose sense of fair play was badly ruffled. 'Now the buyers can pay what they like. We are like lambs facing a leopard. We don't know what the proper price should be. The big guys never come here, so we cannot negotiate. And the small guys . . . even their scales are not set properly, so we don't know for sure how much we are selling.' The farmers were trying to organize themselves into a cooperative, to get some bargaining power. But it was not easy.

Most agreed with the skinny man, who said, 'Growing cocoa will vanish when our generation dies.' Thousands of cocoa farmers were leaving their trees to decay, or clearing the forest to plant maize, groundnuts and palm oil. There had been a big increase in forest clearing, they said. Those that stuck with the business received half of one per cent of the price paid in the shops for a bar of chocolate.

Then they stopped to listen. I realized with alarm that they had invited me in the hope that I could offer some advice. I was from the world outside, after all. Even a local journalist had come to hear my words of wisdom. But I had to admit, I really had none. I was learning about the politics of the powerless.

While the Cameroon cocoa foresters are losing out, the only winners in Africa are larger farms that can cut costs to the bone. Most of those are in the tiny unstable West African state of Ivory Coast, which is now the source of more than 40 per cent of the world's cocoa. There, cocoa is grown in monoculture plantations with no shade and no forest cover. This produces faster instant profits, but at the expense of damaged soils, brutalized ecosystems and the spread of crop diseases. And the crop is often harvested using contract labour brought in from the drought-hit countries of the Sahel region to the north. Frequently, I was told that labour has been a payment for debt, something close to slavery. And sometimes it has involved children, dubbed 'chocolate slaves'. The traders say this practice has now been weeded out. We shall see.

Most of the beans are taken back to Europe and North America for processing. Cargill, for instance, runs huge ships carrying

10,000 tonnes of cocoa at a time into its warehouses in Amsterdam's Zaan district, which handles a quarter of all the world's cocoa. Here the beans are roasted, shelled and ground to make a hot cocoa 'liquor', which solidifies into blocks. These blocks are pressed to squeeze out the yellowy fat content, known as cocoa butter. The rest is ground again to make cocoa powder. The butter is the main ingredient in chocolate (with milk and sugar) and gives it its distinctive texture. The powder is added to chocolate bars for flavouring and is also used as powder for cocoa drinks and in food, from biscuits to ice creams and truffles to cappuccino coffee.

Not all beans are alike. And here is another bug-bear. The farmers in the Cameroon forests told me their high-quality beans once attracted premium prices. Industry insiders I spoke to agreed that Cameroon cocoa, which had been introduced here by German colonists a century ago, was distinctive and once highly prized for its cocoa butter. But in recent years, the traders had taken to bulk ordering with little regard for quality. For them, a bean is a bean is a bean. So the Cameroon farmers get paid no more than the low-grade producers of the Ivory Coast.

What should an ethical chocoholic do? Like many people, I am starting to buy more fairtrade chocolate. Like fairtrade coffee, it is providing a modest helping hand for cocoa farmers without transforming their lives or, in my view, quite providing the fairness promised on the label. (Another way to help farmers, incidentally, is to buy dark chocolate, which contains 70 per cent cocoa and less sugar and milk.) But I must confess that I am still a rather unreconstructed lover of Mars bars and Cadbury's Dairy Milk. And in the end, I think that makes me part of the problem. Too much chocolate in the shops is mundane and cheap enough for us to binge on the stuff. We accept its mediocrity, and ask only for more, at cheap prices. While we do that, the big traders and manufacturers will remain in charge, and the farmers and their forests will continue to suffer.

The disconnect between my world and that of the cocoa farmers of Cameroon is just too great. One young boy, the son of one of the farmers, came up to me on my last day there and asked simply, 'What does chocolate taste like?' Sadly, I didn't even have a bar to give him.

We need to rediscover chocolate as a delicacy and to find new respect for the people who grow it. There are hopeful signs. I notice that in Sussex there is a chain of boutique chocolate makers called Montezuma's, after the Aztec king. And whenever I go to Swanage in Dorset, I drop in at the Chococo company, where they make gorgeous chocolates that cost almost a pound each. They buy fair-trade chocolate from Ghana, Criollo beans (the best, say aficionados) from Venezuela and cocoa powder from the Dominican Republic. They mix them with fairly traded cane sugar from Paraguay, organic cream from Trevor Craig's independent dairy farm in Weymouth, and butter from Bridport, both just down the road. The fillings include raisins from a farmers' association in the Orange River region of South Africa, fairtrade bananas from Uganda, organic dried apricots from Turkey, honey from a Swanage beekeeper and lemon curd from Dorset's very own Janet Pook. It's worth a pound just to read the ingredients. And that's how it should be for the food of the gods.

10

Air Miles: Why Eating Kenyan Beans Is Good for the Planet

We Britons import a third of our food, including 95 per cent of our fruit and 50 per cent of our vegetables. We have relied on foreign food for centuries, of course. Oriental spices kept our food from going rancid. Tea clippers and banana boats have a long pedigree. Slave-grown sugar was the foundation of the British Empire in the West Indies. And we have long feasted on Italian pasta, French wine, Dutch cheese, Spanish oranges and German sausages. But the erosion of import controls, the reduction in subsidies for British farmers, low wages in the developing world and cheap fuel for ships and aircraft mean it is often cheaper to buy from abroad food we would once have grown ourselves. Meanwhile, we have allowed supermarkets to hook us on year-round supplies of fresh fruit and vegetables that were once seasonal British delicacies, like strawberries during Wimbledon fortnight or new potatoes. For such reasons, our food imports are seven times greater than in 1960.

But this trend is starting to worry us. Trust in our food is being undermined by growing concern about everything from African chocolate slaves to Asian bird flu and pesticide-laden grapes from

Latin America. Things may not be perfect on British farms. But how much less do we know about Bangladeshi prawn ponds and Chilean citrus orchards and Brazilian chicken factories? More than half our food imports are of produce we could grow in Britain, like Californian lettuces or Dutch milk or Argentinian pears. And when trucks of British poultry, beef and milk bound for Europe drive past identical trucks bringing identical produce in the other direction, then something surely has gone wrong.

Sustaining each of us for a year involves the transportation of the equivalent of a 12-tonne containerload of food and drink for more than 100 kilometres. Almost one in every three trucks on British roads is carrying food. Bringing food by road to our shops emits 10 million tonnes of carbon dioxide in Britain each year, and another 9 million tonnes abroad.

Then there are air miles. Friends of the Earth reckons that a typical stir-fry today might contain peas from Kenya, baby corn and prawns from Thailand, spinach from California, beans from Morocco and carrots from South Africa, with combined air miles of more than 50,000 kilometres. Every punnet of strawberries air-freighted from California produces emissions equivalent to more than four school runs in the car. Since we import about 5 million punnets a year from the US, that works out at 22 million school runs, or an entire year's ferrying for more than 100,000 children. Only 1.5 per cent of Britain's imported fresh food arrives by plane, of which a quarter is vegetables from Africa. But that 1.5 per cent produces 50 per cent of all our emissions from fruit and vegetable transportation, and 11 per cent of our total food-transport emissions.

Sustain, a green group based in London, has been measuring how much energy from burning fossil fuels it takes to transport our food, and comparing that with the energy we get from eating that food. It requires 66 calories of energy from aircraft fuel to bring you every calorie of food energy in a South African carrot. Chilean asparagus has a ratio of 97 to 1, and air-freighting a

Californian lettuce uses 120 times more energy than you get from eating it. I can't help thinking that a sensible food industry would have got the ratio the other way round.

Organic eating, incidentally, is worse here. As much as three-quarters of our organic food is imported, twice the proportion for ordinary food. Britain is a great place for growing onions, for instance. But not enough British farmers want to grow organic onions. So, more than half of those on sale in British supermarkets are grown abroad. Campaigners for organic food used to argue that energy used up in the extra food miles is generally offset by the low-energy cultivation. Energy savings from growing fruit and vegetables without pesticides and artificial fertilizer are typically around 15 per cent. But one study found that, for vegetables, an extra 400 kilometres in a truck wiped out the difference. And, if the vegetables were being flown, then just 6 extra kilometres in the air neutralized the gains. It is perhaps not surprising that, at the time of writing, the Soil Association is considering stripping its prized organic label from air-freighted food.

But before we ban foreign food, consider this. Many of the biggest energy inputs come not from transport, but from growing and processing crops. And often British production methods are more energy-intensive. We import three-quarters of our tomatoes, mostly from Spain. In season, buying British is clearly the low-energy option. But for the rest of the year, even air-freighting tomatoes from the polytunnels of southern Spain uses less energy than heating a British greenhouse to grow those tomatoes. Likewise, imported New Zealand lamb has only a quarter the carbon footprint of British lamb, even after the meat has made its journey across the planet.

What counts is the total carbon-intensity of agribusiness. A Swedish study looked at the energy needed to bring you a McDonald's cheeseburger. It found the bun required nearly 500 calories; the 90-gram meat burger typically required 2,000 calories (mostly from fodder production for the animal); the leaf of lettuce needed anything from 20 to 1,000 calories (depending on whether it was grown in a greenhouse and on whether it flew to you); the onions and cucumbers were low-energy items; but the cheese racked up another 200 calories. The total for the entire burger could be as much as 5,000 calories. Substantially more than the energy to be gained from eating it.

Often, the cooking is critical. A study of a typical roast chicken dinner found that home cooking was responsible for 46 per cent of the energy involved in breeding and feeding and getting the bird to your plate. By this reckoning, incidentally, ready-cooked chickens are the low-energy option, cutting the energy used by three-quarters.

This is an inexact science, of course. Should such calculations, include the electricity used to heat or air-condition the restaurant, or even the petrol to drive the farm labourers to work? And does it matter how the energy is produced? If a wind farm is generating the power to grow tomatoes in a greenhouse, does that make it OK?

Many people instinctively feel that air-freighting of food to Britain should be shut down. Buy local, they say. We need 'food patriotism' says Conservative leader David Cameron. And several UK supermarkets are sticking labels on air-freighted produce, so that customers can choose whether to buy or not. Fair enough. I am all in favour of informed choice. But my own view is that all this maths raises as many questions as it answers. And for me, just as important as any precise measure of carbon dioxide emissions is the human question. Who gains and who loses in the transactions that bring your food to your plate?

The London think tank the International Institute for Environment and Development (IIED) says that over a million farmers' livelihoods in Africa are supported by British consumers: 'Nowhere are UK consumers more persistently engaged with rural Africa than through food consumption choices.' Harriet Lamb of the Fairtrade Foundation asks: 'What right do we have to quibble about buying coffee or green beans from poor Kenyan farmers because of the air miles involved when we have a lifestyle many times more energy-intensive than theirs?' Good question. I went to Kenya to find out.

When I was young, green beans were an English crop. They were available only in season, and often served in the village shop from a box that had come straight from the field. I knew; sometimes I had filled that box. Growing up in Kent, the garden of England, I often spent summer holidays picking beans. Nowadays those beans are as likely to come from Kenya as Kent. Marks & Spencer and Tesco are full of shrinkwrapped, air-freighted packs of green beans. They are on supermarket shelves within forty-eight hours of being picked.

Most of the beans come from a company called, with no trace of irony, Homegrown, set up and run by a British-born Kenyan called Dicky Evans, before it was taken over in 2008 by the Hong Kong-based Swire Group. Homegrown is a major source of winter vegetables in Britain. Dicky flies about 12 tonnes of beans to Britain each day, as well as courgettes, baby corn and sugarsnap peas. Usually the vegetables travel with cut flowers from his company's big greenhouses around Lake Naivasha in Kenya's Rift Valley. But most of the beans come not from big company farms but from the fields of about 1,000 smallholders.

To find some of those smallholders, I drove two hours east of Nairobi to the sandy hills of Machakos. Trees were everywhere as we wound up narrow roads with farms on either side, many supplying Homegrown. Eventually, we met Jacob Musyoki. Jacob's farm is two terraces dug into the bottom of a steep river valley. They cover about one hectare, the size of a football pitch. Furrows distribute water from a small dam further up the hillside.

In much of Kenya, farming is an old man's occupation. Young men find jobs in the cities. But not here. Jacob is in his late twenties and he sees his future here. 'Homegrown guarantees me forty-five Kenyan shillings [about 34 British pence] for a kilogram of beans.

That is twice what I can usually get from local traders. And the local traders are not always here. Before I joined Homegrown, I made three thousand shillings a month; now it is twenty thousand most months. Even in bad times it is eight thousand.' Round here, he told me, farmers are returning to the land, joining the waiting list to supply Homegrown.

Jacob is not rich, but he clearly reckoned he was on to a good thing. His house had a concrete floor, which is still unusual in these parts. He didn't have a car or a motorbike, but he did have a TV, which allowed him to watch English football. He was wearing an Arsenal cap, so I knew where his allegiances lay. He had two children in primary school, and a wife with expectations. 'Ladies like to be poshed up. She wants my money to help her keep looking young,' he told me with pride. He had paid a dowry for her with profits from his Homegrown sales.

As we walked his fields, Jacob told me his beans took eight weeks from planting to first pick, and harvesting ended after another four weeks. Then he started again. In a good year, his hectare could deliver 4 or 5 tonnes of beans, worth about £1,500. Half a century ago, this area was reckoned to be on the verge of turning to desert. So I asked how the soils were faring. He said he watered the crops three times a week and reckoned the soil was as good as when he started.

In return for Homegrown's good prices, he had to meet the company's requirements, which could be unpredictable, he said. Right now they were demanding 25 kilograms a day from him, and that was hard to deliver. He did not know the reason for the surge in demand, which was that it was November and there had been a cold snap in the UK. People wanted cooked beans and not salad vegetables. But it is a fact of life here that the customer is king. Output has to be geared to the weather in the UK, whatever the weather in Machakos. The orders coming daily from Tesco and Marks & Spencer, Homegrown's biggest customers, had to be met. Come drought or high water, Jacob had to deliver.

Jacob had fulfilled his order for the day and carried his crate from the fields to the road by his house. This is hilly terrain. The house was 200 metres up the hillside. I was exhausted by the climb, so we cooled down beneath his mango and banana trees, and checked the cows he kept to provide manure for his fields and milk for his children. He showed off the padlocked shed where he kept his pesticides, and the sealed pit for disposing of waste chemicals. 'I built all this myself,' he says. 'Homegrown won't take us on until we have done it all.'

Homegrown's smallholders are organized around some 200 local collection depots known as sheds, where trucks arrive daily to pick up the beans and other vegetables. Jacob is part of the Umwe self-help group, who work within a couple of kilometres of the Umwe shed. There used to be twelve farmers in the group but six left, said Jacob, because they could not meet Homegrown's standards. At the shed, Jacob stashed his beans in a store where the air is kept cool, to prevent the beans from wilting, by soaking a charcoal lining with water. It looked a little makeshift, but the technique dates from British colonial times, and every Homegrown shed has one the same. Later Jacob sorted and graded his beans. And at around 3 p.m., the truck arrived to collect the shed's twelve boxes.

One of the surprises at the shed was that all the farmers had mobile phones. They were part of the modern world of just-in-time retailing, and couldn't afford to be out of touch. Homegrown dictates the farmer's individual planting programme, based on expected demand. But the supermarkets, and their customers, are fickle. Week by week, the planned harvest is refined. Every shed is told each night how many beans to have ready for loading the following afternoon. And as late as noon on the day of collection, the retailers may call and alter their order. On occasions, they have demanded 50 per cent more beans.

Jacob's day-to-day 'controller' is the shed's young technical assistant, Patrick Kinyua. He tells the farmers what to plant, when to plant it, when and how much to spray and fertilize, and when to harvest. Patrick showed me the files for each farm. I asked when Jacob had planted and fertilized and sprayed his crop. It was all there, as well as the timetable for future spraying. How much irrigation water had Jacob applied? Patrick had that, too. The records also covered pests found on the beans and any contaminants in the irrigation water. Some farm files noted boxes returned by Homegrown. One was rejected for containing beans with 'curved ends'; another because they 'appeared dehydrated' – the latter, said Patrick, because the charcoal cooler had not been kept wet.

The shed hygiene files contained records of everything from the thrice-daily cleaning of the toilet to the results of the farmers' regular blood and stool tests – aimed to detect diseases or any trace of pesticides in their blood. All this is demanded by British retailers before they will buy from Kenyan farmers.

I visited Umwe with John Simeoni, who was in overall charge of the Homegrown smallholders. John is a maverick. His father was Italian and his mother from Mauritius. They washed up in Kenya, where John became one of Homegrown's first independent farmers. Evans quickly spotted his flair and asked him to build up the smallholder network, which he has done almost single-handed.

Traceability is the key in modern retailing, John said. If a customer anywhere in Britain returns to the store complaining about a pack of shrivelled beans, if M&S analysts discover a toxic pesticide, or – the real fear – if half a town goes down with diarrhoea after eating Kenyan beans from a local supermarket, then, said John, 'we can source any bean back to one farmer, and usually one field within an hour. It's bureaucratic. But it's the difference between being able to sell to supermarkets or not.' The system was last used, he said, when pesticides in some beans were found to have drifted from spraying on a field of tomatoes next door to a Homegrown farm.

I spent some time with Homegrown's smallholders in the hills of

Machakos. I liked them. They seemed independent, cheerful and diligent. They regarded Homegrown as good business. The people in this area are mostly Akamba, former cattle herders who took up farming when their land became overgrazed in the 1930s. Some tribal leaders had served with Commonwealth forces in India during the Second World War, and they came back with new ideas about how to protect their land. Once home, they started digging terraces on crumbling hillsides, capturing the rain that fell on their fields, and planting trees. The results were startling. Since then, the Machakos district has become a textbook example of how to regenerate land suffering from 'desertification'. Jacob and many other Homegrown smallholders are the heirs to what some call the 'Machakos miracle'.

Homegrown has also organized smallholders to grow beans north of Nairobi, on the road to Thika. Here Kikuyu farmers work the land. While the Akamba farms still seem remote and their connection to an international retailing network almost miraculous, here there is abundant evidence of globalized agri-business. We passed a Del Monte pineapple farm where more than 5,000 people harvest and can 300,000 tonnes of fruit a year, and a large tobacco-threshing plant run by British American Tobacco. Up in the hills were tea plantations, mostly supplying Unilever's ubiquitous Lipton brand, and coffee growers for Starbucks.

Here, Homegrown contracts some bigger bean farmers. Pot-bellied John Macharia had a 20-hectare farm that was rough grazing before Homegrown came along. He had a nice house, a car, children through university and a grown-up daughter set up with her own beautician's shop in Thika. All this, he said, was built on the profits of supplying Homegrown. He had fifty labourers to do the work. He paid them 120 shillings – about 90 pence – a day, and provided barracks lodgings that he admitted were substandard and needed upgrading. But even so, he grumbled about the labour rules imposed by Homegrown. One is that no child under eighteen should work on the farm. 'How can kids learn to farm if they don't work in the fields when they are young?' he asked. 'They will all go to the cities and we will lose the ability to farm.'

I didn't take to him. But down the road I met Margaret – a feisty, get-up-and-go entrepreneur. While running the farm, she was supporting five children in school. She had a husband too – a schoolteacher who 'didn't bring in much money'. Margaret had started just thirty months before with less than a hectare. Now she was renting 3 hectares, and grew more than a tonne of beans a month. 'Homegrown take everything I can give,' she said. 'I want to rent more fields, so I can sell them more.' She also grew bananas, mangoes and oranges to feed her family and to hold water in the soils during droughts. And as a treat, she had bought herself a goat for Christmas. The technical assistant at the local Homegrown shed was in awe. 'Margaret's farm is the most productive here because she is a good manager,' he said. 'She does everything on time. She is new but of the thirty-two farms I oversee, hers is the best.'

Back out on the road, John Simeoni was growing concerned. M&S had called in demanding more stock for the next day. M&S did this a lot, he said. 'They don't hold any stock overnight. So they are constantly changing their order on the day.' Evidently, the company's desire to provide its customers, like me, with the freshest produce was making life harder back up the supply chain. Knowing his regular smallholders would not be able to meet the order, John started making calls to his B list. These farmers were not yet guaranteed sales to Homegrown, but were likely to get the nod soon, if they played ball.

But one of them wasn't playing ball. As we returned to Nairobi, he told John he had a better offer that day from one of the freelance buyers who travel the villages operating for other companies. He wanted John to match it. John angrily accepted. He needed the beans. But as he flapped his phone shut, there was one farmer fewer on the B list.

Back at the packing plant on the perimeter of Nairobi airport, the 180 workers on the bean line were ending their day. Mostly women, they had been at work since 7.30 in the morning, topping and tailing beans, disinfecting them in a chlorine bath and then weighing, checking, bagging and labelling them. Much of the work was done by hand, but some things were automated. Like the machine that measured individual beans as they came down the line and picked them out in the right combinations, so that each pack weighed the same.

This wasn't work you would choose. But more than 80 per cent of the workers were permanent staff, which is higher than in much of the UK food-processing industry. And wages were several times the Kenyan average. There could be a lot of overtime, which was a problem for the many women with children. And since final orders from the supermarkets didn't come till noon, when the women arrived on company buses from their homes in the morning, they didn't know when they would finish. The day I was there, it was about 5 p.m., but it could be much later. 'We have rules about not requiring more than twelve hours' overtime a week, and not working after dark,' said Thomas Frankum, the young Brit who ran the plant. 'We sometimes breach those rules, because we have to fulfil the orders.' The simple fact is that women here get home late from work, tired and running risks in the dark after they leave the buses, so that cooks in the UK can keep their beans a day longer in the fridge.

As the sun set over the airport, the trucks were returning from the sheds up in the hills, packed with vegetables for processing the next day. Meanwhile, the previous day's harvest was ready on pallets for the midnight flight to London. After landing, the vegetables go to a large Homegrown warehouse in Stevenage in Hertfordshire, before delivery direct to stores.

I found the Homegrown smallholder operation fascinating. Yes, it could be onerous – partly because of the demands made by UK supermarkets. But a smart group of committed young farmers equipped with mobile phones and advised by trained fieldworkers has made this method of supply a realistic alternative to large plantations. I spoke to Richard Fox, Homegrown's CEO, at his offices in a new commercial development out by Nairobi's old race-course, a relic of the days of Empire and the shenanigans of Happy Valley. Nobody would deny that his first motive was to make a profit. But he was justified in saying that 'in effect we are running a fairtrade operation. We don't pay premiums to communities, but we do guarantee over-the-odds prices to ensure our supplies. Through us, many small farmers get access to foreign markets for the first time.'

Back home, I told this story to greens, suggesting that they could buy Kenyan beans with an easy conscience. 'I don't care what you say,' said one. 'The business is not sustainable. Just look at the air miles.' Well, OK. This is a serious issue. If British customers decide they don't want to buy the green beans with the label saying they flew to the supermarket, then Homegrown's business is doomed.

On the face of it, the statistics don't look good. Emissions from air-freighting beans are 200 times greater than if they had come by ship. But the food-miles issue isn't that straightforward. In summer there are green beans available grown outdoors in Britain, and eating them is the low-energy option. But the energy needed to air-freight vegetables from Kenya to Britain in winter, when British demand is highest, is actually only about 15 per cent more than the energy needed to heat a greenhouse to grow those vegetables here.

But I think the real ethical issue is different. Can it really be right to try to make a tiny reduction in our own emissions by depriving Kenyan farmers of their livelihoods? Think of it this way. The average Kenyan's carbon emissions are one-thirtieth of those for the average Briton. Or to choose the hardest case, let's, for the sake of argument, say Jacob should be personally responsible for the entire carbon footprint of his business, right to the supermarket shelf in the UK. How do things look?

Every kilogram of Jacob's green beans flown to Britain consumes 1.9 litres of aviation fuel, which releases 4.25 kilograms of CO_2. So the carbon footprint of Jacob's typical annual production, taking off a bit for topping and tailing and wastage at the Kenyan end, is about 17 tonnes of CO_2. That is, admittedly, approaching twice the average annual emissions for a typical Briton. But Jacob's farm supports a family of four. So divide by four and the per-capita carbon footprint of his business comes out at about half that of average per-capita emissions in Britain. Surely he has some rights here? Do you still want to boycott his beans?

Many of the people who recoil at the idea of vegetable air miles, and would not be seen dead buying a Kenyan green bean in their supermarket, also want to help poor countries like Kenya through 'trade not aid'. There is a contradiction here. And this is not a trivial issue. Green beans are a major Kenyan export, and 70 per cent of those exports come to Britain.

My sceptical green friends point to other 'sustainability' issues. One is water. Green beans imported to Britain from Kenya soak up, by one estimate, almost 200 million cubic metres of water a year. That is enough, it is said, to provide 10 million Kenyans with daily household water, in a country where millions do not have running water in their homes. Maybe so. But the Kenyan drinking-water problem is largely about pollution and poor infrastructure, not an absolute shortage of water. Shutting down smallholders' farms growing beans for Britain would not put water in taps.

Still tempted to reduce your emissions by cutting out Kenyan beans? Let me suggest that you take the bus to the supermarket, buy a bit less processed food, do something that will hurt you, yes you, not Jacob. As a result of what I saw on my trip, I decided to start eating *more* Kenyan beans. And back home, I did just that at my local M&S. The beans were certainly fresh. They lasted for a week in my fridge. Thomas had promised that if I sent him the tracer code stamped on a pack, he could download the information available on who had grown it. So I emailed him the code: 061104005. Just that.

Good as his word, a couple of days later Thomas replied. My

beans had been grown by Mary Lenkiyieu, who has a tiny farm – more a vegetable garden – covering less than half a hectare. It is in Loitokitok, right on the border with Tanzania. My beans had been sown on 28 September 2006, eleven weeks before I bought them. They were harvested on 28 November, and packed and put in the hold of one of Dicky Evans' aircraft on the 29th.

The records revealed that, along with the beans, Mary grows maize and tomatoes and beans for her family. She was investing her income from Homegrown to buy egg-laying chickens, and a cow to provide milk for her young family, as well as school uniforms and books.

When I started on this journey, I thought that at the end I might concoct an elaborate allegory. Jacob and the Beanstalk, maybe. It seemed quite neat. A generation ago, Jacob Musyoki and his fellow Akamba in the Machakos hills swapped their mothers' cows for beans. The beans grew. Jacob gained some modest riches. Metaphorically at least, he climbed the beanstalk and found himself in a strange land of just-in-time sales to European supermarkets. But then the allegory fell apart. For now, there just does not seem to be an ogre to chase him out of the magic kingdom. Unless, of course, it turns out to be the air-miles crusaders.

One in a Billion:
Severina, the Favela *Queen*

Severina Euega's view is one of the best in Rio. From the clean air of the mountainside, she looks out across some of the bluest waters and most exclusive beaches in one of the most spectacularly sited cities in the world. Her visitors gasp as they walk through her neighbourhood, along Number One Street, catching glimpses of the vistas below. Their surprise is all the greater because they are walking through Rosinha, the largest *favela*, or shanty town, in South America.

Rio's property developers would love to bulldoze Rosinha and cover the hillside with exclusive apartments and hotels like the Sheraton complex, which is down the hill within a stone's throw of the *favela*. But the residents of Rosinha are not for moving. Theirs is a well-established community. Severina came here as a baby forty years ago, and when I met her, she was president of the Women's Association of Rosinha, part of a system of local government within the *favela* that is self-built, like the houses.

The common perception of Rio de Janeiro's shanty towns is that they are hellholes harbouring violence, vermin, drug traffickers and the street children who rob tourists on Copacabana beach. Other Rio citizens claim that the heads of the powerful *favela* associations are drugs barons. Stories circulate of people who stray into the *favelas* and are never seen again. They should, the argument goes, be demolished and their citizens sent back to the countryside or put into public housing. In this atmosphere, extermination gangs kill street children almost at will.

Some of the horror stories about the *favelas* may be true. But visitors invited to Rosinha are in for a few surprises. As well as the spectacular views, there is a friendly and matriarchal community. When we met, Severina was surrounded by children and chickens; a lone pig rooted in a small pen; a samba dress was laid out to dry on a stone wall. She certainly didn't look like a drugs baron. 'We women have joined forces in a struggle to make a better community here,' she told me. 'We need many more facilities. We have just two small health clinics for a quarter of a million people, with one gynaecologist and two paediatricians.' Her association was campaigning for more clinics, better water supplies and refuse collection, another school and for help in improving the worst housing.

Almost 2 million people live in Rio's *favelas*, a fifth of the city's population. Many came, like Severina, from the poor, drought-stricken north-east of the country. While some settlements are new, others were founded during the late nineteenth century. Their inhabitants are essential to the city's economy. Visitors in their air-conditioned buses shudder as they pass the *favelas*. They never realize that the people who served them breakfast at their hotels that morning, and will turn down their beds that night and charge their credit cards when they head for home, probably live in them.

The *favelas* are densely packed and enclosed. But they are far from the chaotic places they seem from the outside. They are as socially stratified as any ordinary town. In Rosinha, says Severina, the poorest families and worst houses are on the upper slopes, which are least well served by water, sewers and electricity, and most vulnerable to the landslides that occasionally bury inhabitants after heavy rains.

Number One Street, Severina's home, is one of Rosinha's highest and poorest neighbourhoods. I reached her house down a ramshackle passageway linked to other 'streets' by stairways. Walking its length involved dodging wheelbarrows, ducking beneath roofs made of crumbling asbestos and leaping over rivulets of sewage seeping down the hillside. The street's communal standpipes do not even have taps, but simply gush water intermittently. Whenever the supply is connected, women rush to collect it in buckets and bowls for washing, or to fill tanks on their roofs. In the areas without taps, I saw tin cans hanging on the edges of roofs to collect rainwater.

More people have electricity in their homes than piped water. Many of the connections are illegal, of course. The local electricians who tap passing power lines are known locally as 'cats'. But most people insist that they pay for their power, often communally, with several families sharing a meter. In fact, the shared meter has become a basic unit of local organization in much of Rosinha, says Severina. It is a mark of trust between neighbours. Other links with the outside world are more tenuous. Severina has a telephone for her work with the Women's Association. And telegrams can be delivered to houses. But postmen deliver letters only to the local church.

Looked at from the outside, the *favelas* of Rio may appear like festering sores on a beautiful city. But from within they are more complex. Yes, they have huge problems. But their human resources are considerable. If I had the task of greening Rio, I think I would start not by razing the *favelas*, but by investing in them and learning green lessons from them. And I would want to find a place for people like Severina in my administration.

Part Three

My Clothes

11

King Cotton: Drought, Diggers and Dirty Secrets

Geoff Hewitt has a big new house and a four-car garage. He has 2,000 hectares of cotton farm and enough trees down by the creek for the roosting kookaburras to wake him in the morning. He lives at Macalister, near Dalby on the Dalby Downs, a four-hour drive inland from Brisbane, the capital of Queensland. People like him made modern Australia: restless, purposeful, a touch idealistic, ever ready to open his door to a visitor.

Out here there are cattle, grain, coal mines and, usually, cotton. But outside on the veranda, listening to the kookaburras laugh, Geoff was explaining to me why, months into the growing season, not a single square metre of his 2,000-hectare cotton farm was planted. Why his high-tech, GPS-navigated tractors, able to steer to an accuracy of 2 centimetres, were idle. And why his plan to sell branded Aussie cotton shirts in British stores like Marks & Spencer was on hold. No rain. It was as simple as that. No rain, so no water in his reservoirs. So no point in planting cotton. 'We've had three and a half inches of rain so far this year. Usually we get twenty-five inches in a year, and it's September.'

Australia is the world's third-largest exporter of cotton. Or was.

For in 2006 the driest continent was in the midst of its worst drought for 1,000 years. Nobody knew if what was happening was natural variability or a product of man-made global warming. By 2008, climatologists were saying whole towns might have to be evacuated. And already a whole industry – the cotton industry, which in a normal year takes a tenth of the country's water – was on its knees. There was no water to take.

Geoff couldn't have been closer to the heart of the crisis. As we looked out across his parched fields, he pointed towards a dried-up creek. 'That is the start of the Condamine River,' he said. 'It is one of the sources of the Murray-Darling, the largest river system in Australia.' The Murray-Darling drains an area twice the size of France, flows all the way to Adelaide and irrigates 60 per cent of Australia's agricultural output. In the good times, four-fifths of the water on Geoff's farm comes from the Condamine. But he is allowed to pump only when there is enough water in the river. And in September 2006, there was no water. So his reservoirs, which can hold 6 million cubic metres, were all but empty.

Geoff hoped for the best. 'This is a land of extremes. We are ready to ride out the tough times and seize opportunities when they present,' he said. But he was fearing the worst. 'We've not had a flood here in ten years. I don't know when we'll see another.' And for now he was making money by hiring out trucks to take coal from the mine over the hill to the railhead.

Aussies are smart and resourceful. But farmers have been selling up on Dalby Downs, said Dan Hickey of Cotton Australia, a service agency for the cotton farmers. Dan spends his days driving across these hills and he has fewer farmers to visit each time. A decade ago, there were 600, he said. Now there were only 350. Some had had only a third of their normal allocation of irrigation water in recent years. Some were getting none.

And yet the farms I saw still seemed oddly wasteful of water. Geoff had some of the most sophisticated, customized, computerized methods available for delivering just the right amount of nutrients to soils. But I was surprised to see that he didn't use a drip irrigation system which would have allowed him to make more efficient use of his water. He said the cost of installing drip irrigation would be too great and the benefits too small. 'Even with drip, we would still have had no water for the past couple of years, and the extra cost burden would have put us out of business,' he said.

But the biggest losses were from his reservoirs. Geoff captured all the rain that fell on his land. Yet, he admitted, 'We lose about 1.4 metres of water to evaporation from the surface of our reservoirs in a year.' His largest reservoir, covering 31 hectares, had a bank only 4 metres high. I calculated that, depending on how much rainfall he had, he must lose between a tenth and a third of his water to evaporation. He agreed that was 'probably pretty close to the mark'.

The Australian cotton industry is always a whipping boy when the rivers run low. The farmers are aggrieved. But I didn't find it surprising. Just 1,500 cotton farms use more than the country's 7 million householders. And they only seem to care about their profligacy when the water runs out.

Geoff's farm looked pretty big to me. But it was tiny compared to what, so far as I can establish, is the world's largest cotton farm, a couple of hours down the road near Dirrabandi on the border with New South Wales. You can spend a day just driving round the edge of Cubbie station. The entire farm, which until twenty-five years ago was a cattle ranch, stretches 40 kilometres in one direction and 20 kilometres in the other. Nearly half is now irrigated. Its reservoirs, which like Geoff's take water from the Condamine, can store more water than Sydney Harbour. The thinking is not that the reservoirs will fill every year, but that when the big flood comes (if it comes), the farm can take all the water available. Then they hope they can use most of it before it evaporates.

Station manager John Grabbe has a simple philosophy. 'I firmly believe we have a responsibility to absolutely maximize production from the water we are entitled to divert.' He is as good as his word. After a programme to reduce evaporation by deepening his reservoirs, he followed up not by giving water back to the river, but by increasing the acreage under irrigation by 50 per cent. Grabbe complains about being singled out. He takes only 15 per cent of the flow of the Condamine, he protests, and less than 1 per cent of the entire flow of the River Murray system. But that is still a lot for one cotton farm.

I had planned the trip to Dalby Downs expecting to see the cotton that made my shirts growing in the fields. That plan was derailed by the drought. But everybody told me that normally there would have been cotton that would end up in M&S or other British stores. Geoff said, 'We sell cotton from this farm to Paul Reinhart, who I know sell our quality cotton to M&S. Every bale is tagged from this farm, so we should be able to trace it.' Cotton Australia had gone further: 'Together with Marks & Spencer, we have traced out the supply chain from gin-yards in Australia to spinners, knitters and weavers in Indonesia, Thailand and Korea, garment manufacturers in China, Vietnam and Bangladesh, and from there to European stores.'

But when I enquired further, neither M&S's chief cotton buyer Graham Burden nor the Australians could be sure of the precise journey. It became a deepening mystery. For almost a year, both sides promised to try to firm up the link. I had an email from Burden saying that he had tracked back some products to Indonesia, a major outlet for Australian cotton. He was 'drilling down to the next layer' to make the final connection. But he never managed it. Allan Williams of the Cooperative Research Centre for Cotton, which was doing the research for Cotton Australia, was working from the other end. But he too hit a brick wall. It seemed that no grower knew for sure where his cotton ended up, and no retailer knew where his cotton originated.

As in other major commodity industries, like coffee and cocoa, international trade in raw cotton is concentrated in the hands of a few companies. They include Dreyfus, Cargill and Dunavant (the largest) in the US, Reinhart in Switzerland, Plexus in Liverpool and the newcomer Chinatext in China. The problem, as Geoff put it, is that these traders have no interest in putting the growers in touch with the markets. 'They might cut out the middleman if they knew how the supply chain worked.'

There is a real problem here. In some industries a transparent supply chain is emerging. But not in cotton. I felt I had a right to know where my cotton came from. And Australian farmers were similarly aggrieved that nobody knew about their quality cotton. They have a programme called Best Management Practice, or BMP. Begun in the 1990s amid scandals over the misuse of pesticides on Aussie cotton farms, BMP has helped clean up toxins in the industry. It is, said Geoff, one of its most ardent advocates, a voluntary toolkit for farmers, covering soil and water management, chemicals spraying and fertilizer application. He showed me the paperwork involved. Now the farmers wanted to sell BMP cotton as a brand at premium prices. Not organic; not fairtrade; not GM-free; but top quality. 'We want a label on every shirt,' he said. It could be done, if the traders cooperated.

I had my doubts about the 'sustainability' of Aussie cotton, given its clearly unsustainable water use. But anything that starts a debate on those issues sounds like a good thing. In any event, a few more years of drought and Geoff would have to become a full-time coal haulier, sell his nice house – or make better use of his water.

But I was still waylaid on my journey: unable to establish a link between my wardrobe and the cotton fields of, well, anywhere. I needed to know more about the industry. World cotton production is around 25 million tonnes a year (the equivalent of fifteen T-shirts for everyone on the planet). *Homo sapiens* collectively spend more than half a trillion pounds a year buying clothes, with cotton the main ingredient. This would keep the GDP of Mali ticking over for almost 200 years. Every year Britons spend about £800 each on clothes. Well, I don't; but you may.

Most of the cotton for all this comes from seven countries: the large mechanized farms of Australia, the US and Brazil; the millions of small farmers who dominate in China, India and Pakistan; and the huge state monopoly of Uzbekistan in Central Asia. Despite being major producers, China, India and Pakistan export little raw cotton. This is because they spin most of what they produce and turn it into clothes within their national borders. As a result, cotton exports are dominated by just three countries: the US, Uzbekistan and Australia. It is these countries that supply the raw materials for the other big players – the low-wage 'sweatshop' garment-makers – who take advantage of the fact that no automated processes have yet been found to replace the work of human hands and sewing machines.

The cotton industry has always had a bad reputation for abuse of human rights. From the days when cotton was one of the prime products of the British Empire, it has been associated with slavery. And the stain lingers in places like Uzbekistan, where state compulsion to go cotton picking is routine, and in Pakistan and India, where child labour remains common. But today there is equal concern about the environmental impact of producing this apparently natural product.

One issue is pesticides. While occupying just 2.5 per cent of the world's croplands, cotton uses a tenth of all the world's chemical fertilizers and a staggering quarter of all the insecticides, mostly to fight off two pests: whitefly and bollworm. In India, half of all the country's pesticides are sprayed on to its cotton fields. The health effects of this are poorly quantified but undoubtedly substantial, with thousands of field workers thought to be dying of pesticides poisoning in India alone each year. When a chemicals factory burped a toxic cloud over the Indian city of Bhopal in 1984, with many thousands of deaths, it was making pesticides for cotton farmers.

Then there is the crop's huge demands for water. Cotton grows best in hot, sunny regions – typically deserts. Three-quarters of all cotton production round the world requires artificial irrigation – more than any other major crop. From the Yellow River Valley of China to southern Pakistan, from the headwaters of the Murray-Darling to the dried-up Aral Sea, cotton empties rivers and lowers water tables on a scale achieved by no other crop.

How is this reflected in the clothes I buy? A T-shirt, for instance. Britain imports almost half a billion T-shirts each year. About eight each. They often cost little more than the price of a beer. Yet to make the cotton for the average 250-gram T-shirt requires 80 grams of fertilizer, 3 grams of active ingredient in pesticides, and between 2,000 and 7,000 litres of water, or upwards of thirty bathtubs full. For one T-shirt. The market ignores this. Far from reflecting these environmental concerns in high prices, world cotton prices have been on the slide for more than a decade.

Two factors keep prices low. First the spread of Monsanto's GM cotton, engineered to resist the bollworm. This cuts pesticide use. But, in the past five years, the increasing popularity of GM cotton among farmers has raised yields by 20 to 30 per cent, flooding the market at a time when demand for cotton has been static because of growing consumption of man-made fabrics like polyester.

The world cotton industry is also seriously distorted by state subsidies for cotton farmers. Subsidies inflate production and so depress market prices. By most measures, Australia is the only country that does not top up the income of its farmers. Elsewhere, as much as a fifth of all cotton growers' earnings come from governments. The biggest subsidies come from the US government. The largest recipient in recent years has been Tyler Farms, which covers 16,000 hectares of the Mississippi delta in Arkansas. Its owners pocketed almost $37 million in the decade to 2004. As an Oxfam study of impoverished West African cotton growers pointed out, 'This one farm receives subsidies equivalent to the average income of 25,000 people in Mali.'

So far I haven't mentioned cotton's carbon footprint. This turns out to be large, but surprisingly, much of it arises not from making your T-shirt, or even transporting it round the world, but from using it – more particularly from washing and drying it. Growing the cotton for that shirt generates about 1 kilogram of carbon dioxide, mostly in making agrochemicals and water pumping. Turning that cotton into a shirt accounts for another 1.5 kilograms at spinning and knitting and garment factories. Transporting the cotton between those factories and ultimately to your home takes perhaps a further half a kilogram, though quite a lot hangs on whether you drive specially to the shop to buy it.

After that, if you are a fairly typical user, you will machine-wash that T-shirt twenty-five times before throwing it away. If you wash at 60 degrees, then tumble-dry and iron the shirt, it will emit about another 4 kilograms of CO_2. That is more than the energy used in producing and delivering it to you, and gives your T-shirt a lifetime footprint of 7 kilograms of CO_2 or twenty-eight times its own weight.

We can take this further. Some analysts have put the 'social cost' of CO_2 – that is the amount of damage it does in changing the climate – at £125 per tonne. On that basis, a typical T-shirt causes about 90 pence worth of damage to the climate during its lifetime.

This study was funded a few years ago by M&S, and it does seem designed to point the finger at consumers. Who washes at 60 degrees? Isn't 50 degrees more usual? Do we all routinely use a tumble drier? And who on earth irons their shirts every time they wash them these days? So you can cut that footprint substantially. M&S, which is now cuddling up to its customers rather than accusing them, has a full-page advertisement in my paper as I write, pointing out that by washing at 30 degrees rather than 60 degrees, we can save 40 per cent of the energy bill. Hopefully, it will also soon add that hanging your washing on the line to dry will save even more.

M&S has also looked at the energy footprint of a viscose blouse. Viscose is a fibre made from wood. It takes twice as much energy to make viscose as to grow cotton, but less to turn it into a garment. So far they are level pegging as they leave the shop. But because you can wash viscose at lower temperatures and it drip-dries in a jiffy, the carbon footprint of the viscose blouse from day-to-day use can be as little as a tenth that of a cotton T-shirt. It might be going a bit far to suggest, as one headline writer did, that viscose can save the world. But it could help. Personally I hate viscose. But I'll cool-wash cotton, I don't own a tumble drier and I *never* iron shirts, even cotton ones. So I hope I am not too bad.

12

Behind the Label: Bless My Cotton Socks

Searching for some new socks in Marks & Spencer one day, I noticed, buried way down low, a small collection of fairtrade cotton socks. They cost twice as much as the other pairs, but I bought them. The label made me feel that the other pairs were unfairly traded. In fact, I felt so good about the purchase that I went back and picked up an £8 fairtrade T-shirt. But, apart from the feel-good factor, what extra was I getting for my money? More to the point, who was getting my extra money? Armed with the product codes from several recent purchases, plus M&S's shop slogan promising to go 'behind the label' to tell customers where their clothes come from, I talked to M&S's chief cotton buyer, Graham Burden, at the company's west London HQ.

M&S turned out to be a bit hot and cold on going 'behind the label'. They wanted to do it when they had a good story to tell, but not when they didn't. Graham was not keen for me to pursue the origins of a pair of £9 jeans made up in Bangladesh. But he was keen to make the introductions for me to follow the trail of my fairtrade socks and T-shirt. And it is a good story.

It was still dark when I got off the sleeper train from Mumbai.

Surendranagar station was in the middle of nowhere in the near-desert Indian state of Gujarat. But I stepped into a pre-dawn hubbub. It was the end of the Eid festival, and the platform was packed with people returning home. I eventually found my host, Dilip Chhatrola. We took a pre-dawn truck-stop breakfast with drivers wrapped in blankets against the chill, and headed north for the small agricultural town of Rapar. The highway was full of Tata trucks bringing raw materials from the huge seaport of Kundla to factories making steel girders and ceramics and much else. But as we approached Rapar, the sun's first rays caught the white of cotton in fields ready for harvest. In the town, the morning rush hour mixed bullock carts with motorbikes. A camel was pulling a cement mixer. This was more like India.

I had come to see organic cotton being grown under fairtrade rules. My contacts this cold desert morning were from Agrocel, the company training the farmers in organic ways and buying their cotton to make into my socks and T-shirt. Curiously, Agrocel's small depot in Rapar was stacked high with agricultural chemicals. They included organophosphates like methyl parathion and dichlorvos – one with the alarming brand name of Doom. These are lethal products, especially in villages where protective clothing is virtually unheard of, where farmers have nowhere secure to store their chemicals, and where many cannot read the instructions on the labels. This was the enemy, surely?

Agrocel, it turns out, is an offshoot of a larger Indian company best known for its pesticides. But it has been changing tack. The Rapar store manager said, 'We sell pesticides, but we explain to the farmers at the same time why they should switch.' It sounded like greenwash, but I was wrong. In this corner of Gujarat, Agrocel has established one of the world's largest farmers' associations for producing organic cotton, and recently won certification from the Fairtrade Foundation. In the villages around Rapar, 560 smallholders were growing organic cotton and receiving a premium price from Agrocel in return.

We set off to meet them. Each described how, after attending Agrocel classes, they had given up on that company's chemicals and begun composting farm waste, recycling cattle dung on to the fields, and using natural plants to ward off pests. They ground up seeds from the local neem tree to make an oil that killed aphids and the dreaded bollworm, for instance. 'Before, I sprayed endosolfan every week,' said Amarsi Chhandha in Bhimasar village. 'It cost me a lot. But neem oil is cheaper and safer and works well.' Most farmers also planted crops that attracted pests away from the cotton. Marigolds were popular, and not just as a pesticide. Everywhere I went, farmers' wives garlanded me with elaborate wreaths of the bright yellow flowers.

This reliance on natural pesticides was very impressive. Whenever I had met cotton farmers before, they had told me their crops failed without a constant chemical dousing. But here they were adamant that organic methods worked. Ranabhai Dungarbhai, a numerate and articulate farmer, said, 'Before Agrocel came here, I sold to local traders who paid less and often paid late. I used to get about twenty rupees for a kilo of seed cotton straight from the field. Now it is about twenty-four rupees, and the price is guaranteed.' His yields had initially fallen when he switched to organic, but they recovered and were now just 7 per cent down. But he wasn't worried, because without pesticides to buy, his farm costs were down 20 per cent. So he was better off. He planned to spend his improved profits on a new house for his three young children.

The big problem for these farmers was not pests but water. Gujarat is dry, and cotton is a thirsty crop. One farmer in Padampar told me that a generation ago his father could bring water to the surface in a bucket, but now he ran electric pumps round the clock to haul it on to his fields from 100 metres down. 'We have to dig deeper every year,' he said. Organic farming was helping. 'The soils are better and hold more water,' said Ranabhai. He used to irrigate once a week, but now turns on the pumps only every ten or twelve days. But the water tables still kept falling. One village was taking steps to increase the water supply. Touring the Padampar village, I saw ponds and earthworks dug by hired JCBs to capture the monsoon rains and pour it down wells to recharge the underground reserves.

Who was paying for this muck shifting? Agrocel. Besides the premium price paid to farmers for organic cotton, it also pays an additional 13 per cent to village associations for community projects. And the people of Padampar had invested most of the £20,000 they received in the previous year on schemes to catch the rain. They could not have done this without Agrocel, they said. The community premium – equivalent to £10 per head of its population – was more money than the village got from the government.

The community cash was being spread widely. Virtually everyone in the villages benefited. At Padampar school, teacher Babubhai Klor came in on a public holiday to show me three shiny new taps. For the first time his 360 pupils had drinking water in the school. Then he showed off the school's small herb garden. And we went into the classroom, where he opened a cupboard to reveal two small microscopes, a tray of test tubes, a torch, a pinhole camera, some tiny solar cells and a miniature windmill – all paid for with the communal premium. I began to feel good about my cotton socks. The fairtrade premium was making a real difference.

Agrocel's main office is at Mandvi, four hours' drive away from Rapar. There, I asked Hasmukh Patel, the charismatic head of the fairtrade project, why an agrochemicals company was sponsoring organic farms? He said the parent company, Excel Crop Care, was one of the philanthropic enterprises set up by self-styled Indian visionaries after independence from Britain in 1947. Its founder, G. C. Shroff, had dreamed of uplifting peasant farmers through selling them pesticides. Back then, access to farm chemicals was seen as the route to prosperity for the rural poor. This was before Rachel Carson's book *Silent Spring*, published in 1962, sounded an environmental warning about pesticides. Nobody spoke then about a 'pesticides treadmill', and the health hazards were largely unknown.

But Shroff later saw the light. So he has sent out his top lieutenants to help farmers grow organic cotton and to find markets for their produce. Bishopston Trading Company, a co-operative clothes shop in Bristol, started buying Agrocel cotton to be spun and woven on handlooms in southern India. Agrocel also got help from the Shell Foundation, a charity set up by the petro-chemicals company to help poor farmers with the problems of globalization. This was fascinating. Two companies whose prime business is selling agrochemicals had got together to found one of the world's most successful organic enterprises.

After going organic, Hasmukh spotted the growing market for fairtrade products. And now business is booming. Demand far exceeds supply. The week before I flew to India, M&S had announced that it wanted to buy one-third of all the world's fair-trade cotton. A couple of weeks before I showed up, M&S's local buyers had been in the Agrocel office asking to purchase 6,500 tonnes from Agrocel's 2007 harvest.

That caused a big laugh. Agrocel is growing by 40 per cent a year, but the order was still four times higher than its expected production for the year. 'M&S pushed and pushed,' Hasmukh said. 'We told them our first priority was our small, regular customers. Whole villages in India depend on our cotton to make clothes for people like Bishopston. M&S may be big, but they are newcomers.' In the end, he promised to sell them 300 tonnes. 'One day we may be able to meet M&S's demands,' he said. 'But not yet.'

Many fairtrade cotton suppliers are facing similar dilemmas. They crave the big contracts, but fear the major brands could disappear as fast as they have arrived. And even if they stay, they may end up subverting the fairtrade formula. Hasmukh is optimistic, however. He believes that the communal premiums could be the key to long-term success. 'They have really encouraged farmers to share expertise, through the associations set up to manage the money. We also find that women in the villages are taking a big part.' He saw two major threats. One was GM cotton, which is spreading fast through India. The other was the shortage of water, which a surge in demand for even organic, fairtrade cotton could make worse. In that sense, the fairtrade cotton boom may contain the seeds of its own destruction.

Maybe in the long run, it is too dry in Gujarat for cotton farming of any sort. But at least the farmers seemed to be making informed choices about their water.

India is the world's third-largest cotton producer, with more land under cotton cultivation than any other country. Its big industrial combines invest in high-tech spinning, knitting and weaving plants. Welspun is the world's biggest producer of fabric for babies' nappies. Arvind in Ahmedabad is one of the world's biggest manufacturers of denim, churning out a staggering 30,000 pairs of jeans a day for brands like Levi's, Lee, Diesel and Wrangler. But I was following my personal footprint, the trail of the cotton that went into my fairtrade socks and my fairtrade T-shirt. And that took me east to the state of Madhya Pradesh, in the heart of India's cotton belt.

Here, on the banks of the River Narmada, among traditional handloom weavers and thousands of sari stores, I visited Maral Overseas, a large integrated cotton operation, covering hundreds of hectares. Maral is a global company, growing its own cotton, buying in more from across the globe and employing thousands of workers to make yarn and clothing. It turned Agrocel cotton into yarn for my socks, and produced my fairtrade T-shirt from start to finish.

Maral, like Agrocel, has a tradition of Hindu philanthropy. Its campus has free food and clinics open to the entire community. The on-site farm grows vegetables and fruit for the factory kitchens, and has a herd of cows living in a cowshed as well air-conditioned as its guest rooms. The cows supply the canteens with milk, and their dung fertilizes the vegetable gardens. Every cow has a name: Yamuna, Kamini, etc. The bull doesn't.

Maral funds a local school that is so good that children come from 40 kilometres away to attend. I was introduced as a guest of honour at one morning assembly by the principal, Mr Panda – a small, bustling, improbable man with a sharp business suit and a punkish quiff of hair. The uniformed students stood smartly to attention. It all felt like a scene from a Gilbert and Sullivan opera.

The company also has 1,200 farmers of organic cotton under contract. This, incidentally, gave the lie to claims I heard elsewhere that Agrocel's organic cotton farming was only possible because of some peculiarity of the local cotton. The project's mastermind, Surendra Kumar Tiwari, took me round the farms. This was no monoculture. Interspersed with the cotton, I found parsley and aniseed, coriander and brinjal, chillis and ginger, papaya and tomatoes, runner beans and gilki, which is like a courgette, red onions and chickpeas and turmeric. There were Mahua trees, whose flowers produce a traditional alcoholic drink. The farmers had planted lemons and potatoes round the fields to attract birds that eat the pests.

As we sat beneath his mango tree, farmer Sitaran Giadi twiddled his fine moustache and told me profits were good. His children go to university. 'I left education when I was thirteen,' he said wistfully. Other farmers had sent their children off to engineering college, or bought more cattle or dug more wells or arranged better marriages for their children. 'Living standards have improved since we went organic,' everyone agreed at an outdoor meeting. Most now had TVs in their homes and about a quarter had motorbikes, though mobile phones were still rare.

One farmer's wife took me into her bedroom to show me a small wooden chest where she kept gold jewellery. It was clearly like a bank to her. It reminded me that the people of rural India have, collectively, the largest stash of gold in the world. Cotton, the 'white gold', was paying to buy real gold.

Maral is a huge operation. Less than 1 per cent of its cotton comes from these farms. And as M&S's biggest supplier of organic and fairtrade clothes, it shares in the problem of where to find the certified cotton to make those clothes. Agrocel cannot meet the demand, so they are going further afield. The Maral warehouse turned out to be full of bales from Cameroon, which has established a beachhead for fair trade. Maral had recently imported 1,500 tonnes of fairtrade cotton from West Africa, enough to meet M&S's needs for six months.

Maral produces more than 35 tonnes of yarn a day, a big part of which is bought by M&S. Most of the operation is automated. But even so, more than 600 people work in the four spinning sheds, cleaning the cotton, combing and compressing and then spinning the fibre, and loading it on to giant bobbins, each with more than 100 kilometres of yarn. Maral's forty knitting machines turn 9 tonnes of this yarn into fabric each day. The fabric is washed and dyed and cut into shapes on huge cutting machines. Then, for the first time, I heard a hubbub created not by machines but by human voices. Some 900 people on two shifts, armed with sewing machines and shears, turned those oddly shaped fragments of fabric into clothes, like my fairtrade T-shirt.

There were some pretty unpleasant jobs here. I watched women making buttonholes all day. Then I found a small side room where a dozen young men were sitting cross-legged on the floor separating collars that had been made in bulk by machines. They pulled a thread and tore a collar away, time after time after time. Afterwards, there was ironing and metal checking and folding and tagging and packing.

Maral sells branded goods to Timberland and Cotton Ginny, Marlboro and Sainsbury's and Cecil, as well as M&S. My fairtrade T-shirt was made here in its entirety, put on a hanger in the dedicated M&S storage area and loaded into a container for the journey to Mumbai port and London. But it turns out that Maral has only a bit part in the saga of my other fairtrade item, my socks. There is a long way still to go to my sock drawer – a journey that made me ponder whether Maral's role was altogether sensible. This fair trade ultimately seemed pretty mad.

My socks, produced several months before my visit, had been made with Agrocel cotton. But by the time of my visit, Agrocel was being overwhelmed by orders. Because Agrocel could not supply enough cotton to Maral, most of the fairtrade socks by then in stores contained cotton grown on farms in distant Cameroon. That cotton was trucked to Cameroon's coastal port of Bonaberi (the same port that exports cocoa for my Mars bar). Then it was shipped round the Cape of Good Hope to Mumbai, for a sixteen-hour drive to Khalbujurg, along one of the busiest and scariest 500 kilometres of road in India.

But the cotton didn't spend long in India. After being spun into yarn, it was put back in a truck and driven all the way back to Mumbai, where an Israeli company called Delta Galil took charge, as the yarn went on another long sea journey, this time through the Suez Canal to Turkey. Near Corlu, west of Istanbul, a firm called Aloha dyed the yarn. After that, Delta took it back to Istanbul and knitted it into socks, before trucking those socks across Europe to Delta's warehouse in Northampton. That was a journey of maybe 12,000 kilometres. All for a pair of socks. As this book goes to press, every pair of M&S fairtrade socks makes that same journey.

What lies behind these convoluted journeys? Price, of course. It makes economic sense to ship these products back and forth across the planet in order to find the cheapest place for each stage of manufacture. Maral is competitive in some areas, but not in others. You see, hard though it may be for us in the West to believe, Indian labour is comparatively expensive in the cut-throat world of global textiles, and it cannot compete for many labour-intensive activities.

Maral is technically a very efficient plant. It can hold its own in the high-tech carding, spinning and knitting operations. It is a cheap place to make yarn. But other stages in the process use more labour, and Maral pays its unskilled workers 120 rupees for an eight-hour day, and its skilled workers may get double. That works out at between 18 and 36 pence an hour. And at those wages, it cannot compete these days with sweatshops in some other countries, like China and Bangladesh.

Maral can hang on to some fairtrade and organic goods, like my T-shirt, because customers will pay more and the extra wage costs can be absorbed. But, for the rest, for the cheap, throwaway fashion of the high-street stores, it is in trouble. Maral's managers told me that three-quarters of its yarn, which is produced with automatic plant, is shipped out to sweatshops for the labour-intensive activities involved in turning that yarn into garments. They just could no longer compete for that business.

Unwilling to pay Maral's wage rates, the big brands in Europe and North America are switching much of their business to the very cheapest factories paying the very lowest wages. 'H&M buys mostly from Bangladesh now, and M&S is increasingly doing the same,' Maral's managers told me.

Even M&S? That company used to have a reputation for buying where quality was best. But twice in recent years it has come close to collapse because of uncompetitive pricing. So it has transformed itself into a prime player in what economists call the 'race to the bottom'. When price is all and the customer wants a £3 T-shirt, then, if the cutters and sewers and ironers and packers come cheaper in Dhaka, that is where they will be employed. So, fascinated as I was by my fairtrade organic detour, it was to Dhaka that I went next.

13

Trouser Snakes: The Strange Truth of Dhaka's Sweatshops

Five women lived in the room altogether. Three of them, Aisha, Akhi and Miriam, lined up on one bed. I sat on the other. There was just space between the beds to dangle our legs. The room had corrugated iron for roof and walls. There was a black-and-white TV flickering in the corner and a fan overhead to make the hot evening bearable. 'We've lived here for two years,' said Akhi, the most talkative of the women. They worked shifts of eleven hours, and sometimes more, in a nearby garment factory in Dhaka, the capital of Bangladesh.

I had travelled to Dhaka to find out who made the jeans I was wearing, and the numerous other cheap garments labelled 'Made in Bangladesh' on sale in stores across Europe. I anticipated finding the unacceptable face of the Bangladeshi garments industry, and discovering where sweatshop labour was even cheaper than in India. I was right on both counts. But I also discovered a strange flowering of female emancipation. These three young women, and hundreds of thousands more in this teeming city, were the first in countless generations of their families in conservative, rural, Muslim Bangladesh to have any sort of economic independence, any sort of personal rights beyond those allowed by their husbands. Life here was better than in the rice paddies and prawn farms. It was freedom and wealth, of a sort. And they were rather proud of it.

I had found Akhi and her friends by ducking beneath a flyover in the Mohakhali district of Dhaka, one of the city's many garment-manufacturing zones, then taking a dark lane down beside the railway tracks towards a food market and entering a warren of alleys through an unmarked door. There were eighty-four families packed in here, each occupying a single room. This was typical of where the seamstresses and occasional male co-workers of Dhaka's huge garments industry live.

Aisha, Akhi, Miriam and the two other absent women each paid 500 taka a month for their room. Or £3.60. You wouldn't expect much for that money. But on wages of 1,660 taka a month, it was all they could afford. The overcrowding was severe. Men were showering in the alleys from hosepipes; children rushed about. The women got up early to cook breakfast and food to take to work. They had to because the four gas burners outside their room were shared by nine rooms, inhabited by forty people. 'We all start work at the same time, eight a.m.,' said Akhi, 'so we have to start cooking at four a.m.'

I could not visit their factory, but I saw others like it. Dark, dingy sweatshops up narrow flights of stairs, often with bars on the windows and blocked fire exits. The noise of sewing machines could be deafening; the managers could be intimidating; the drudgery unimaginable. When I met the three women, it was about eight in the evening. They had just got home after their eleven-hour day. One of them hemmed trousers, another sewed collars on to shirts, the third put in zip fasteners. Day in and day out. They didn't even get to swap jobs for the sake of variety. Their managers couldn't see the point of that.

'Officially we get one day off a week, but if there is extra work we have to carry on working,' said Akhi. In Bangladesh, there is a legal maximum of fifty hours a month overtime, and employers are not allowed to require women to work after 8 p.m. But sometimes, she said, they worked all night and could clock up a 120-hour week. I had no way of checking these figures, but no reason to dispute them. These were ordinary workers telling me their ordinary stories.

Who do they cut and sew and press shirts and jeans for? You and me, of course. The biggest customer at Aberdeen Garments where two of the women worked was H&M. Hennes & Mauritz is a Swedish company 'known for their inexpensive and fashionable clothing offerings', as Wikipedia puts it. My daughter agrees. She buys a lot from H&M. And H&M buy around half of its cotton textiles from Bangladeshi garment makers. Most analysts believe the company is the biggest European customer in the whole of Bangladesh. So my daughter will very likely have something from Aberdeen Garments in her wardrobe – purchases that are part of my financial footprint, even if I don't wear them.

I asked these women what they thought about H&M, expecting an angry reply. But no. The garment workers constantly swap notes about working conditions, and H&M have a better than average reputation. The company pays more attention to workers' needs, the women felt. So it was disturbing to hear claims that even H&M, for all its goodwill, was being hoodwinked.

The buyers – the brands' representatives in Bangladesh – make regular inspections of the factory, the women said. But 'they always inform the owners first. Before they come, the managers come through the factory with megaphones. We are told to prepare the factory, to clean up. And they instruct us what to say to the buyers about working hours and holidays and conditions. We have to lie about holidays especially.' I asked about other brands. Of one, they said, 'They are only concerned about the product.' There was one factory where that company was the only customer. 'That is the worst factory in Mohakhali.'

Most of the 4,000-plus garment factories in Dhaka have

uplifting English names. Harvest Rich and Sunman Sweaters, Glory Garments and Niagara Textiles, Life Garments and the Abba Group, Imperial Knitting and Melody Garments and Fashion Club International. Some companies do their best, I am sure. But overall, this is a world of corner cutting, subterfuge and threats. In recent times, the women said, buyers have threatened to withdraw business after reports of workers being sacked without reason. So the factory managers found a way round the problem. 'They demanded that we sign a resignation letter. If they later decide to sack us for any reason, and if there is a protest about it, they will show the resignation letter to the buyer.'

I heard dozens of similar stories, both scandalous and petty. One supplier to Gap, JC Penney and Wal-Mart converted a storeroom into a crèche when buyers came visiting, and told women to bring in their children for the day. Government inspections? Nobody had any experience of them. Not surprising, perhaps, since I was repeatedly told that most of the garment factories were owned by leading politicians, their friends and families.

Khorshed Alam writes reports on the companies for Western NGOs and retailers alike. He said most brands had little idea what was going on, and many did not really want to know. After a well-publicized scandal about alleged use of child labour, he investigated the Harvest Rich company. Its buyers included M&S, Tesco, H&M, Sara Lee and Reebok. 'Many of these brands had sent in social auditors to check conditions and interview staff, but when I read the audits they all said different things. It was as if they were writing about different places.'

I talked to workers who had come to the Awaj Foundation, an NGO providing advice on labour issues. Some said that if they took a day off sick, they would be refused admittance to the factory and then fired for non-attendance. One was excluded for taking five days off work when her husband died. Others had no contracts of employment at all. One man said he was sacked for refusing to sign a blank sheet of paper. Others for speaking up about conditions, or saying the wrong things to buyers. They reeled off the brand names that their employers contracted for. Wal-Mart and Gap, H&M and M&S, Sears and Asda.

But the women also told me about their former lives in rural Bangladesh. The three women in the Mohakhali slum all came from villages around Dhaka. Akhi had seven brothers and sisters. Back home there wasn't enough land, and certainly not enough work, to support so many. So the families sent their young women to find jobs in Dhaka. Out of their meagre earnings, Aisha and Miriam, sisters-in-law, together sent home 4,000 taka a month (about £30). The alarming truth was that these women, for all their pitiful surroundings, were the rich ones in their families. And it confirmed what I heard in the prawn villages around Khulna – that a job in a garment factory in Dhaka was an aspiration.

Aisha and Akhi both had children back in their villages, looked after by their mothers. They said they hoped to go back one day. But that seemed an idle hope. Most don't go back, and these women already seemed caught between two worlds. I noticed a cheap bag hanging on a hook at the back of the room. 'GUCCI' it said in large letters on the front. It was a fake, of course. But unlike their mothers and sisters back in the village, these women had heard of Gucci. They aspired. Even their tiny black-and-white TV showed them a world they badly wanted. What else was there to dream of when making clothes for Western consumers than about joining them?

But the economic gap between their world and ours is huge. In 2006, the Bangladesh government raised the minimum wage across the country for the first time in a decade. It was now 1,662 taka a month – a bit under a dollar a day. Or 5 pence an hour. No wonder the likes of M&S are moving there. Why pay 18 or even 36 pence an hour when you can pay 5 pence instead?

But even 5 pence was proving too much for some Dhaka garment makers. After the rise in the minimum wage, many were simply delaying monthly wages to maintain cash flow. I met Jakir, who had just been sacked from his job ironing and packing T-shirts for a garment factory that sold to NKD, a German discount clothes company. The factory was owned, he said, by a well-connected former captain of the Bangladesh cricket team. Jakir's crime was to lead a delegation complaining that wages for February would not be paid till 30 March, and February overtime not till mid-April. He said there was a lot of overtime pay due because the workers were routinely forced to work a fourteen-hour day and sometimes nineteen hours 'because of the contract pressure'. I later checked NKD's website. Its T-shirts retailed at 5 euros.

Child labour is largely banished now from the factories that Western buyers know about. But it persists on a small scale among the sub-contractors that the factories call on to meet customers' deadlines. During my visit to Dhaka, I saw a locked-up building right next to an NGO in Shyamoli, a middle-class suburb. My host said it was a sub-contracting garment factory that operated from time to time. The workers appeared to be children. He often heard their voices amid the sound of machinery, in the middle of the night. He had never been inside, but materials for garment making often came in and out of the building. He seemed nervous about intervening, and didn't know who the children worked for.

Nazma Akter, the founder of Ajay, said some buyers were sympathetic about the obvious exploitation of both children and adult workers. Certainly, European brands occasionally sack suppliers exposed as using child labour. But, he said, 'in the end they are not serious. Price comes first. Every time the buyers make another order, they want lower prices. First it is the £5 T-shirt, then the £3 T-shirt. That is unethical.' The system, she said, is run 'so that everyone down the line is well enough off to have a nice house and a car – except for the women who make the clothes. Sometimes I even feel sympathy with Bangladeshi manufacturers, the way they are leant on by the Western brands.'

Soon after, I spoke to a top manager at one of the main garment makers. She said, 'These big-brand companies have corporate social responsibility departments, but the people who place the orders don't talk to them. We see it here all the time. The CSR people come in and stipulate basic standards. Then the next day the buyers come in and drive down prices and bring forward deadlines. These two things are usually completely incompatible. While the buyers are in charge, all this talk from the CSR people is just corporate window dressing, however well-meaning the people involved might be.'

The truth is that retailers talk about little else but price. How they are moving from Sri Lanka or India or Mauritius to Bangladesh or Cambodia or China to take advantage of lower wages. The only limitation seems to have been the quota systems set up in European and North American governments to protect their own domestic industries. But the quotas are now being abolished. And the 'race to the bottom' in the mass marketing of cheap clothes is intensifying.

Nazma dismissed Western hand wringing, and said she thought that it would be pressure from within that would ultimately clean up the industry. But she pleaded with customers in Europe not to respond to the obvious injustice with boycotts. The jobs, poor as many were, empowered women. 'Women are becoming an economic force. This is the first time they have had jobs outside the home. They are independent decision makers. They can come and go; nobody stops them. They are the economic backbone of the Bangladesh economy now.' Western consumers, she said, should be demanding better conditions for the women of Dhaka, and above all should be willing to pay the higher prices involved. And retailers should stop competing on price. But please, she said, 'don't stop buying.'

Most of the garment workers I spoke to agreed. Like many other workers I met on my journeys for this book, they had a good sense of their worth, and how they were being let down by the obsession of Western consumers with ever lower prices. Shuktara, who came to Dhaka eight years ago, told me, 'Our pay in a month is less than the price that you pay for a pair of jeans.' That was about right. Her pay works out at £15 a month. Sitting next to her, Nosrul, who came to Dhaka twelve years ago, chipped in. 'In our factory, there are between eighty and ninety workers. In an hour we make a hundred and twenty pairs of trousers.' So it takes a bit less than an hour for one worker to make the trousers that will eventually be sold for the price of her salary for a whole month.

Bitter? If so, Nosrul hid it well. 'We just want the customers in Europe to know that we would like them to pay more for their clothes so that maybe we will get paid more too.' I can't imagine myself being so sanguine.

Caught up in the human stories, I had lost track of the story of my jeans. I had bought a pair of Blue Horizon jeans for £9 in Marks & Spencer a few months before. Made in Bangladesh. M&S bought them from a company called, coincidentally, Spencer's Apparel, part of the large Medlar Group. The fabric that made the jeans came from the Nassa Group, which was Wal-Mart's 'International Supplier of the Year' in 2002. But M&S didn't want to give me an introduction to the companies, and without that the companies weren't interested in talking to me. So I asked Khorshed about them. They weren't the worst, he said, but not the best either. Just one of the pack in the race to the bottom.

I wanted to follow where my jeans came from back to the cotton fields. And here came a surprise. Bangladesh's largest garment makers want to cement their position in the market by making their own fabric. So they have been scouring the world for supplies of cheap cotton. In the past three years, Bangladesh has become the largest consumer of cotton from the Central Asian state of Uzbekistan.

14

White Gold: My T-shirt, Slave Labour and the Death of the Aral Sea

It is an old story, but with an unpalatable new twist. One we should be ashamed of. The world knows all about how, under Josef Stalin, the Soviet Union harnessed the rivers that flow into the Aral Sea, extracting their entire flow to irrigate fields of cotton. It knows how the cotton fields that clothed the Soviet Empire were worked by what amounted to slave labour, with millions of people, including schoolchildren, teachers and doctors, press-ganged into harvesting the 'white gold'. And it knows that this social holocaust was accompanied by an ecological holocaust as the Aral Sea, once the fourth-largest inland sea in the world, dried out.

All that was supposed to stop when the Soviet Union collapsed in 1991. Four years after Moscow's retreat, I joined officials from the World Bank and UN Development Programme at an international conference in Uzbekistan, the biggest cotton producer in the old Soviet empire, where they signed up with the governments of the region to an International Fund for Saving the Aral Sea. Schoolchildren were invited to the meeting to spray the delegates with flowers and declare their happiness that the sea was going to return – and that their days of forced labour were over.

Little did they know. When I returned a decade later, not only had the sea not returned, but the plight of the people and the entire local environment had deteriorated. The enforced labour continued, and even less water reached the sea than before. Wherever the money from the international fund went, it did not go into reviving the sea. And now we are to blame. For the cotton that once clothed the Red Army is now clothing us. Today it is to be found on the shelves of most high-street stores – and on your back and mine. Yet retailers who pride themselves on their ethical and green credentials – and who can give you precise details about the source of their 'fairtrade' cotton – profess to be blind to this tyranny.

Since the collapse of the Soviet Union, the assault on nature and the citizens of Uzbekistan has intensified. Islam Karimov, the former strongman of Soviet Uzbekistan, remains in place, and seems to have been emboldened by the departure of his Moscow masters. Most years, no water at all makes it to the Aral Sea down the Amu Darya, which once carried more water than the Nile. Cotton still employs 40 per cent of the Uzbek workforce, including hundreds of thousands of schoolchildren. And complaints about human-rights abuses have intensified. One story in the *Sunday Times* began: 'When Fazliddin Akhrorov was ordered by officials in the central Asian republic of Uzbekistan to give up his studies and pick cotton for three months, he at first refused. Threatened with expulsion from his institute, he was taken away. Within three weeks the healthy sixteen-year-old was dead.'

Uzbekistan is the world's second-largest cotton exporter, after the US. Most of its 800,000 tonnes a year goes south by train to the Iranian port of Bandar Abbas, and then by ship to south and east Asia. Of the 400,000 million tonnes of cotton imported by Bangladesh, half comes from Uzbekistan. That makes Europe, the biggest consumer of clothes from Bangladesh, the main destination for Uzbek cotton. Craig Murray, who was British ambassador to Uzbekistan from 2002 to 2004, reckons that a quarter of the cotton garments on sale in British high streets and shopping malls contain Uzbek cotton.

We are rightly concerned about the sweatshops of Bangladesh and elsewhere. But we seem profoundly indifferent to the people who grow and harvest the cotton. I wanted to put that right. I don't know for sure that the cotton in my £9 jeans came from Uzbekistan, but I can surmise that it probably did.

I travelled the length of Uzbekistan, from Tashkent to the Aral Sea. What struck me most was that the old Soviet system persists, but is living on borrowed time. The nation is straining ever harder to deliver its cotton harvest, but the actual output is less every year. The reason is that the infrastructure is decaying, and the environment is deteriorating. Evidence of the decay since the departure of Commissar Cotton appears round every corner. Canals are filled with weeds, sluice gates are broken, and concrete water channels leak into the ground.

The Russians prided themselves on levelling the fields to prevent waterlogging. Few farms do that any more. So the water builds up, leaving behind salt in the soil. Salt is toxic to cotton, so every winter the fields have to be flushed clean. These days, around half of all the water taken from the rivers is used not to irrigate crops but to flush the salt from soils before the spring planting season. Meanwhile, with drainage systems overwhelmed, huge lakes of salty water are forming in the deserts. I spotted one that took an hour to drive past. The Aral Sea has not so much been dried out as dissipated into a thousand desert sumps.

But the worst consequences of the country's continued addiction to growing cotton were at the end of my journey, in Karakalpakstan. This is the Uzbek province that once bordered the Aral Sea, before the tide went out. It had the country's seaside resorts and a huge fishing fleet operating out of Muynak. Now, you can walk north for 100 kilometres from Muynak before you find the sea. Not that anybody does; it is a new and unexplored desert.

Karakalpakstan was once a green and pleasant land, the delta of the Amu Darya, once called the Oxus. Even twenty years ago, it still grew large amounts of cotton. But now the water is all taken upstream. Little water reaches the delta, and virtually none makes it to the sea. The province is turning to desert. On the delta, half of the old cotton fields have been abandoned. State farms have gone bankrupt and found no buyers. Tamarisk is returning to the fields, and the population is migrating, or going back to the old ways – herding cattle.

Nothing I saw here was new. Everything was old Soviet issue. The cars were old Ladas. Soviet automatic cotton-picking machines lay rusting in scrapyards. More work for the children. I came across the site of a large Soviet tractor-parts factory in the town of Kanlikov. Today it is empty and the railway sidings that once brought raw materials are covered in weeds. Each year, locals said, there are fewer tractors and more donkeys.

The Uzbeks were told that, after 1991, capitalism would bring investment and efficiency. The truth seems to be the opposite. There is no investment; efficiency has deteriorated; concern for the environment appears even less than before. The only surviving Soviet skill seems to lie in propaganda. During my visit, the evening news announced with a fanfare that Karakalpakstan had met its cotton production target for the first time since 1993. What the newsreader never mentioned was that the target had been halved in that time.

Uzbekistan takes from nature more water per head of its population than any other nation, bar its smaller cotton-growing ex-Soviet neighbour, Turkmenistan. Yet I visited communities in Karakalpakstan where people had nothing to drink except water from irrigation canals. And that water was the uncleansed effluent from upstream farms. The water – indeed the entire environment of Karakalpakstan – is laced with salt. It is in the water, the soil, the food and the air. As a result, anaemia has become endemic, infant mortality is soaring and cancers of the oesophagus are the highest in the world. Since Soviet times, life expectancy has fallen from sixty-four to fifty-one. Local gynaecologist Oral Ataniyazova told me that in many villages on the delta the farm water was so salty that cow's milk added to tea curdled. And sometimes babies will not take their mother's milk from the breast because it too is salty.

Without the moderating influence of the sea, the climate has changed. Summers are hotter but shorter. Winters are colder and longer. People often harvest the last cotton in November, desperately trying to reach their quotas with frozen fingers on frosty mornings. Rainfall has declined and the region is increasingly ravaged by dust storms. An estimated 70 million tonnes of dust from the exposed seabed blows across the land each year. It carries a cocktail of salt and pesticides brought to the sea in past decades in drainage water. Those pesticides include DDT and lindane, which are banned in Western countries but still poison the air here.

'The entire population of Karakalpakstan has been chronically exposed to salt and farm chemicals,' Oral told me. 'We have researched the literature but can find nowhere like this anywhere in the world.' At a meeting of farmers in the delta town of Chumbai, one weatherbeaten man, the manager of a state cotton farm, looked at me gravely and said, 'We are all affected. There is a lack of good blood. All the women have it. Many children are born deformed here. My daughter and son were both in hospital for six months.'

Cotton has become a curse to Uzbekistan. A curse maintained by Western markets for cheap cotton clothes. 'We don't need cotton; we need fruit and vegetables,' Oral said. 'Then both the sea and the people could recover.' Maybe it will happen. The cotton industry is probably dying. Everywhere I went in Karakalpakstan, people said that when they had spare cash they bought cattle. That is what they did in the old days before cotton. The herds are growing. As I turned back from Muynak and headed for Tashkent, the roads that once hummed with tractors from the cotton farms were full of cattle coming home from grazing on the abandoned fields.

The people may be giving up on cotton, but the government is not. At least not yet. Instead, the country's élite is trying to get rich on it. The nation's cotton exports are all controlled by a series of exporting agencies, with names like Uzimterimpex and Uzmarkazimpex and Uzprommashimpeks, each of which shipped more than 250,000 tonnes of cotton in 2004. The agencies are privately owned and controlled by state officials and people close to the government. According to former ambassador Craig Murray, the agencies rip off the farmers, who receive only a thirtieth as much as similar farms in neighbouring Kazakhstan.

The International Crisis Group, an NGO, discovered that the agencies often work through offshore companies registered in the British Virgin Islands or Cyprus, laundering cash from their cotton trades with the big global brokers into underworld accounts. At all events, the cotton profits seem to translate into shiny new buildings in Tashkent and shiny new Western cars for top officials in the agencies.

If I can put this simply, our obsession (yes, my obsession too) with ever cheaper jeans is not just helping to sustain the dreadful conditions in Bangladeshi sweatshops, it is also helping enslave Uzbeks, desecrate their land and finish the emptying of the Aral Sea. And while the Bangladeshi sweatshops do have the saving grace of helping rural women take the first step on a long road to emancipation, I can see no similar justification for propping up the Uzbek cotton farms. They are bad, bad, bad.

I learned all this during a week-long visit to Uzbekistan, escorted by locally based researchers from an international agricultural research institute. Their status gave the scientists some independence and safety from intimidation by the government there. But it seems that few of the cotton traders or retailers who buy up the country's cotton harvest have taken the trouble to make a similar journey. Thomas Reinhart, who runs the cotton trader Paul Reinhart, told the *Sunday Times* he had never heard of the use of child labour in the region. 'We buy our cotton from government agencies and don't know what happens out in the fields.' Well, I reckon he damned well should. It isn't hard. And he has a large staff in the country to do it.

One in a Billion:
Nellie, the Flower-stall Girl

Nellie put on her platform shoes, tottered past the display of multi-coloured condoms decorated with animal heads, thanked me for one of the better tricks of the week and headed out again to sell her body from a flower stall in the Manila night. I went home to bed. Our encounter was only an interview, held in the offices of ReachOut, a clinic for prostitutes in the Philippine capital. But it revealed much about why the country remains a demographic nightmare. Nellie told me about a city where the mayor had banned contraceptives from clinics. About a country where the half a million abortions each year were all illegal – and where even the Muslim clergy were more liberal on family planning than the Catholics, led then by the aptly named Cardinal Sin, Archbishop of Manila.

Cardinal Sin is gone now. He retired soon after my visit and died in 2005. But his legacy is pervasive. Thanks in part to his influence, the country has some of the highest rates of unwanted pregnancies on Earth. And fertility remains above three per woman, when most of the Philippines' Asian neighbours are below two.

What went wrong? From the pulpits and the nation's tabloid press, church leaders inveighed for decades against contraception. And unlike in most Catholic countries, the clerics inspire real fear among politicians. The church under Cardinal Sin helped push out Ferdinand Marcos in 1986, and has flexed its muscles ever since. The UN Population Fund, which has spent more than half a billion dollars on contraception in the Philippines in the past two decades, was forced by church hostility to pull out of more than half of the twenty-one provinces.

Family planning has been an underground movement here. Its practitioners adopt many disguises. 'Reproductive health' clinics are the most obvious. Then there are lunchtime staff-training programmes, adolescent clubs and discussion groups for rickshaw riders. I visited an agricultural development programme that encouraged women to adopt family planning under the guise of helping them set up piggeries, onion fields and fish farms. I met Aurora Silayan-Go, who was running the Foundation for Adolescent Development. It was, she admitted, a cover for providing youngsters with contraceptives and advice on sex and health. At a teen club in the town of Cavite, she told me, 'Because this is a club – you can play chess here – it is easy for kids to come without being seen by their parents going to a clinic.'

The need for such centres remains urgent. Private surveys have revealed that a fifth of 15–24-year-old young women in the Philippines have had an abortion. Every health worker I spoke to agreed that back-street abortionists were killing thousands of women every year. They all wanted abortion legalized. But none would speak up, for fear of the attacks on their organization that would follow.

The national government spent not a cent on contraceptives. And local officials often harassed foreign aid agencies and local activists who did. People such as Dr Junice Melgar. She supplied contraceptives to the Manila shanty town of Apelo. She worked from a tiny clinic built on a former garbage dump, sandwiched between a sewage-filled canal, a rusting store for liquefied gas and a big new fundamentalist pro-life church. In this world of dank alleyways and garbage scavengers, monogamy is a myth, marriage rare, rape endemic and abortion rife. Here, sterilization and injectables remain the contraceptives of choice, the women said, because their men need never know.

But times may be changing. I met Benjamin Martinez, mayor of Balayan, a poor church-dominated market town south of Manila. He is a classic product of macho, nepotistic Philippines politics. He was ushered into the mayoral chair at the age of twenty-seven when his father, the incumbent, dropped dead six weeks before polling. His brother was the town's head priest and opposed all 'artificial' family planning. So did the provincial governor, his father-in-law. Yet Martinez chose to use his mayor's development fund – a big slab of municipal revenue normally spent on highly visible infrastructure projects contracted to the mayor's favourite companies – on 'reproductive health' clinics and a cadre of some 500 health volunteers.

The services were in such demand that many women health volunteers were themselves winning elections to neighbourhood councils. 'Reproductive health is a political gold mine,' Martinez told me. 'I may run for Congress next.' In the event, the people of Balayan have kept re-electing him mayor; he has been in the post for more than a decade.

Meanwhile, back at the ReachOut centre in Manila, they were restocking their shelves with bizarrely shaped condoms in a city where neither prostitutes such as Nellie nor abortions officially exist. In a city where I saw twelve-year-old boys and girls selling themselves at the same flower stall as Nellie, under the eyes of a police-run protection racket. And in a city where the clinic's newest client was a nineteen-year-old girl in her fifth pregnancy. Welcome to Sin's City.

Part Four

The Chinese Dragon

15

Computing Power: Mice, Motherboards and the New Emperors of Suzhou

You will never have heard of Sammy Cheng. I hadn't. But we are all in touch with him. Probably more of us touch his products, and do it more often, than any other physical object coming from one place. For Sammy – an ebullient, shirtsleeved raconteur in the buttoned-down world of Chinese businessmen – runs the factory that makes two-thirds of the world's computer mice. It also makes a third of the world's webcams; has a virtual monopoly in track-balls, the upside-down alternative to the mouse; and claims a half-share in the worldwide market for remote controls. And how many of those do you have around the house?

Sammy runs the main manufacturing base for the Swiss computer peripherals company Logitech. Its 6,000 employees work on the fringes of Suzhou, one of China's most ancient and loved towns, famous for its Confucian gardens and waterways. But Suzhou is also just fifty minutes by train from the mega-city of Shanghai, and is in the middle of what is fast becoming the world's largest urban area, stretching from Shanghai across the delta of the River Yangtze. And if you wanted to bring the world's computer manufacturing industry to a halt, shutting down the power station at Suzhou would do it. For on Suzhou's outskirts, now dwarfing the ancient town, are two giant purpose-built industrial cities. And besides making Logitech's indispensable computer plug-ins, Suzhou hosts factories that make a quarter of the world's laptop computers, a tenth of its scanners and nearly half of all its PC motherboards.

I went to Suzhou to see where my computer world came from, but also found myself plugged into Sammy's world. Sammy is Taiwanese – the son of an air-force colonel and an electronic-communications expert, who both fled mainland China in 1949 when the Communists took over. Now he is back, and so are large numbers of his engineering mates. Virtually all the companies that have made China the heart of world computer manufacturing have their headquarters in Taiwan. And Sammy was bursting to introduce me to his compatriots and to give me a snapshot of their takeover. But first, my mouse.

Logitech is Swiss-owned but with headquarters in Silicon Valley, California. It was one of the Suzhou pioneers, establishing its main manufacturing base there more than a decade ago. That is almost medieval times in the footloose world of computer electronics. Now it churns out 70 million mice a year – under its own brand name and for almost everybody else as well. I watched them stamping the names of Dell and Acer and Hewlett-Packard and many more on to the mice as they came off the production lines, one every three seconds. And Sammy was gearing up for the release of the world's first mass-produced 3D mouse, for Christmas 2007. 'Our philosophy is to have more than fifty per cent of any market,' he said with calculated immodesty. 'That's why we have had double-digit growth here in both output and profits for the last thirty-four quarters.'

Keeping the mice flowing is a high-wire act. The mouse may seem like a simple peripheral, but Sammy has 400 suppliers, and if any one of them goes down, he is in trouble. Luckily most of the suppliers are local, with 90 per cent manufacturing within 50 kilometres. For instance, his capacitors, the tiny energy-storage devices needed in most electronics kit, are made by the billion by Yageo, the Taiwanese market leader, just across town. But the two most high-value components for bestselling mice come from abroad – chips from Motorola's plant in Malaysia and optical sensors from Agilent in the US.

Suzhou is a boomtown. Driving down the main street, Sammy said that 'there were no cars here three years ago, and look at it now.' But real wealth is rare. While a handful of senior Taiwanese managers earn Western salaries, their more junior Chinese managers are on about £13,000 a year, and the 5,000 or so production-line operators earn less than £1,000. Once a paragon of socialist equality, China now has the biggest income gap between rich and poor anywhere in the world.

The eighteen-year-old girls who run the assembly lines are delivered by agents from the country's poorer provinces, like Anhui and Wuhan, which is where Sammy's parents came from. They are part of the estimated 100 million members of the greatest, and among the most compliant, mobile labour forces of all time. Most live in cramped Logitech dormitories, eight to a room. For recreation – between shifts where they make trackballs and webcams for the world's computerized youth – the girls have basketball and table tennis.

Touring the plant, I waited in vain for one of them to look up from their work. Just once, a plump face caught my eye. It was partly flirtatious, but mainly bravado. The girl knew she was alone in acknowledging the rare foreign visitor. In her glance, I imagined she knew she was being exploited, but also that she had found freedom of a sort from the stifling world of the Chinese peasantry. Freedom, at any rate, to glance at foreigners.

Logitech may dominate the market in sexy computer peripherals, but the real heart of a computer is the primary circuit board, or motherboard, where the microprocessor and central memory are housed. The world's largest manufacturing centre for motherboards is virtually across the street from Logitech. Asustek makes almost half the world's motherboards, 60 million a year, on a campus of breathtaking size that employs 85,000 people. 'It's not a company; it's a whole town, an entire society,' said Sammy enviously, as we drove up to one of its six heavily manned gates. There are no factories in England today one-tenth the size of Asustek's operation here in the ancient city of Suzhou.

You may not have heard of Asustek. It is one of the many 'ODM' companies that rule here. ODM stands for original design and manufacture. Besides making motherboards, they design and manufacture the computers that are sold under Western brand names. They are the key to Taiwanese success in the world computer business. The first ODMs were Taiwanese companies manufacturing the first laptop computers, and the business model has spread to dominate the rest of the industry. Buy a Hewlett-Packard or an IBM or an Acer, and the chances are that Asustek has not only made the motherboard, but also assembled, packaged and shipped the entire computer from here. I am writing this book on an Acer, almost certainly from Suzhou. Asustek also makes the 'bare bones' of market-leading Dell computers, though Dell finishes them off, customizing them to order at its own plant. And if Asustek didn't make your computer, then probably one of its ODM rivals, like Quanta or Compal, will have.

Sammy introduced me to his friend David Chen, another cheery Taiwanese and Asustek's procurement vice-president. The two men had worked together years before for the Dutch electronics company Philips. These days, David runs a logistical nightmare that puts even Sammy's work in the shade. He has to ensure that components from 1,800 different suppliers always turn up in time for assembly – including mice from Sammy.

The Asustek complex contains six separate factories. Factory six, the largest, employs 20,000 people. I had only an afternoon, so I went round plant number one. It was hardly small. It has sixty-eight production lines, making motherboards for all the major PC brands, including the top four: Dell, HP, Acer and IBM. On the lines, the basic task is to plug and solder resistors, capacitors and other electrical components on to the boards. Some of this work is mechanized, using big machines from the German manufacturer Siemens. But many of the larger components are inserted by hand.

As at Logitech, this is the work of China's most marketable resource: bored, methodical, nimble-fingered eighteen-year-old girls fresh out of school. Besides plugging in the components, some girls do hand-welding. They have simple textile face masks, and lead is no longer used in the solder. But the pungent solder fumes spread down the production line. David said many of the fiddly repetitive tasks being carried out by the girls were 'hard to do by machine'. Managers at other assembly plants told me there were machines up to the job, but girls were cheaper. At any rate, said David, 'We only use women for these jobs; they have better fingers than men.'

Asustek has a reputation as the lowest-cost ODM. It works its machines and its staff hard. The basic shift is eight hours, and operators work a six-day week. But, rather than running three shifts, Asustek has two shifts plus routine overtime. That may be as little as two hours in the low season, but it stretches to four hours in the high season, in the run-up to Christmas, when there will be operators on the production lines twenty-four hours a day. It might be worth bearing in mind next Christmas that a computer bought around then may have been made by people in the twelfth hour of their shifts.

As in many low-wage industries, the workers depend on overtime. Sammy told me, 'People leave if they don't get overtime. It is the only way they can save.' But the truth is that people leave anyway. Constantly. I asked how long the operators at Asustek stayed.

'We have a turnover of ten per cent,' said David.

'Ten per cent a year – that's amazingly good,' I said.

'No, not a year, a month.' So most people leave after less than a year. Despite inducements like free train tickets, huge numbers of the girls never return after going home for the Chinese New Year.

Wasn't he worried that women were so keen to leave his employ? Sammy intervened: 'These jobs are one of the starting points for rural girls setting out on a career. When they leave, they get other work in the city, restaurants for instance.' In which case, why do so many leave at New Year? While some girls stay in the city to find other jobs and send money home to their families, many do not. The image of tens of thousands of girls going home to their families and never returning told its own story. A story of young women lost and disillusioned in the vast regimented confines of a factory like Asustek. Enslaved, we should remember, to the demands of Western brands and consumers. My Acer PC, which I confess I bought largely because it was cheap, is a critical part of that process.

David was more concerned about the practicalities of staff turnover than the ethics. Asustek has to find and train 7,000 new operators every month. It has recruiting agents touring schools in almost every province in China. Sammy likened this to army recruitment. The logistics of running Asustek took my breath away. Every morning, 800 buses show up at the plant bringing in workers from dormitories and digs across town. Just getting food for the canteens is a problem, David said. 'Before last New Year, we tried to do a special meal, but nobody could supply forty thousand chicken legs, so we settled for cake.' Let them eat cake.

Suzhou is expanding in two directions: west to Lake Taihu, China's third-largest lake, and east towards Shanghai. The western park, known as the Suzhou New District, is cheap and basic. Rents are low and this is where the companies with large payrolls like Asustek set up. The eastern Suzhou Industrial Park is more prestigious, but higher-rent. It looks rather like Singapore, all glass and trees and wide boulevards – probably because it was designed jointly with the government of Singapore. This is where the swish apartment blocks are congregating, where the city authorities have recently relocated, and where education campuses and science parks are being installed in the hope of attracting more high-tech, R&D-based firms, like software companies and nanotechnologists.

The city claims to have six billion-dollar investment projects on the go out here. It is a maze of foreign brands: buying, selling and manufacturing. Tesco and Siemens, BOC Gas and Knorr, Pfizer and Sony, Epson and Sanyo, Alcan and Bosch and Wal-Mart. If China escapes from the low-wage sweatshop origins of its industrial revolution to become a fully fledged consumer society, then this is how it will happen.

Keep going on the expressway east of Suzhou Industrial Park and you get to the Kunshan export-processing zone. Here another Taiwanese ODM, Compal, makes almost a tenth of all the world's laptop computers. It produces for Dell, IBM, Hewlett-Packard, Acer and many other brands. My trusty Toshiba, companion on many a trip, came from here. 'Logitech sell them webcam modules,' said Sammy as we headed in to meet another old mate, Compal vice-president Mage Chang.

Compared to Asustek, this place is modest. Just 22,000 employees. But it is hugely productive. Compal, one of the earliest laptop manufacturers, turns out about 1,000 machines a year for every one of its workers at this plant. That works out at a retail value of about $1 million a head, of which each employee ultimately sees about $600. But Mage told me margins were tight, with the big brands demanding ever lower prices.

The immediate competition was literally over the back fence, where another ODM called Wistron, a spin-off from Acer, employed a workforce almost the same size as Compal's to make almost as many laptops. Rivalry was intense. Compal was, at the time of my visit, world number two in laptop manufacture, behind Quanta, whose main operation is in Shanghai. But it was only a whisker ahead of Wistron. Mage told me he regularly looked over the fence to count the number of container trucks leaving his rival's yard. He might have been joking, but I don't think so.

Compal is, like Asustek, a major supplier of bare-bones computers to Dell, which turns them into complete custom-built machines at its assembly plant 700 kilometres to the south in the port town of Xiamen. I followed the bare bones there. I was thinking of buying a Dell laptop next time.

Dell famously claims to ship completed computers, made to order, within twenty-four hours. And it seems to be true. You might imagine that means holding lots of stock. But not so. Dell buys $16 billion worth of bare-bones computers and components from Chinese companies every year – a spend exceeded only by Wal-Mart. Yet at its Xiamen plant, it holds no stock at all. Instead, it instructs its suppliers, like Asustek and Compal, to bring what Dell needs to the city and hold it in warehouses close by. Every two hours, Dell sends out new orders for parts, which it expects to be delivered to its premises within thirty minutes – 'just in time' for assembly.

I watched. Assembly begins, rather like a cafeteria, with a large pile of pink plastic trays. Each receives a piece of paper detailing the individual order – even a Dell production line is not paperless. Then components are loaded on to the tray, and the full tray is sent for assembly. A few hours later, after software is installed and tests run, the completed computer is packed up into a box at the other end of the building, addressed and shunted through a hole in the wall straight into a container for dispatch.

Interestingly, Dell does not use a conventional production line, in which workers pick a product off the conveyor, do their single task and pass it on. Instead it has 100 production 'cells' in which single workers perform most of the assembly in less than ten minutes. They have to be better trained than on a conventional line, but the job is more interesting. And they are slightly better paid, at a bit over £1,000 a year. Staff turnover, Dell said, is lower as a result. Oh, and guess what. At those pay rates, they appoint as many men as women to the operator jobs. And their fingers seem to be as nimble as girls'.

*

China makes 80 per cent of the world's PCs and laptops. But the brains behind this remarkable dominance is Taiwanese: men like Sammy and David and Mage, and bosses back in Taipei. Whatever the label may say, it is they who design and manufacture your computer. Today eight out of China's top ten exporters are Taiwanese ODMs, supplying big Western electronics brands. They have $12 billion invested in Suzhou alone.

Many of the Taiwanese engineers and entrepreneurs who run these companies worked first for Western electronics companies in Taiwan, like RCA and Philips. As Sammy tells it, as each of these companies shut down, the thousands of engineers they had trained set up their own companies: Asustek, Compal, Acer and its offshoot Wistron, Flextronics and Hon Hai, the owner of Foxconn, which manufactures iPods for Apple. The companies moved to mainland China to take advantage of low wages, but their top management is still dominated by Taiwanese.

As many as a million Taiwanese electronics managers now work on the mainland. They form a kind of economic occupying force that must be worrying for China's leaders in Beijing. And despite superficial rivalry, Sammy says there is a common bond among the ODMs. 'The top management were colleagues and schoolmates. We all served in the Taiwanese army. It's a team culture,' he says. 'If we need parts, we will call each other up.'

Sammy has done well. Not content with homes in Taiwan and Suzhou, he has set up his family in Canada, where his wife lives in Vancouver and his children are at universities in Toronto. He visits them monthly en route to his reporting sessions at Logitech's headquarters in California. His family's escape from China is complete.

But others are left behind. And some are victims of the helter-skelter economic growth. Across the road from Logitech's plant in Suzhou, there are row upon row of mean twelve-storey apartment blocks. They accommodate the thousands of farmers whose land has been concreted over to make way for the new factories. The farmers are allocated menial jobs in the city. Dozens of villages have been wiped off the map already. And the municipal authorities are in the process of extending the Suzhou New District by 200 square kilometres, an area almost the size of Birmingham. That will take it down to the beautiful Lake Taihu. But already the pollution from the factories is playing havoc with the lake's ecosystem. It has triggered a recurrent plague of algae. In 2007, the government declared the lake a natural disaster and hastily vetoed plans for the construction of a new prestige residential area on its shores.

But the industrial development continues unabated. At the end of my day at Logitech, Sammy drove me down to the lake where, whatever the new edicts, they were still building golf courses and condominiums. On the way, we drove through the old town of Dongwu. It is famous for its silk embroidery, but is rapidly becoming a building site. And judging by the maps drawn up by the municipal authorities, it too is scheduled for elimination.

16

Zhangjiagang: The World Capital of Rainforest Destruction

Zhangjiagang is not far from Suzhou. It is a major port on the River Yangtze, and imports more tropical hardwood timber than any other port in the world. Day and night, the ships cross the South China Sea and come up the foggy channel of the Yangtze, past the mega-city of Shanghai and wharfs where Europe's waste paper is imported, before unloading their cargoes of okoume from West Africa, or meranti from Borneo, or teak from Burma, or merbau from Indonesian Papua, or greenheart from Guyana, or bintangor from Papua New Guinea.

Two million cubic metres of tropical timber are unloaded here annually. Zhangjiagang is the new world capital of rainforest destruction. The place where, as they joke in China, the forests of Borneo are laid out end to end and turned into flooring for new apartments in Shanghai and Beijing. Except that in truth as much of the timber is exported again as stays in China. For in the past decade the 'workshop of the world' has also become the floorboard fabricator, plywood maker and joiner of the world.

China is by some way the largest buyer of timber on the planet. It is also the world's leading exporter of plywood, wood flooring and furniture, where it has more than a third of international trade. The Tropical Forest Trust, which works with European retailers to green their timber supplies, estimates that half of all the internationally traded tropical hardwood passes through China, and two-thirds of that passes through Zhangjiagang.

I don't buy too much wood personally. My last purchase of furniture was a solid beech desk made in North Yorkshire from timber probably blown down by the 1987 hurricane. My computer sits on it. It will see me out. But I am guiltily aware that I also have a wooden table and bench out in the garden. They were probably made in China or Vietnam, from timber hacked down who knows where. And there are the kitchen units, which have what looks like a tropical hardwood veneer. Gulp. Campaigners say that if I don't know where timber like this comes from, I should assume that it was logged illegally. I am in receipt of stolen goods – stolen from the rainforests.

At Zhangjiagang, local merchants happily show you round the vast timber yards, where there are street signs to prevent you getting lost. Many of the merchants have no calling cards, only cellphone numbers, which they scrawl on to the logs with a marker pen. Xiufang Sun, a market analyst for the non-profit research group Forest Trends in Beijing, knows the port well. She says there are about 140 importers and dealers working full time there. Most have no idea where the logs they buy come from, she says, though they must know they have often been illegally felled. But so far as they are concerned, that is someone else's responsibility. The wood was dead on arrival. They simply want to sell as fast as they can, to make room on the dockside for the next load coming in on the next tide. And they have plenty of clients, as the rash of five-star hotels in the port underlines.

Most of the timber coming out of most of the countries from which Zhangjiagan imports is reckoned by reputable international agencies to be logged illegally. Sometimes this may be on a technicality. But often it is sheer brazen corruption and transgressing of basic laws designed to protect the forests and their inhabitants.

A short way up a delta creek from Zhangjiagang is a small town called Nanxun. It is not on most maps, but it calls itself the hardwood-flooring capital of the world. With reason. In the past half-decade it has gone from being a small, local woodworking centre into the largest producer of wood flooring in a country that exports half the world's flooring. It has some 200 sawmills and 500 floorboard manufacturers. They are lined up along the creek. Here, planks from Zhangjiagang are cut, planed and varnished to make flooring for the world.

Much of the flooring is made of merbau, a tropical hardwood from the island of New Guinea prized for its strength and durability. It also makes great outdoor furniture and decking. The London-based Environmental Investigation Agency (EIA), an NGO which has tracked the merbau trade in detail, says one log of merbau from the Indonesian part of New Guinea is imported to China every minute of every working day.

One of the largest manufacturers of merbau flooring in the town is Zhejiang Fangyuan Wood, which produces 2 million square metres of flooring a year. Half of this, it says, is destined for export. This merbau trade is largely illegal, says the EIA. Not in Chinese law, let me make absolutely clear, but in almost everybody else's. The EIA calls it 'the world's biggest timber-smuggling racket.' And it says China is 'the largest buyer of stolen timber in the world.'

China's emergence as a timber superpower is recent. Only a decade ago, it was virtually self-sufficient in wood. Then two things happened. First, in 1998 there were major floods on the River Yangtze. More than 2,500 lives were lost and millions were left homeless. The government blamed the floods on deforestation of the river's upstream catchment in provinces like Sichuan, and it swiftly banned all felling of the country's surviving natural forests. The ban was 100 per cent effective. Four years later, I was in the mountains of Sichuan, north of Chengdu. Locals told me the roads there used to be bumper to bumper with trucks carrying logs. But now they were empty, except for the occasional bicycle. Huge timber-processing works stood empty.

But at the same time, China's wood-products industry was taking off. It needed timber. So the country erupted like a typhoon on to the world timber market. Within four years of the domestic logging ban, it had gone from nowhere to importing 16 million cubic metres of logs. It was the world's largest importer, unseating Japan, which had held the position for several decades. The majority of that timber was softwood from the Russian far east. But the country had also become the biggest consumer of tropical hardwoods. Today it buys 70 per cent of all the hardwood leaving South-east Asia, and increasing amounts from central Africa.

First, China tapped Indonesia, especially the rainforests in Borneo and Sumatra. I was in Borneo in 1999 and watched the process at first hand. Every week, thousands of labourers arrived on ferries from Java, where the country's economic meltdown had put them out of work. They were taken from the ports by truck to remote forests, handed chainsaws and given £3 a day to cut down the trees. Groups of up to 200 men were living rough in the forests, felling trees. I saw several teams of Javanese men jammed in trucks driving up and down the new trans-Kalimantan highway.

In places, the first timber they cut was used to make crude railways across the thick peat swamps. Only then could they bring out the timber in quantity. The pace of deforestation since has been breathtaking. One of the largest rainforests on the planet, covering an area larger than England, has been stripped bare in the past decade. At least half of the logging was illegal. A great deal of the timber went to China. Is some of it in my garden bench?

The Indonesian government has recently clamped down on the export of logs. It is trying to protect some at least of what is left of the country's forests. But it doesn't have the authority of its Chinese counterpart. Many generals and police chiefs and ministers and local officials continue to grow rich either by logging themselves or taking bribes from those who do.

Merbau is one of the most valuable timbers in the Indonesian forests, especially in Indonesian Papua, a remote region where loggers have moved as the pickings become thinner in Borneo and Sumatra. The EIA says several shiploads of merbau leave its waters every month, headed for Zhangjiagang. Much of this arrives with documentation saying it came from Malaysia, from where log exports remain legal.

The Indonesian crackdown has pushed up prices. A cubic metre of merbau can now cost £250. But as the trade has got hot and the logs have got expensive, Papua New Guinea has taken over from Indonesia as the timber pirates' forests of choice. Papua New Guinea is now China's biggest source of tropical hardwood. And the place, some say, where the immorality of the trade is mostly clearly on display. Through remote harbours along its huge coastline, one of the poorest countries in the world is emptying its forests of merbau and other valuable tropical hardwoods like bintangor, which is a favourite veneer for plywoods. Four out of every five logs that leave these shores end up in China. About 80 per cent of Papua New Guinea is still covered in forest, but more than half is licensed for logging. Current estimates are that the country's forests will be logged out in fifteen years.

The logging of Papua New Guinea is now a huge business. Timber is the country's main export earner. Fortunes are being made in this former South Pacific backwater. And about 40 per cent of the logging business in Papua New Guinea is run by the Malaysian firm Rimbunan Hijau. This thirty-year-old company is owned by Tiong Hiew King and his Chinese-Malay family. Tiong has been ranked as South-east Asia's twentieth-richest man. Today, his company is one of the world's largest loggers and timber traders, with subsidiaries in the Solomon Islands, Cameroon (where it has 140,000 hectares of logging concessions), Gabon (550,000 hectares) and Equatorial Guinea (320,000 hectares). The company is noted for its intensive logging methods.

Tiong has established what many see as a virtual stranglehold on Papua New Guinea's logging industry. Industry analysts say Rimbunan Hijau and its network of subsidiaries and related companies own twelve of the top thirty concessions and are responsible for more than half of the 2 million-plus cubic metres of logs exported each year. The Tiong empire also has the country's largest sawmill, at Kamusie in the remote western province, and its only veneer mill, at nearby Panakawa. It also owns one of the country's two major newspapers, the *Nation*, as well as having interests in fisheries and shipping, insurance and mining, finance and IT, retailing and palm-oil plantations.

While there is plenty of legal logging, the World Bank estimates that 70 per cent of the timber from Papua New Guinea is illegally logged. The government in Port Moresby insists that the logging operations are fully licensed and that forestry laws ensure 'sustainable' operations. It says independent audits for the government confirm this. However, Forest Trends examined sixty-three of these audits and concluded that they show nothing of the sort. 'The overwhelming majority of commercial logging operations are illegal', with logging rates far in excess of any that could be sustainable, and few benefits accruing to the locals. Forest Trends says there is 'corruption at the highest level of government and throughout the bureaucracy. Conglomerates with logging and export interests are reported to provide funds for political parties and individual politicians . . . In return for funds, companies are able to buy the right to log particular concessions and they are virtually exempt from the rule of law.'

We are part of this. The link from the forests of Papua New Guinea to the timber yards and workshops of China is clear. But so too is the onward path of products to the DIY stores of Britain. Papua New Guinea's timber is in much British plywood in particular, says Forest Trends' Xiufang. Greenpeace, in a study published in 2005, established that at least three major forest concessions in Papua New Guinea supplied plywood to major builders' merchants in Britain, via China. I have on my desk an off-cut of bintangor-faced plywood that made the journey from the Xuzhou Zhongyuan, a large plywood and board manufacturer based in Pizhou, north of Shanghai, to Britain. Since getting it, I have been looking closely at my kitchen units. The veneers do look very similar, I am afraid.

Since the Greenpeace report, several British companies have announced that they would end imports of plywood from China. But I found it still widely available. Britain was in 2006 by far the largest European market for Chinese plywood. The British Tropical Timber Federation advised its members against buying timber sourced from Papua New Guinea, because it will almost certainly have been logged illegally. But that is hard for a timber yard to comply with when the timber products are simply labelled 'Made in China'. And harder still for you or me buying plywood or furniture or flooring. In late 2008, environmental group WWF reported that, whatever the rhetoric, Britain remained the second largest importer of illegal timber.

Scott Poynton, head of the Tropical Forest Trust, says things can change if a 'chain of custody' can be established for timber. He says the big DIY stores have the commercial muscle to demand that Chinese timber mills find out and reveal where their timbers come from. Concerned customers, he said, should be looking for the label of the Forest Stewardship Council, which certifies sustainably logged timber. But even where that is not available they should be demanding that their timber suppliers can show the origins of their timber.

Making that happen in practice should become easier as agglomeration in the industry leads to the formation of larger timber combines in China. Timber combines with names and reputations to defend. Take plywood. Major Chinese companies in the plywood business include Happy International, which is based in Hong Kong and produces everything from plywood and veneer to parquet flooring and table-tennis bats. Another is Shanghai

Xingaochao, owned by Tao Xinkang. Tao set up a furniture workshop in Shanghai in the late 1970s. Today he has 20,000 employees and produces over a million cubic metres of plywood a year. He has been listed among China's twenty richest entrepreneurs. Because of their size and visibility, such companies are easier to hold to account than small fly-by-night operations.

There are other important players in Scott's 'chain of custody' companies further up the supply chain, nearer to where the deforestation is taking place. A lot of Happy International's logs, for instance, reach China via ships run by Pacific King Shipping of Singapore. A company prospectus that I found on the Internet says: 'Our group's vessels are mainly engaged in the transportation of logs from the Solomon Islands, West Africa, Papua New Guinea and Southeast Asia to PRC [People's Republic of China] and India.' It said the company shipped $19 million worth of logs in 2005. It is not illegal to do this.

Knowledge of illegal logging may be widespread, but guilt is hard to pin down. The paths taken by tropical timber, even in a simple journey across the South China Sea, can involve many layers of agents and a great deal of paperwork. But Poynton says he has special mistrust of the middlemen of Singapore and other ports along the route from the forests to China. There is, he says, a small island off the coast of the Malaysian Borneo province of Sabah where the local Chinese Chamber of Commerce is 'notorious in the trade for issuing phoney certificates of origin for millions of cubic metres of stolen Indonesian wood, and possibly also from Papua New Guinea. The traders pay the chamber of commerce to issue the certificates as the ships go sailing by.' In such an environment, establishing a traceable chain of custody is still going to be a hard task.

17

The Great Mall: Toothpicks to Placentas, Everything Must Go

A young niece of mine has taken to declaring whenever she picks up a toy: 'It seems to me that everything comes from China.' Even eight-year-olds read the labels, it seems. And those toys, some Christmas presents from me, do all come from China. It's not just toys, of course. It's everything: big and small, smart and stupid, adult and juvenile. For the bottom-end stuff, I recommend a visit to Yiwu in southern China – about four hours' drive from Shanghai. Forget the Great Wall: this is the Great Mall, the tat capital of the world. Or, as they put it there, 'the largest wholesale market for small commodities on the planet'.

On a visit there, I recognized things that have been cluttering up my house for years, things that turn up in every car-boot sale and Christmas stocking – and every charity shop just after Christmas. Toothpicks and tennis rackets; mothballs and candles that sing 'Happy Birthday'; clogs and car jacks; walking sticks and rat traps; Russian dolls and fake African carvings. If you want to go to one place where the world's stuff comes from, go to Yiwu.

Yiwu is a town of about a million people. Not big by Chinese standards. They have a hundred that big. But this is where the world's retailers come to fill their stores. Where 80 per cent of the world's Christmas decorations reach the global market, and 60 per cent of children's toys. Christmas is made in China and sold in Yiwu. Every day in the run-up to Christmas, more than 1,000 containerloads of goods sold in its markets leave the city. The taste of much of it is frankly appalling, from the mantelpiece clocks with Crucifixion scenes behind the hands, to the replica toy guns, to the aisle after aisle of children's clothing in migraine-inducing yellow and pink.

The city is dominated by a series of covered markets, each the size of Wembley Stadium and occupied by thousands of tiny booths. Many appear to be selling the same things. But the accumulation is stunning. The city fathers claim there are 50,000 booths selling more than 300,000 product lines. There are whole stores dedicated to selling different sorts of babies' dummies and dusters and Halloween witches and purses and keyrings and things to hang in car windows. There is an entire market devoted to socks, though I couldn't find a pair I liked.

And outside the covered markets, it is more of the same. God help you if you want to buy groceries. Instead, there are whole streets, whole neighbourhoods, dedicated to selling individual items. If you want to buy a belt, you have a choice of a million, at least. Then there is bra street, zipper street, plastic-products street, timber street, computer street, stationery street, necktie street, artificial-flowers street, towel street, scarf street, calendar street, picture-frame street, and Christmas-crafts street. To name but a few.

Up near the prestige international market there are street after street of shops full of beads: plastic and wood and stone and glass, all different sizes, in bags and buckets and no doubt by the containerload if you ask. There are single shops containing a million or more beads, and the entire neighbourhood cannot contain fewer than a billion. Probably there was one for everyone on the planet, certainly one for every woman.

Yiwu is the biggest bazaar in the world. It has so many shops and booths that the main street is devoted not to department stores like in any other town, but to selling shelving systems and shopping trolleys. By one estimate there are some 8,000 permanent foreign buyers in the city, constantly scouring the stalls for produce to ship home. There are so many Middle Eastern buyers that the city has its own Arab quarter. In the international market, there is a constantly changing display of the Commodity City Price Index. When I was there helmets and ties were down, but locks and baby food were up. There seemed to be a run too on Father Christmases playing the saxophone.

Where does Yiwu get all this stuff from? Why does Santa do his shopping here? Because the province around it, Zhejiang, has made itself into the world capital for making . . . stuff. Suzhou may make the computers; Zhangjiagang may turn the world's rainforests into furniture, flooring and plywood. But round here they seemingly make everything else. There are large factories, but also millions of peasant farmers and their families running backyard workshops. Most of these cut-price capitalists have huddled together. Towns you have never heard of have captured great chunks of the world market in specialized and not so specialized products.

Take Qiaotou. It has 200 factories making 60 per cent of the world's buttons and zips. That works out at 15 billion buttons and 200 million metres of zips – enough to stretch halfway to the moon. The president of the Great Wall Zipper Group proudly remarked recently that 'There is almost nowhere else in the world that makes zips.' Without Qiaotou, the world's flies would be undone, and much else in disarray. Around 70 per cent of the world's reusable cigarette lighters come from nearby Wenzhou. The Tiger brand is made here by some 300 small workshops. Meanwhile another town, Cixi, makes a similar proportion of the world's disposable lighters, as well as millions of electric irons and air conditioners and washing machines, and billions of ball-bearings.

Nowhere in the world makes more drinking straws than Yiwu itself. The city also makes 3 billion pairs of socks a year, but is rather put in the shade by Datang, half an hour down the road, which makes 8 billion pairs. One in three of the world's socks comes from here. Datang is the base for the Zhejiang Stocking Company, started in the early 1990s by Dong Yong Hong, a former schoolteacher who began by selling at the roadside. She got big, but much of her output is subcontracted to legions of home workers in the town.

Meanwhile, a billion or more people round the world are wearing shoes made in Wenling. One in every three men is reckoned to have a tie in a drawer somewhere from the 300 million made annually in Shengzhou. Hangji, in the eastern suburbs of Yangzhou, is the purveyor of 3 billion toothbrushes a year. Here are 1,600 backstreet producers and one giant, the Sanxiao Group, recently renamed Colgate-Sanxiao. Elsewhere in Yangzhou, there are 3,500 households engaged in producing the cheap disposable bits and pieces you find in hotel rooms, like slippers and folding combs and shampoo and shavers. Oh, and there is a toy factory with 40,000 employees. It has probably filled the toy cupboard of my niece. All this and more comes via Yiwu.

On the outskirts of Shenzhen, I stumbled on the world's largest market for fake oil paintings. At the Dafen Oil Painting Village, 8,000 painters work in 800 studios night and day to churn out imitations of the great masters – and some other sure-fire sellers. I have often wondered where those sorry paintings on the walls of hotel bedrooms come from; now I know. In one street there was a shop full of Mona Lisas; another with wall-to-wall Warhol Marilyn Monroes; another specializing in Canalettos; and a fourth with identical portraits of George W. Bush. Further down the street, I met a real artist who couldn't understand why punters flocked to buy the fakes rather than his original watercolours. The trouble was he charged twenty times more.

*

It felt and looked like a large black prune. But you can't be too careful. 'What is it?' I asked.

'It's a birth sac – a placenta,' came the stallholder's reply.

'What animal?'

A brief smile. 'Oh, a human. You take it for women's problems, and to make you more beautiful.'

I hurriedly put it back on the market stall. I had heard of women frying their own placenta for a post-delivery breakfast. But other people's afterbirths? That sounded more like cannibalism than medicine. But China sells everything.

I was in the heart of Hehuachi, the traditional-medicines market in Chengdu, capital of Sichuan province. A giant hangar the size of a couple of football pitches was packed with stalls selling herbs and spices, potions and animal parts of every description. Some of it would not have been out of place in a Western street market on a Saturday morning. But there was much that was more exotic. Immediately around me there were hedgehog pelts reputed to cure rheumatism, dogs' kidneys that promoted sexual arousal, newts to treat stomach ache, and dried snakeskins for dunking in wine as a tonic.

There were all manner of deer and antelope parts – feet and tails, horns and penises – jars of caterpillar fungus incongruously labelled in English, and boxes full of tiny crabs and dried sea-horses, which, the stallholders insisted, would bring me 'youthfulness'. Other delicacies on sale nearby included bat faeces, pangolin scales, seal genitals, the tiny fallopian tubes of frogs, toad venom, cuttlefish bones, dried geckos and leeches arranged in rows like so many chocolate bars on a sweet counter.

Hehuachi is one outpost of a fast-growing trade in traditional wild medicines that appears to have no limits. Based in China, it is spreading round the world. Many Westerners have tried to dismiss traditional Chinese medicine as a witch's cauldron of false remedies and bogus aphrodisiacs. But the truth is different, says Rob Parry-Jones of Traffic, which monitors China's trade in endangered species on behalf of conservation groups such as WWF.

Many potions have been found successful in epidemiological trials, he says. Research conducted for WWF at the Chinese University of Hong Kong has found that both rhino and saiga-antelope horn are potentially lifesaving cures for fevers and convulsions, for instance. (A flat contradiction of statements put out by WWF over the years.) And Western drug companies have isolated a surprising number of active ingredients in Chinese medicines for use in their products. The Chinese treat gallstones with bear bile. Western firms have discovered that bear bile contains tauro ursodeoxycholic acid, which in tests dissolves gallstones. (Confirming the smartness of Chinese pharmacology, the only Chinese bear whose bile does not contain this acid is the giant panda, which is also the only bear from which the Chinese do not extract bile.)

Likewise, a 1,500-year-old Chinese treatment for malaria uses a daisy called artemesia, or wormwood. Its active ingredient is artemisin, which has recently been adopted by Western doctors. It works by reacting with the high iron concentrations in the malaria parasite, releasing free radicals that kill it. Another plant used in China to fight asthma contains ephedrine, a stimulant prescribed in the West for the same condition. And Western doctors recently patented a version of a Chinese remedy for eczema that uses the root of the peony shrub, apparently to strengthen the immune system.

The foremost chronicler of China's pharmacological history, Cai Jing-Feng of the China Academy of Traditional Chinese Medicine in Beijing, is also a doctor trained in the Western tradition. He says that the philosophies behind the two traditions are very different. Western doctors generally treat the disease or the diseased organ, while the Chinese tradition is to treat the whole body to bolster its defences. But whatever the philosophy, the treatments are often much the same.

Even the ancient Chinese medical ideas that Western scientists find most difficult to cope with, such as the notion of opposing forces of yin and yang within the body, turn out to have a physiological reality, said Cai. The yin and yang conditions diagnosed by Chinese doctors correspond to what Western doctors identify as disturbances in chemical messengers in the hormone system known as cAMP and cGMP. 'When Chinese doctors describe yin and yang as being out of balance, Western doctors see a change in the ratio of the two chemical messengers,' says Cai. 'In the yang condition, cAMP is low and cGMP is high. In the yin, it is the reverse.'

In China, you are what you eat. And more and more Chinese are using traditional medicines as food. Whatever the potential risks from overdosing on active ingredients, the prevailing view is that the richer you get, the more 'health food' you should eat.

The soaring worldwide demand for Chinese medicines is becoming a major threat to the survival of wild products, from obscure herbs to bears and tigers. Conservationists once hoped that the demand for Chinese medicines would decline because they would be seen increasingly as old wives' remedies. Now it seems the old wives' remedies do work. So groups like WWF are changing tack, demanding that threatened herbs are cultivated rather than being gathered from the wild, while substitutes are found for animal products like tiger bones and bear bile.

It will be an uphill task. Economists have put the total value of the booming Chinese-medicine market in wild products at between $6 billion and $20 billion annually. I never did find out the going rate for human placenta.

One in a Billion:
Ely, the (ex-) Slave Owner

I was in Mauritania, the West African desert state. It is an odd place, one of the strangest and least connected to the outside world that I have ever been to. Its main natural resources are a big iron mine in the interior and, offshore, one of the world's great fisheries (see Chapter 5). In between the two, its sand dunes and shanties and nomadic tent cities and grand air-conditioned houses are full of fiercely independent people living odd quasi-tribal lives. One of the most cultured and pleasant people I met there was Ely. Or that's what he called himself.

Ely was a tall, athletic government official. And from a good family. That was generally how you got government jobs in Mauritania. We shared a car ride through the desert in search of fishermen for me to interview. He was chaperoning me and a couple of other journalists because the higher-ups, having invited us into the country, didn't want to let us explore on our own. Human-rights groups were reporting that slavery, which was only abolished in Mauritania in 1981, secretly persisted amid the dunes and in the grander houses. They didn't want us stumbling on anything embarrassing.

So I was both surprised and amused when Ely announced that his family had, until recently, owned several families of slaves. He badly wanted me to understand how good it was being a slave, and how tough it was being a slave owner. And yes, he did lapse into the present tense at times.

He conjured up an image of slave owning as a social service. 'You have to clothe and feed and house them. It's quite expensive,' he said as our four-wheel-drive bounced down a dusty track towards a fishing village. 'You can't throw your ex-slaves out into the desert, whatever the government says. They get old. We don't have slaves any more. It is illegal. But some families want to be slaves, because they couldn't survive on their own.' After the government ban, he said, it was very hard to persuade some slaves to take up their freedom.

He laughed as he explained that the son of one of his family's slaves was now a senior government official, head of protocol for the prime minister. 'So the former slave is my boss!' Better that than slaves who stay put.

Ely had a white Moor father. His paternal grandfather was the family patriarch. 'He's a big man; we depend on him.' His mother is black. 'I'm café au lait,' he said with practised ease, and went on to explain the role that race plays in his country. The rulers are Moors, followers of Islam. But not all Moors are the same. There are white Moors – made up of Arabs and Berbers – and black Moors. Most former slaves are black Moors. But 'even blacks had slaves.' That made Ely chuckle.

There was, he assured me, no stigma in being an ex-slave or from a former slave family. In fact, those considered to be the lowest of the low in Mauritania were the blacks from the south of the country. They had never been slaves. But they suffered from something even less likely to get them into polite society – not being Moors. The way he put it, being a black slave (or former slave, of course) was a sign of distinction in Mauritania. Perhaps it is.

At any rate, not being a slave, and therefore not being owned by someone of importance, was potentially dangerous. A decade before, hundreds of southern blacks were killed in a pogrom that went on for weeks. Many more fled over the border to Senegal – a black, and much more civilized, country, it seemed to me. Ely regarded this as water under the bridge. 'It's all over now,' he said. 'Those that were thrown out have been told they can come back if they wish. They can have their property. Former officials can have their jobs back.' They didn't seem to be queuing at the border.

But having established the pecking order at the bottom of society, it was important to find out who was who at the top. In 2007, Mauritania for the first time staged democratic elections that got a clean bill of health from international observers. The country is still effectively run by a caste of Moorish Koranic scholars called *marabout*, however. They hold enormous sway across many Muslim countries in West Africa, but nowhere more than in Mauritania.

Some *marabout* run large estates out in the desert and have huge and loyal followings. Many of those estates are worked by young boys, lured from their homes by promises to their parents that they will receive schooling. Shades of more slavery, it seemed to me. Or debt slavery. And it is sometimes by this route that children from West Africa became traded across borders. The 'chocolate slaves' on the cocoa estates of the Ivory Coast often came from Mauritania.

Some *marabout* set up as international prophets. A taxi driver later told me they targeted black Americans, persuading them to invest in the desert fiefdoms as a route to finding their 'roots' in Africa. I had visions of black Americans being conned into funding a new form of slavery. That may be a little unfair, but native Africans often seem very dismissive of their brothers across the water – and it seems to be tied up with the fact that their ancestors were slaves. But this was another bizarre lesson, for a white liberal like me, in the dangers of making easy assumptions about race.

The confusions kept coming. Ely and I finally got to the remote fishing village. The people there, the Imraguen, are called by one reference book 'the smallest black ethnic group, still held in Arab bondage.' But Ely insisted that the word Imraguen just meant fishermen. Some were former slaves, he agreed. But some were high-born white Moors.

I never did find out why rich white Moors went fishing. Maybe in reality they were the boat owners, sending young men to take part in illegal fishing, dicing with death among the European trawlers hoovering up the country's fish off the Mauritanian coastline. But they don't talk about a lot of things in Mauritania. Especially if it touches on the time – just yesterday, really – when many were slaves, and some were slave owners. And maybe still are. Like that nice man Ely, whose smile and wave I still remember.

Part Five

Mines, Metals and Power

18

My Beer Can: Giant Footprints in Bloke Heaven

I can't say I drink beer out of a can by choice. Give me a glass or a bottle any day. But like most of the world, I have got used to the sound of the ring-pull, the feel of aluminium against my lips, and the slightly metallic taste of drinking whatever is inside, whether beer or Coke or iced tea. Even so, I wonder how this seemingly innocent, if sensorily flawed, activity impacts on the planet.

Aluminium is the most abundant metal in the Earth's crust, but it is only rarely found in a form that can be abstracted and purified – so rarely that Napoleon III once gave a banquet in which special guests got aluminium utensils, while the hoi polloi had to make do with gold. But modern extraction and processing methods have eased the shortages, and today it is the second most widely used metal, after iron but ahead of copper.

Aluminium is handy stuff. It conducts heat and electricity, melts at a relatively low 660°C, and resists corrosion. It is also lighter, stronger and softer than most other metals, so it can easily be drawn into wire, rolled into sheet or cast into any shape you want. And it is pretty. For more than a century, the cool sheen of aluminium has been seen as modern, an ideal material for stylish design in everything from furniture to electronic goods to jumbo jets to, well, the humble can. Aluminium was the most distinctive metal of the twentieth century. But it also helped create another defining feature of the twentieth century – greenhouse gas emissions. For it takes a very great deal of energy to turn the ore into pure aluminium. The amount of electricity needed to make one drinks can will run a TV for three hours. And the world uses 250 billion cans a year. I went to Australia, land of the tinny and one of the biggest producers, to explore the footprint of my beer can.

The story starts at Weipa on the Gulf of Carpentaria in northern Queensland. This is the homeland of the Alngith people and, until the miners showed up in the 1960s, one of the last untouched wilderness areas in Australia. Since then, the miners have turned the wilderness into one of the largest single man-made sores on the planet's surface. The mining area established by Rio Tinto, the world's second-largest mining business, stretches for more than 100 kilometres and has engulfed three aboriginal communities. All told, the company has a licence to strip-mine 2,600 square kilometres of the bush and remove more than a billion tonnes of aluminium ore, called bauxite. That is enough to make around 250 cans for every person on the planet. Right now, a tenth of all the world's bauxite comes from here.

Digging up the ore is easy. It comprises a layer of red pebbles about 4 metres thick beneath about half a metre of soil. Huge digging machines scrape away about 10 square kilometres of bush every year, much of it virgin woodland, to remove some 24 million tonnes of pebbles. Rio Tinto puts back the soil afterwards, and vegetation will slowly recolonize the mines. But the new land is several metres lower than before.

After washing to remove soil and low-grade ore, some 16 million tonnes of bauxite a year goes to the Lorim Point Wharf, where it is loaded on to bulk carriers for a five-day ride round Cape York, Australia's northernmost point, and through the Great Barrier Reef to the port of Gladstone on Queensland's east coast. No vessels have yet hit the reef, which is a World Heritage Site. There would be an outcry if they did.

Gladstone wallows in another ecological mess, created as the town annexed once extensive mangrove swamps across a river delta. It has a nice harbour, where you can take boat trips out to the southern end of the reef. But it also has a cement works, a nickel refinery, a nitrate factory, and a mothballed operation for extracting oil from local shales. And it vies with Newcastle, down the coast in New South Wales, and Richards Bay in South Africa for the title of the world's largest coal port. Some 68 million tonnes a year come here by rail from mines in the Queensland interior. Burning that coal ultimately puts into the air about 200 million tonnes of carbon dioxide a year.

Most of Gladstone's coal goes to fuel steel works in the booming economies of east Asia. But not all. For Gladstone also has Queensland's largest coal-fired power station. And most of the power from the station is consumed by the masters of the town: Rio Tinto. For, where Queensland coal meets Weipa's bauxite, Rio Tinto has created in Gladstone the world's largest bauxite-processing operation.

Getting off the plane, I met Rick Humphries, head of climate change at Rio Tinto Aluminium. He is from the new school of big-industry environmental executives: cheery, anxious to proclaim that he once worked for Greenpeace, and at pains to be candid. 'Aluminium processing is responsible for half of Rio Tinto's carbon footprint round the world,' he began. 'And it is mostly because of operations in this town.' We set off to check out the footprint, beginning at the waterside, where we watched a bucket-grab offloading red bauxite pebbles from the RTS *Pioneer*, a ten-year-old Japanese bulk carrier. The 60,000-tonne cargo was enough to keep production going for about two days. A conveyor took the pebbles to one of two refineries, where they are turned into aluminium oxide – alumina, as it is known in the trade. From there, the oxide is smelted into pure aluminium ingots.

Rick calls Gladstone 'bloke heaven'. There is beer (in aluminium cans, of course) and fishing in the bay (from aluminium boats), and lots and lots of blue-collar jobs. But at the refinery, after my safety induction, I met technical manager Anne Duncan. She smiled at my surprise. Female faces are rare in the town, rarer still inside the factory gates. Anne hadn't planned on a career making blokes' beer cans. She trained as a nuclear engineer but 'I showed up for my first day's work on the day the Chernobyl reactor blew up, so I had a better idea and decided to retrain as a chemical engineer.' Anne is the daughter of one of the leading academics in the aluminium business, John Duncan. My files contained a fading photocopy of a paper he wrote years ago on the life cycle of the aluminium can.

Anne drove me round the refinery. It is not the kind of place you would walk round: big and with an undergrowth of pipes and cables and vats and boilers as dense as any mangrove thicket. The bauxite pebbles from the conveyor are milled here into a powder of various aluminium-containing minerals. The powder is boiled up with caustic soda shipped in from the US (1 tonne of caustic for every 8 tonnes of bauxite), and the resulting liquid is drawn off into tanks where, after a few days, crystals of aluminium oxide form. To be turned into pure metal, the aluminium oxide goes to one of several Rio Tinto smelters scattered round the world, in New Zealand, Tasmania, Wales – or direct by conveyor across Gladstone to Australia's largest aluminium smelter, on Boyne Island. I took the short route.

Smelters are huge electrical furnaces, and this single plant uses as much energy as a city of a million people. The aluminium oxide is melted, dissolved into a conducting fluid, and then electricity is transmitted through the thick, hot mixture from giant carbon terminals, known as anodes. The electric current is a staggering 150,000 amps. It strips the oxygen from the aluminium and bonds it to carbon from the anode, making carbon dioxide and a sludge of pure aluminium.

The sheer scale of the operation took my breath away. It takes place in three cavernous smelting halls, each about 900 metres long. Inside them are 13,000 anodes, each weighing more than a tonne and the size of a child's coffin, arranged into 500 cells that smelt hundreds of tonnes of molten aluminium at a time. Over the road is another factory almost as large, dedicated to making the carbon anodes from coal tar, pitch and coke. To make them fit for conducting the vast amounts of energy, they are baked at more than 1,100°C for fourteen days.

The smelting process, known as the Hall–Héroult process after its nineteenth-century inventors, is largely enclosed. The operators would fry otherwise. But occasionally I could see the fiery glow as remote grabs lifted a spent anode out of the molten liquid. Humans were like tiny ants in the hall. We occasionally veered away from walls of heat coming from red-hot spent anodes standing to one side, cooling. Don't touch, said Alan Milne, the production manager. We hardly needed reminding.

The pure molten aluminium is eventually poured into moulds. The cooled ingots head off round the world to be turned into all manner of goods. A lot of it goes to China. Gladstone aluminium may well be in my computer, my digital camera, my phone and my printer. Gladstone also helps make European Airbuses. So I probably flew to Australia courtesy of this extraordinary inferno. The whole process had the feel of something primordial, or at least a throwback to Victorian engineering. Alan agreed. 'This plant is relatively new, but the process hasn't really changed in a hundred and twenty years, since it was invented.' Aluminium may look sleek and modern, but it is made in a way essentially unchanged since the horse-drawn carriage.

Making aluminium has a huge environmental footprint. There is the wrecked wilderness of Weipa, of course. Then the two giant refineries converting bauxite to aluminium oxide create 5 million tonnes of waste slurry that is thick with both iron from the bauxite and caustic soda. Caustic soda is extremely alkaline. It burns. To neutralize the slurry partially, Rio Tinto mixes it with 17 million tonnes of seawater a year before pumping the resulting 'red mud' into reservoirs several kilometres wide, which are scattered across the delta. They dominate the view as you fly in and out of Gladstone. 'We still don't know what to do with them,' admitted Rick. The iron could become a valuable resource one day. But nobody has yet found an economic way of extracting it. So there it sits.

Meanwhile, everyone hopes the reservoirs do not leak and contaminate the rest of the delta. That would be curtains for the remaining mangroves. The big fear is that one of the cyclones that regularly form in the ocean off Queensland makes landfall here. A full cyclone hasn't hit Gladstone for nearly a century. But on the wall in the smelter control room is a large map constantly updated to show passing storms. One day . . .

And while we wait for the cyclone, Gladstone has a daily impact on the whole planet through its great, galumphing carbon footprint. Aluminium smelting requires more energy than any other metal process. Worldwide, the industry accounts for about 2 per cent of electricity consumption. The Boyne smelter takes a constant supply of 900 megawatts of power, fizzing down four power lines from the Gladstone power station. The power station couldn't be worse. It is thirty years old, burns coal and has a thermal efficiency of around 30 per cent. That is pathetic by modern standards. It means that less than a third of the coal burned actually makes useful energy. As one joker put it, Gladstone power station is a giant machine for converting coal into carbon dioxide – with a little electricity as a by-product.

The Boyne smelter also produces its own carbon dioxide as part of the production process. Adding both the power and production sources together, Boyne emits 17 tonnes of carbon dioxide for every tonne of aluminium. In 2005, the smelter was responsible for almost 10 million tonnes of carbon dioxide emissions. Looked at another way, the smelting of aluminium to make every beer can here generates 260 grams of CO_2 – enough gas to fill 300 cans.

The electricity demands of aluminium smelting are so great that smelting companies will locate almost anywhere to get cheaper supplies. Rio Tinto plumps for Queensland coal at Gladstone. But its reliance on coal – which produces more carbon dioxide than other fossil fuels – is unusual and an increasing public-relations liability. Globally, more than half the power for aluminium smelting comes from hydroelectricity. This started when the US built the Grand Coulee and Bonneville dams on the Columbia River during the Second World War to make the aluminium for 60,000 fighter aircraft. They helped turn the tide on the western front. Ever since, many of the world's largest dams have been built to meet the smelters' bloated demands for power.

The construction of those dams has been the source of bitter disputes. To provide the power for Rio Tinto's smelter in Tasmania, the island's government filled Lake Pedder, one of the country's greatest natural treasures, to twenty-five times its natural size. UNESCO later described this as 'the greatest ecological tragedy since the European settlement of Tasmania.' The Ghanaian government flooded an area of its country the size of Lebanon to generate power for the Kaiser Corporation's smelter. Brazil inundated 2,400 square kilometres of Amazon jungle to create the Tucurui dam, which powers smelters at Vila do Conde and São Luis. Canada's controversial dams on the Indian lands of Quebec power Alcan's smelters in the province. And it goes on. Alcoa, the world's largest aluminium producer, has just finished a controversial new dam in Iceland that captures meltwater from Europe's biggest glacier to power a smelter built largely with Polish labour on Iceland's east coast.

Clearly there are serious downsides to many hydroelectric dams. But as concern grows about global warming, fossil fuels look even worse. About 30 per cent of the world's aluminium is still smelted using coal, and Rio Tinto does more of it than almost anyone. This makes Rick's job as the company's climate supremo a bit sticky. 'We'd like to do more with renewables,' he told me. But the reality, he admitted, is that Rio Tinto has no intention of giving up cheap fossil fuels. At Gladstone, it has a long-term contract to take power from the city's power plant. It half-owns the plant and gets power for about half the rate paid by other industries.

But Rio Tinto is hedging its bets. It is planning to build a new smelter in Abu Dhabi that could handle a lot of Weipa's output. It will be powered by local natural gas. Sandeep Biswas, managing director of the company's aluminium operations, says 'The Middle East is fast becoming a key region in the global aluminium-smelting business.' Why? It is a no-brainer, says Rick. 'They are outside the Kyoto Protocol.' Australia joined the US in reneging on the Protocol, so when I visited it had no targets for cutting its emissions of greenhouse gases such as carbon dioxide. But most people expected it to join. And months later a new Labour government announced just that. Fearful that it will face a tax on its emissions, Rio Tinto is preparing to make a speedy exit to countries that will be spared targets. Places like Abu Dhabi.

This is – how shall I put it? – not fully consistent with Rio Tinto's claims to be taking a greener outlook on life. Natural gas may be better than coal. But burning fossil fuels to make electricity to smelt aluminium is a rogue activity that should be shut down.

Should I boycott aluminium cans? Maybe. But wait. Could there be a path to redemption for aluminium? For one thing, aluminium is light. Everywhere that it replaces steel, for aircraft wings or drinks cans loaded on a truck, it saves energy and hence CO_2 emissions. Of course, that gain has to be balanced against the emissions from making the aluminium in the first place. But one study found that the extra carbon dioxide generated by making aluminium to replace steel in cars is offset by the reduced emissions from the lighter vehicle within the first 25,000 kilometres – and after that it is downhill all the way.

In addition, aluminium is an ideal metal for recycling. Aluminium smelting uses so much energy that its producers have long since understood the virtues of 'mining' waste metal for new manufacturing. Since the Hall–Héroult process was developed in the 1880s, it has produced more than 700 million tonnes of aluminium. But only 200 million tonnes of that has been discarded. The industry estimates that the rest is still in use somewhere. Metal originally smelted for the first bicycles or modernist furniture at the start of the twentieth century, or as canteens for soldiers in the trenches of the First World War, is now in modern aircraft or computer casings or window frames – or my drinks can.

The industry plays this green card for all it's worth. Quite right too. Recycling aluminium takes only a twentieth as much energy as smelting new metal. So I set off to find out what happens when I chuck a can into a recycling bin.

Usually it ends up at Europe's only dedicated aluminium-recycling plant, at Latchford Lock on the Manchester Ship Canal near Warrington. Novelis, the international company that owns the plant, reprocesses 35 billion cans a year from around the world, almost a third of them at Latchford. Novelis is also the largest producer of aluminium sheet for drinks cans. It is 'closing the loop.' Old cans are making new cans.

My taxi ride to Latchford Lock ended in a forecourt filled with bale after bale of squashed cans. I snooped around for a few minutes among the Stella and Murphy's, Coke and Sprite, Bulmers and Heineken, Foster's and Cobra, till I found the general manager Mike Killen. He said the yard held ten days' supply – 200 million cans altogether. In the boardroom we opened cans of Sprite. Latchford's aluminium recycling opened for business in 1942 as part of the war effort, Mike said. At the same time as the US began big-time smelting at Grand Coulee, the plucky Brits were handing in their aluminium saucepans to be turned into fighter aircraft. The Battle of Britain, they say, was won at Latchford.

From the forecourt, cans go up a conveyor into the plant. I threw on my Sprite can. First it was broken into fingernail-sized pieces by a giant hammer; next a magnet removed any steel; and a blast of super-heated air stripped off the paint and lacquer. Then came the centre of the operation. The two furnaces can each hold 90 tonnes of aluminium, or almost 3 million shredded cans. Here the aluminium melts. A quick stir, and the molten metal is poured into moulds where a shower of water cools and solidifies it into new ingots. Each is 9 metres long, weighs over 26 tonnes and contains the molten remains of 1.6 million cans.

Looking at the ingots, I could have been in Gladstone. The same sleek slabs of pure metal. Better, said Mike. 'We supply the cleanest can bodies in the world – even better than from primary ingots.' Latchford keeps one furnace dedicated to cans, and the other to everything else. This preserves the distinct alloy preferred for cans, which contains small amounts of magnesium and manganese. Out at the back, a truck was ready to drive the next ingot, containing my old Sprite can, to Goole on Humberside. From there it went by barge across the North Sea and up the Rhine to the world's largest aluminium-rolling mill, outside Düsseldorf. The metal from my can might have come back to supply UK can makers in Wrexham or Wantage or Wakefield, from where it may have reappeared on my local supermarket shelf or in the pub fridge within six weeks. Equally, it could have gone to a Spanish bar or a Greek taverna or a Warsaw grocery store.

In 2006, Western Europe passed a milestone. For the first time, more than half of all cans sold came back for recycling. But, while Norwegians hit 93 per cent, and Finns and Swiss 88 per cent, the Brits managed a paltry 41 per cent. Britons are among Europe's biggest users of drinks cans, but we are among its most reluctant recyclers. More than 3.5 billion cans a year fail to complete the recycling loop and end up instead in British landfills or back alleys or littering the countryside. That is almost as much as the rest of Western Europe put together. It's a little-noticed scandal. The energy required to smelt fresh aluminium for those 3.5 billion lost cans could power about half an hour's viewing on every TV set in the country, every night of the year.

Besides being an ecological crime, this is also a failure of the market. Because cans are cash. Novelis pays a bit over one penny for a used can. Aluminium cans make up only 1 per cent of the contents of our dustbins (that's not counting the metal bin itself, of course), but they represent 25 per cent of the potential cash-recycling value. For years, environmentalists have rightly seen aluminium smelting as a pariah industry. But if the British beer can could be 'mined' to the extent that the Scandinavians achieve, then its image could be transformed. If we recycled all our aluminium cans and foil and milk tops and electronics boxes and the rest, then we would scarcely need to mine the metal any more. Aluminium could be the 'greenest' metal out, rather than the most polluting. As I left the Latchford plant, I added another can to the bales in the forecourt, and waved it goodbye.

19

Shock and Ore: Where My Metal Comes From

Remember the 'limits to growth'? Almost forty years ago, apocalyptic environmentalists warned that we were about to run out of resources. Copper and tin and other key metals were going to disappear within a few decades. The Massachusetts Institute of Technology predicted that a scramble for the last metals and oil would prove so costly that 'the industrial base will collapse'. Civilizations would crash. Well, it hasn't happened yet. The prediction of an exponential rise in demand for resources proved false. Prices of key metals fell rather than rose, and a new optimism took hold. If metals ran low, we would always find more, or technology would create substitutes. The road to continued economic growth was clear.

But now the rapacious demands of surging economies like China are beginning to undermine this optimism. At current rates of demand, there are thirty years of antimony and silver left, forty years of tin, and sixty years of copper. The date of peak oil production may be close. And, most worrying perhaps, a whole suite of new metals has become vital to the twenty-first century – many of which are in short supply even as they are being exploited for the first time.

Our world now depends on indium, with a projected thirteen years of supply, on gallium and hafnium and terbium and ruthenium and, thanks to the mobile phone, tantalum. The –iums are in charge. Of course, technology may come to our rescue again, cutting our requirements, finding alternatives or increasing mineable reserves. But then again it may not. Or not always. The question is being asked again: are we running on empty?

For thousands of years, through the Iron and Bronze Ages to the Industrial Revolution, metals have been the benchmarks of our economic progress. Finding metals has driven many of our conquests. The Romans first came to Britain to extract tin. Gold and silver drew Europeans to the New World. Two-thirds of all European investment in Africa prior to the 1930s went into mining. And not too much has changed today. Mining is the world's fifth-biggest industry. The biggest mining corporation, the Australia-based BHP Billiton, formerly Broken Hill, has a turnover of $125 billion, roughly the same as Finland. Close behind are Rio Tinto and Anglo American, both headquartered in London.

The biggest rock-shifting businesses are iron, which removes more than a billion tonnes of ore a year, and copper, which removes 7 billion tonnes to make just 16 million tonnes of metal. Most copper now comes from a handful of vast mines. Utah's century-old Bingham Canyon mine is the largest man-made hole on Earth, 4 kilometres across and 1.5 kilometres deep. During the Second World War, Bingham supplied a third of all the copper used by the Allies. But the world's biggest source of copper today is Chile. The country has two-fifths of known world reserves (enough to keep us going for twenty years), and 8 per cent of global supplies currently come from the Escondida mine in the Atacama Desert in northern Chile, which removes 350 million tonnes of ore a year.

Mining has a big and brutal footprint on the land. Over the past century, the industry has displaced 100 million people, and laid waste innumerable precious natural habitats. The extraction and refining of ores often requires toxic substances, like cyanide and mercury, that pollute land and rivers. A tonne of mercury is released into the Amazon for every tonne of gold extracted there. Worldwide, metals smelting pollutes the air with more than 100 million tonnes of sulphur dioxide, the main cause of acid rain.

And, while most human economic activities reduce their footprint with time as they become more efficient, the mining footprint just keeps on growing as the available ores become less concentrated. At the start of the twentieth century, copper mines like Bingham Canyon were extracting ore with a metal concentration of 3 per cent or more; by the end of the century, that figure was down to 0.6 per cent. Tungsten is now taken from 0.25 per cent ores, zinc from 0.05 per cent and gold from 0.02 per cent or less. The holes in the ground, not to mention the spoil heaps and tailings reservoirs, grow ever larger. The ecological and social havoc often increases.

Some talk about the ore taken from the earth as the materials 'rucksack' of everyday products. By that they mean that every item we own made from stuff hewn from the Earth carries with it a 'rucksack' of all the waste ore that had to be mined to produce it. This book started with gold. My wedding ring took 2 tonnes of ore to produce. So its rucksack weighs 2 tonnes. Modern mobile phones weigh about 75 grams, but their materials rucksack is 75 kilograms. My watch clunks along with 20 kilograms, heavier than most grandfather clocks of old. And my PC computer has a 1.5-tonne rucksack. That's a lot of computer. To make a tonne of aluminium typically requires 4–6 tonnes of bauxite ore. A tonne of iron requires the mining of 15 tonnes, and a tonne of copper a staggering 420 tonnes. My personal annual materials rucksack, as a typical European, weighs nearly 50 tonnes.

How does this 50 tonnes break down? On average, 15 tonnes in my rucksack comes from extracting fossil fuels like coal. Another 12 tonnes is accounted for by metals – of which copper at 2 tonnes, and iron, tin and gold at one tonne each, are the biggest components. Then come construction materials such as stones, sand, gravel and limestone, which make up a hefty 9 tonnes. After that biomass, including our food and other crops like cotton and timber, takes 6 tonnes. Behind those come losses of soil to erosion, which is estimated at 4 tonnes, excavation and dredging at 3 tonnes, and non-metallic industrial minerals (everything from diamonds to phosphate rock for fertilizer) at 2 tonnes.

This analysis, from the Wuppertal Institute in Germany, does not include water, which I return to later. Suffice to say, my rucksack should also, strictly speaking, include most of the contents of an Olympic-size swimming pool.

What do we use these laboriously extracted materials for? Most iron makes steel, and most steel is used to create the structures within which we live and work – homes, offices, factories and cars. There is more steel than anything else in cars and planes, though aluminium is catching up. Getting on for half the world's copper goes into electric cables, plumbing and heating systems in buildings. About a third goes into phone systems. Then there is lead, two-thirds of which goes into car batteries. Zinc, chromium and nickel are all widely used in alloys to make corrosion-resistant, stainless or just plain shiny steel. Tin goes into cans, solders and alloys like bronze.

Some materials are only found in economically viable quantities in a few places. South Africa has 88 per cent of the world's platinum, 40 per cent of the world's extractable gold and 35 per cent of its chromium. Most of the rest of the world's chromium is in Kazakhstan – a fact that inexplicably escaped Borat's attention. China has 60 per cent of our antimony, which is widely used in the ubiquitous electrical conducting devices known as semiconductors, and in flame retardants. There may be only thirty years' supply of antimony left. China also has 30 per cent of our tin and 20 per cent of our zinc.

All this makes resource politics interesting. We know all about oil politics. And the world of blood diamonds has become notorious. But what about phosphate politics? Phosphates are an essential nutrient in soils. Plants need phosphate to grow as much as they need water. It takes a tonne of phosphate to produce every 130 tonnes of grain. There are no substitutes. If natural phosphate is in short supply in their soils, as it often is, farmers must add phosphate rock. To that end, the world mines 140 million tonnes of the stuff a year, mostly from the US and China (which both consume most of what they produce) and Morocco. Or rather, and here is the rub, Morocco and the neighbouring desert state of Western Sahara, which Morocco annexed in the 1970s.

Morocco and its neighbour have more than 60 per cent of all the world's known economic reserves of phosphate – reserves that may run out by the end of the century. Morocco's hold over this critical resource may explain the world's reluctance to demand independence for the Western Sahara. Meanwhile the Moroccan royal family, through a process somewhat euphemistically termed privatization, has retained personal control of most of the country's mining operations for phosphate through their firm Omnium Nord Africain. Right now, much of the world continues to grow its food thanks to the favour of one North African royal family.

Prices of most mainstream metals have surged through this decade, as China in particular has sucked in supplies. Many old mines have been reopened. From Congo and the copper belt of Zambia, to Indonesia and Peru, peasant miners have given up working on farms (where world prices have been in freefall) and switched to scrabbling through the rubble and tailings of old mines to find low-grade ore to process in makeshift smelters and refineries.

Meanwhile, the world is growing increasingly dependent on a range of metals that most of us never heard about in our school chemistry lessons. This is not what we were promised in the days (oh, just a couple of years ago) when people said that the information age would reduce our dependence on physical resources like metals. We cannot escape that easily. Our dependence hasn't gone away, it has just changed. We have new metals fixes.

For instance, twenty years ago we decided to clean up the smog-producing chemicals in car exhausts by fitting catalytic converters. They filter out the pollutants using two metals: platinum and palladium. World demand for both has soared as a result, and catalytic converters take almost half current supplies. South Africa is the world's dominant source of platinum and, since it has most of the world's reserves, is likely to remain so. Meanwhile, more than half of the world's palladium comes from Siberian mines. The metal is mostly refined at notoriously polluting metals smelters at Norilsk on the edge of the Arctic Circle. These smelters are the biggest concentrated source of sulphur dioxide pollution on the planet. For hundreds of kilometres round Norilsk, the trees are dead because of the acid they generate. In effect, we are destroying huge areas of Arctic tundra with acid rain so that the rest of the world can keep its city air clean. I can't say that makes me breathe easy.

Modern electronics, meanwhile, is adding to the list of obscure metals on which we depend. Ever heard of the ruthenium rush, the bismuth bonanza or the indium stampede? Nor had I. But my office is full of these metals, and metals prospectors are scouring the world looking for more. Indium, for instance, is a soft metal that can be made into a very thin coating. It is built into a billion consumer devices a year, mostly the LCD displays of TVs and mobile phones. From early 2003 to 2006, indium prices increased eightfold to $800 a kilogram because of fears that economic sources (the metal is largely a by-product from zinc mining in China) might run out within a decade or so. Indium is also an ingredient in a man-made material called indium gallium arsenide which is vital to a new generation of photovoltaic solar cells. With gallium also in short supply, the boom in the new solar cells could be shortlived. There is growing concern about supplies of lithium. Demand has been booming because the metal is used in lithium-ion batteries for mobile phones, but now these batteries are likely to become the mainstay of a global push towards electric cars.

Meanwhile, demand for bismuth (currently mostly produced

in China) is surging because of its use as a safer substitute for lead in the billions of tiny drops of solder applied to consumer electronics goods. Its price has doubled, while that of ruthenium, used in resistors and disk drives, rose sevenfold during 2006. Ruthenium is found in the Ural mountains of Russia and can be extracted from spent nuclear fuels. Then there is hafnium. It is in big demand as a substitute for silicon compounds in computer chips, and could be gone by 2017. And terbium, one of the rarest of the 'rare earths', is a vital raw material for the boom in low-energy fluorescent light bulbs because it glows with a green light. The biggest reserves are in clay in southern China. They could be gone by 2012.

In an age of scarcity, hotspots of valuable materials become so hot that, particularly in poor countries, nature's bounty becomes a curse. It seems to stymie economic development, cripple governments, fill the pockets of rebels and all too often pay for protracted civil wars.

Take Angola. Its rich resources make it potentially one of the wealthiest countries in Africa. But it has become synonymous with squandered wealth. After independence in 1975, it descended into civil war. Initially the US, Russia and South Africa armed the combatants. But when the Cold War ended and the superpowers lost interest, the local combatants kept going by plundering natural resources. The main rebel group, led by the late Jonas Savimbi, invaded northern Angola to grab the diamonds littering the river beds. This way Savimbi raised several billion dollars to buy arms. Meanwhile, the government in Luanda sold off the country's huge offshore oilfields to big oil companies so it could fight back.

In Afghanistan, the Taliban and the Northern Alliance have kept operating over the past decade, whether in government or not, by selling emeralds, timber and opium. Afghan opium poppies currently have a 90 per cent world market share. In Colombia, rebels have prospered from cocaine sales and used the threat of sabotage to extort hundreds of millions of dollars from oil companies. And in Cambodia, the friendless Khmer Rouge kept going through the early 1990s by selling rubies, sapphires and logging rights in their jungle terrain.

Once, environmentalists warned about the risks of conflicts when resources ran out. But in truth conflicts are more likely where there are abundant natural resources. Michael Renner of the Worldwatch Institute, a Washington DC think tank, calculates that a quarter of all conflicts around the world are either fought over, or largely funded by, the looting of lucrative natural resources. Today's rebels are often more interested in liberating diamonds than in freeing repressed peoples. Worse, they finance their start-up costs by selling the spoils of war in advance.

'Booty futures' have become the currency of conflict, as wannabe warlords sell resource rights to foreign corporations, mercenaries and governments. In Sierra Leone in the 1990s, rebels got off the ground by selling diamond futures to Charles Taylor, a warlord and subsequent president in neighbouring Liberia. When the rebels got within 30 kilometres of the capital, Freetown, the government hired mercenaries by offering them the same diamond fields.

Since the end of the Cold War, rebel groups can no longer expect funding from superpowers jockeying for strategic advantage. And abstract ideologies have become less potent. Moreover, particularly in the poorest states, globalization and the rise of the free market are reducing the power of governments. They control far less of their national economies. At the same time, rebels find it easier to sell their booty abroad. As a result, even successful rebel groups may conclude that there is little to be gained by seizing the reins of government when the rewards are few and when perpetual conflict maximizes the potential for pillage, extortion and exploitation of labour.

David Keen of the London School of Economics argued in an influential essay, 'Economic Functions of Violence in Civil Wars', that 'we tend to regard conflict as a breakdown in a particular system.' In fact, he said, it represents 'the emergence of another, alternative system, of profit and power.' If he is right, then the crucial resources we need to run our lives will increasingly fall into the hands of criminals and warlords. And the future for an ordered, stable world looks bleak indeed.

What should we do? How can we maintain our supplies of diminishing resources and reduce the minerals curse? One answer is recycling, turning waste products into the new mines. We can no longer chuck scarce metals in the landfill. If we do, we will soon have to mine the landfills. Or even street dust. That is a serious proposal, incidentally. Platinum from catalytic converters can reach concentrations above one part per million in street dust, which makes it a richer resource than currently commercial copper ores. And palladium fall-out in the soils around Norilsk is so heavy that it too may soon be worth extracting.

The world has always recycled some metals. Gold and silver, for instance. In the Middle Ages, church bells were melted down for bronze cannons in wartime – and afterwards, to celebrate victory, the cannons were turned back into church bells. Today, the economic case for recycling is becoming ever stronger. The world is not short of copper, but it makes more sense to recycle used metal than to mine the remaining ores. About 30 per cent of the world's copper consumption is currently met by recycling. Likewise, as we have seen, most aluminium gets recycled. Again, there is no urgent shortage of bauxite, but recyling it makes sense, given the very large energy savings. Other metals with significant recycling rates include nickel (35 per cent), chromium (25 per cent), lead (72 per cent), zinc (26 per cent) and tin (26 per cent).

Iron too – or rather the usual end product, steel – has also long been recycled. Between 70 and 90 per cent of all the steel waste in North America and Europe goes for recycling. Modern electric arc furnaces take only a third as much energy to produce recycled steel rods or sheets as to make new. As the environmentalist Lester Brown puts it, 'In the new economy, electric arc steel mills will largely replace iron mines.'

*

My water footprint is huge, and so is yours. I have written a previous book about our use and abuse of water, so this is just a summary. But I still find the stats extraordinary. I drink only a couple of litres or so of water in a day, most of it in tea and coffee. We don't have a water meter in our house, but I reckon that, as a fairly average British water user, even after cooking and washing and flushing the toilet, I don't get through more than 150 litres a day. But that is just the start of my water footprint. The scary numbers come when I look at the water it takes to grow my food.

To grow enough wheat to make a round of toast takes 150 litres. So my daily consumption is doubled, just to make some toast. A single portion of rice in my curry needs 100 litres; a pint of beer to wash it down takes 250 litres. But for meat-eaters and even dairy-product guzzlers, the news gets worse. Growing grain to feed enough cow to deliver a single litre of milk requires up to 4,000 litres of water, and it takes 11,000 litres to generate a quarter-pound hamburger.

For food grown in Britain, much of this water comes from rain-fall, which at least makes it cheap. But increasingly Britons are buying food from distant lands, where rains are scarce, rivers are being emptied and underground reserves pumped dry. So my water footprint becomes a global concern. The corn in my break-fast cereal probably comes from the American Midwest, where the underground water reserves are drying up fast. Increasing amounts of my meat come from cattle raised in sheds where they are fed with irrigated alfalfa, an extremely thirsty crop. Even home-grown chickens are fed soya from Latin America.

If my sugar is grown by cane farmers in India, then, according to a UN report, those farmers often 'use huge quantities of water in places where there is little rainfall . . . the poor farmers are left to fend for themselves.' In Israel, 70 per cent of the country's water is used to grow export crops like tomatoes that turn up in my supermarket; meanwhile Palestinians on the West Bank are told they cannot sink new wells to meet basic household needs because there is a water shortage.

And other farm products like cotton or leather take a huge toll. My pair of leather shoes takes at least 8,000 litres of water to raise the animal and turn its skin to leather. The cotton in my shirt takes around thirty bathtubs of water to grow. And if that cotton comes, as it may well do, from Uzbekistan, then it will be helping empty the Aral Sea.

Water is a renewable resource, of course. Ultimately nature will recycle it, through evaporation and rainfall. We are still drinking the same water that the dinosaurs bathed in. But today humanity is extracting water from the natural cycle on such a scale that it is often not available when we need it and where we need it. If a farmer has no water, then it is little compensation to know that it is raining somewhere else.

Two-thirds of all the water that humans take from nature is used for agriculture. By some estimates, 10 per cent of that agricultural use of water – about 1,000 cubic kilometres of water, or twenty River Niles – ends up in international trade. The water is not traded, of course; but the products of its use are. Economists sometimes call this 'virtual water'. And as countries across the world run short of water, this trade in the virtual stuff is increasingly important. The phrase is a bit of an abstraction, I agree. But it does show how water is becoming an increasingly vital resource, and those who have it have something of increasing value.

The biggest virtual water trades are in beef, soya, wheat, cocoa, coffee, rice and cotton. All of them are global commodities that are often grown in poor, dry countries to meet the demands of people like me in richer – and often wetter – countries. So whenever I eat Thai rice, or burgers made from Costa Rican beef, or wear clothes made of Uzbek cotton, or sweeten my coffee with Indian or South African sugar, I may be emptying rivers or denying some farmer the water he needs to feed his family. Among the world's top ten exporters of virtual water are drought-stressed countries like China and India.

Britain is the world's number-three net importer of virtual water. We take 47 cubic kilometres a year, roughly the flow of the River Nile. According to UN virtual water analyst Arjen Hoekstra, Britain's national water self-sufficiency is lower than any other nation outside the Middle East, bar Switzerland, The Netherlands, Belgium and Malta. Only 30 per cent of Britain's overall water needs, including crop growing, are supplied within its own borders. That makes my own personal importation of virtual water more than 700,000 litres, or 700 tonnes.

My own total water use, incidentally, is around 2,000 tonnes a year, or 100 times my own weight every day. If everybody in the world had the same requirements as me, then that would work out at 13,000 cubic kilometres of water, which is only slightly less than the total amount of accessible water flowing down the world's rivers in a year. No wonder they are starting to run dry. The natural water cycle may renew our water, but it does not do it fast enough to meet our demands.

I find it a shocking thought that the world is running up against real global limits on the supply of nature's most basic resource: fresh water. I could, at a pinch, live without indium and copper and tungsten and aluminium and iron and the rest. I could not live for one day without water.

20

Footprints in the Snow:
Finding the Last Oil

George Tagarook, the Stratocaster-playing Inuit heart-throb of
Kaktovik, was proud of his three gleaming fire engines. He showed
them off on the driveway of his fire station in the small town on
the north coast of Alaska, where he was both fire chief and vice-
mayor. Across the road were a new school, clinic, post office and
power plant. 'All this,' he said proudly, 'is built with oil money.'

Kaktovik lies within Alaska's huge Arctic National Wildlife
Refuge. To the south is pristine tundra. To the north are the great
ice floes of the Arctic Ocean. But a half-hour flight to the west lies
North America's largest oilfield, operated by BP around Prudhoe
Bay. For three decades, more than 1,000 wells here have been
pumping up to 2 million barrels of oil a day from beneath the
tundra, and sending it down an 800-kilometre pipeline to Valdez
on the southern shore of Alaska. From there, tankers take it to
refineries around the world.

Prudhoe Bay is one of a series of remote regions of the planet
where the fossil-fuel industry has implanted its giant footprint.
One of the places that keep the world's petrol tanks full and homes
heated. One of the places that keep me travelling round the world.

One of the places, too, that are responsible for heating the planet's atmosphere. And the extraordinary wealth generated by Prudhoe Bay is the reason why George can have three fire engines in a town of 2,000 people where they have only four fires in an average year. Interviewing George was part of my inquiry into my oil footprint in remote parts of the world that few of us get to visit.

But George was worried. Oil production at Prudhoe Bay was falling, he said, as wells were exhausted. Revenues had been slipping, and he needed new fire engines. 'Without oil, this place will go down,' George told me. And in August 2006, after my visit, production was shut down altogether for a while, following the discovery of corrosion in the pipes and oil leaks on to the tundra around Prudhoe Bay.

Like most people in Kaktovik, George wants the US government to lift its ban on oil prospecting within the wildlife refuge and allow the oilmen to move east to keep the oil and money flowing up here on the Arctic shore. With talk that the world is close to the start of a long-term decline in oil production, the case to open up those reserves is being heard loud and often. But there is also a huge international campaign to prevent a further giant oilfield being opened up on this pristine tundra, where the caribou and polar bears are already threatened by climate change. And in that battle, Kaktovik is on the front line.

The lives of George and the other Inuit at Kaktovik and in other towns along the north shore have been transformed by oil. But not entirely destroyed by it. The second-biggest industry on the coast, after oil, is traditional whaling. There are eight old whaling families in Kaktovik. Each September, they set off in search of the three whales that the International Whaling Commission allows them to catch. The harvest is cut up and stored in underground ice cellars, and shared among the community – Stratocaster players and all.

On a bright Sunday morning, at Kaktovitch's tiny Pentecostal church, the Reverend Isaac Akootchook announced to the congregation, many of whom work for the oil companies, the date for the next distribution of whale meat and muktuk (a prized cut of skin and surface blubber). In his younger days, he said afterwards, he had been a whaler. He caught the largest whale ever landed at the village harbour – a 17-metre beast.

Isaac said whaling was once the heart of the community. But things started to change in the 1950s, when the US military established an airfield and an early-warning radar post to spot Russian bombers flying in over the Arctic Ocean. He was among those thrown off the original town site to make way for the airstrip. The town still contains disturbing hints at how the military has in the past treated its hosts. One sign in the community hall read: 'If you remember having been subject to human radiation experiments, please contact . . .' Another asked for the help of polar-bear hunters in providing bear organs for a study of chemical contamination.

But that legacy pales beside Kaktovik's current Faustian pact with big oil. Oil revenues course through the local economy. Average incomes here are far above those in non-oil towns in the state. And some years ago, the town invested some of its oil revenues in buying control of almost 100,000 hectares of Arctic refuge that are believed to be rich in oil. The Inuit want permission to start pumping.

That's the official line, anyway. But I found a lot of whispered opposition. 'This place is very divided about oil,' said Carla Kayotuk, who runs the town store. Many fear what oil is doing to the environment. Isaac is against opening up the reserve because any expansion of the industry will damage whaling. Others fear the effects on their society. Alcoholism is one problem. Alcohol is banned by the town, but people say travellers recoup their air fares by smuggling in bootleg booze. The community occasionally evicts unruly people: four in the last three years. The exiles end up down the coast at Nuiqsut, described to me as an Eskimo 'sink settlement'.

Outsiders who have been long-term residents, especially those sceptical about oil's benefits, say they feel frozen out of the town's affairs. They are rejected as not being Inuit. And yet many of the town's leading families are far from pure-bred. The oldest citizen, eighty-nine when I visited, was Nora Agiak. She remembered travelling across the Arctic ice on dog-drawn sleds. She still wore mooseskin moccasins and a jacket of wolverine fur. She claimed to speak no English, yet neighbours said she was the daughter of a Scottish whaler. Kaktovik is not a town at ease with itself.

The Inuit are not the only people up here with an ancestral claim to the tundra. I flew to see a community 200 kilometres inland, on the southern edge of the wildlife refuge, that takes a very different view of big oil. Arctic Village has an airstrip, but no road, no hotel, no domestic plumbing and certainly no fire engines. The people here are Gwich'in, North American Indians, and their lives remain much more communal. But the politics of oil is bringing the outside world in.

The timetable on the communal noticeboard listed the visitors that week: two environment groups, some press, a team trying to sell the village solar panels, and a couple from the Isle of Man on a world tour. Next up were some Congressmen. But the first item on the board, in preparation for the visitors, read 'village clean-up' – no doubt the reason for the huge pile of drinks cans behind the house of Sarah James, head of the Gwich'in inter-village committee, which was set up to fight the oil companies.

Why are they rejecting this wealth? Arctic Village is one of a dozen communities of Gwich'in strung out along the migration route of a huge herd of caribou known as the Porcupine herd, after the name of one of the rivers they cross. The traditional ways of the Gwich'in are built around an annual hunt of the 110,000-strong herd as it moves from the snowy fastnesses of northern Canada, through the mountains near Arctic Village and on to its summer calving grounds on the coastal strip of northern Alaska near Kaktovik, where the cottongrass grows richest and the ocean breezes keep the vicious local mosquitoes at bay.

For thousands of years the caribou have survived grizzlies,

golden eagles, wolves and human hunters. The oil industry has already eaten into grazing grounds around Prudhoe Bay. So far, the pastures of the Porcupine herd to the east are untouched. But the 7,000 Gwich'in people believe that if the oil companies expand into the wildlife refuge, the herd will disappear – and their own way of life too will be lost. 'We are caribou people,' said Sarah. 'That is how we identify ourselves. That is how we feed ourselves.'

Though different in many ways from the Inuit of Kaktovik, this community too is fractured. 'The current generation is lost between two worlds,' said village schoolteacher Mary Groat, who has since left Arctic Village. There is the world of the elders, underpinned by the Gwich'in language and the caribou hunts, and the world they see on TV or when they go to college in Fairbanks.

'Caribou hunting is now the main tradition we have left,' Mary said. Many people send dried caribou meat to their exiled relatives in the cities. Caribou meat was Sarah's parting gift to our party. It is their nutrition, the wellspring of their communal culture, and their tie to the landscape. A young Gwich'in village official, Roland Tripp, sat in front of one of the council's computers. 'We need cash, of course we do. But our caribou are more important to us than money. And if the oil companies come to the refuge, we will lose the caribou.' Sarah put things more simply. 'We need the caribou herd like the Amazon Indians need the rainforest. It is our lives and culture.' But that is to romanticize. The truth is more complex. At the communal barbecue, caribou meat and fish were supplemented by hamburgers, pasta and a neverending supply of sugary biscuits.

It was late June. My visit had been timed so I could see the Porcupine herd on its pastures. But the timing had gone awry. The herd was a month late. Heavy snows in the mountains – caused, paradoxically, by warmer winter weather – had delayed their migration. We camped on the edge of the coastal plain, and saw the first males come by. The females were straggling behind, often dragging newborn calves across rivers swollen by melting snow.

This had never happened before, Fran Mauer of the US Fish and Wildlife Service in Fairbanks said later.

There were many tears in Alaskan schools that month. The children had 'adopted' caribou cows fitted with radio collars and were receiving regular updates on their progress towards the pastures. But a quarter of the adopted animals died, along with many of their calves. Among them was Gus-Gus, a calf being followed by the children at the Arctic Village school.

Most biologists I spoke to in Alaska were convinced that the Porcupine herd was already under severe pressure from man-made climate change, caused in part by burning the oil from Prudhoe Bay. But now the animals face the ultimate threat – the appearance of oil rigs on their grazing grounds. Can they survive such an invasion? Nobody is sure. The greatest caribou herd on the planet, responsible for one of the last great mammal migrations, could be doomed, and with it the lives of its hunters. It was time to go and see big oil.

Flying west from Kaktovik along the Arctic north shore in a four-seater bush plane, bumping through a rainstorm late in the evening, I first saw the pipelines, then roads, and finally the lights and flares of Prudhoe Bay itself. This is a major industrial enterprise in the middle of the Arctic. Hundreds of millions of dollars are invested here. After landing at Deadhorse airstrip, I met BP's resident biologist, Ray Jakubczak. He said the local caribou herd don't mind the oil developments. He stopped the car. We watched a caribou dodging the trucks going to the wellheads, before ambling under the main pipeline linking the field to the port of Valdez in southern Alaska. It didn't seem too upset. 'If we get permission to develop in the refuge, it certainly won't be a wilderness any more,' Ray conceded. 'But the wildlife will be fine.'

Later, when I met caribou biologist Ray Cameron at the University of Fairbanks, he choked in disagreement. 'Yes, you saw caribou round the oilfields. But they are not from the Porcupine herd, and you only saw males. The females and their calves keep well away from roads and oil developments. Around Prudhoe Bay they can do that because the coastal plain is wide. But further east, which is where the Porcupine herd have been calving for thousands of years, and where BP wants to drill, the plain is much narrower. There is less room for them to hide.'

BP says any future developments would have a much smaller 'footprint' than Prudhoe Bay. There would not even be road links. Everything would go in and out by helicopter. But even so, the north slope is a precious place. BP's recent record of oil spills up here does not command confidence in its ability to keep its footprint small, whatever the blueprints. And nobody knows how the Porcupine herd would respond to its presence. It would be shaming for the herd to be destroyed for a few months' supply of oil to the world. And to hell with George's fire engines.

Whatever its failures at Prudhoe Bay, BP's footprint in Alaska is dainty compared to the way the bogs and forests of West Siberia have been trampled by Russia's quest for oil and gas. I have travelled to this region twice: once in the 1990s and again in late 2005. What was once the world's largest swamp – frozen solid in winter but with thick, bouncy peat bogs in summer – has been brutally scarred by big oil, Russian style.

Once, we could blame that on Communism. In 1926, in one of the most notorious statements of Soviet intentions towards nature, Stalin's favourite writer Vladimir Zazubrin declared: 'Let the fragile beast of Siberia be dressed in the cement armour of cities, armed with the stone muzzles of factory chimneys, and girded with the iron belts of railroads. Let the taiga be burned and felled; let the steppes be trampled. Only in cement and iron can the fraternal union of all peoples, the iron brotherhood of man, be forged.' And so it was.

Notions of an iron brotherhood may have passed into history. But not a lot else has changed. Now, Russia's new generation of capitalist oligarchs is continuing to trample the taiga. And, increasingly, it is Western consumers who are the market for the oil and gas coming out of here. The West Siberian oilfields now rank close behind Saudi Arabia. And the region is second only to the Middle East in its reserves of natural gas, which come down a vast network of pipes to keep much of Western Europe warm in winter. West Siberia's hydrocarbon reserves make up about a fifth of what the planet has left.

On my first visit, I landed at a Siberian city called Noyabr'sk, one of the major centres of the Siberian oil industry. Only incorporated in 1982, Noyabr'sk has a population of 100,000. Most of them are Ukrainians shipped in during the latter days of the Soviet Empire. I visited with Western oil engineers brought in during a fit of glasnost to advise on the future development of the oilfields. During many hours of helicopter flights, we saw a landscape where the main features till two decades before were reindeer tracks. But now it was covered with pylons, oil pipelines, drill rigs, a network of endless roads laid through forests or on wide embankments across lakes and bogs, and narrow straight gashes that marked the routes taken by old seismic surveys. No attempt had been made to run these different pieces of infrastructure along common corridors. Instead they snaked independently across the land, dividing nature into millions of fragments, each only a few hundred metres across at most. It was as Zazubrin decreed.

Pollution was everywhere. We flew through clouds of black smoke from gas flares and burning pools of waste oil. Our experts estimated that a tenth of all the oil pumped to the surface was lost before it left the oilfields. Our expedition visited one drilling pad unannounced. The pumps were pumping, but there was nobody there. The rig was surrounded by blackened forest where waste oil had poured into a creek and plastered tree foliage. We could see sheens of oil glistening on the lakes and bogs all around.

Nowhere on Earth, the Western experts concluded, has such a large hydrocarbon resource been exploited so quickly and so wastefully. The region round Noyabr'sk had 12,000 oil wells – ten times more than the Prudhoe Bay oilfield. They had been drilled from several thousand large concrete drilling pads. Often the pads were less than 500 metres apart, each requiring its own roads, pipe, power lines and waste dumps for the millions of tonnes of polluted water generated during drilling. Modern methods could replace twenty or more well pads with a single drilling point, the Western oilmen said. But their Siberian counterparts were 'like cowboys, taking the cheapest and easiest oil in the cheapest and easiest way.'

The huge oilfields around Noyabr'sk were, at the time of my visit, owned by a state company, Noyabr'skneftegas. They supplied one of the world's largest oil refineries in the Siberian city of Omsk to the south. In 1999, both the oilfields and the refinery came under the control of Roman Abramovitch, the soccer-loving Russian tycoon who now lives in Britain and owns Chelsea Football Club. The reserves of the new company, Sibneft, are believed to be greater than those of Exxon, and the refinery's 'light sweet crude' is sold to Europe for jet fuel and low-sulphur diesel for cars and trucks.

Often, when I fly out of Heathrow or Gatwick or change planes at Schiphol or Frankfurt, my plane will be fuelled with Sibneft's oil from the bogs around Noyabr'sk. In 2005, Abramovitch sold Sibneft at a profit of several billion dollars to the huge state energy conglomerate, Gazprom. So whenever I go and watch Chelsea take the pitch at Stamford Bridge, I reckon I am watching the team that Noyabr'sk's oil built.

Our trip to Western Siberia was extensive and, so far as I am aware, unique for independent outsiders. We flew north-east from Noyabr'sk, dropping in on an abandoned Stalinist labour camp called Gulag 501 Construction Enterprise. Half a century ago, it housed political prisoners brought to work on an abortive railway project along the Arctic Circle, known as the Great Stalin Railway. Now it held only ghosts. We continued to a tiny town called Krasnoselkup on the banks of the River Taz. Here they hunted sable and squirrel, fished the rivers and logged the forests. I was offered the pelt of a big brown bear for $1,000. They didn't believe me when I said I could never take it home, because Customs would impound it and arrest me.

Russian engineers had just started drilling outside Krasnoselkup. The main test rig was 100 metres from Devil's Lake, a major centre for wildlife. The deputy mayor Alexander Laetov told me how the exploratory drilling was frightening away the reindeer and poisoning fish. (We weren't helping. Our ex-military pilot spotted a bear and chased the terrified animal through the wet landscape. It was like a scene from *Apocalypse Now*.)

We met a small tribe of native Selkup people camping on the banks of the River Taz. There are only 4,000 Selkup left in the whole of Siberia. They told the story of their centuries-long march north in the face of advancing Russians. In the woods they showed us their shaman's sledge-load of sacred objects. Among them were arrowheads and metal ornaments in the shape of birds and snakes, made, they said, in the days when the Selkup were a great people and smelted iron. But they and their reindeer were on the retreat once again as the oilmen moved in.

Since that visit, Gazprom has moved into Krasnoselkup in force. The area around Devil's Lake is now called the Yuzhno-Russkoye oil and gas field. Roads and pipelines and the rest of the infrastructure needed for a major gas field are being constructed. Production begins in 2008. The gas will go down a pipeline across Russia and beneath the Baltic Sea to northern Germany.

Krasnoselkup's website boasts about the huge investment going into the town. But it is silent on the steps, if any, being taken to protect the lakes and rivers and wildlife that were still there in profusion when I visited. This will be Noyabr'sk all over again. Nor can I find any information on the fate of the Selkup community I visited, but it is hard to believe that they have not moved north yet again.

Krasnoselkup is turning out to be a major gas find, bigger than the existing main gas-producing area a couple of hundred kilometres to the west, around Novy Urengoi. The two areas together make Gazprom probably the largest gas company in the world. And Gazprom doesn't let anyone forget its power. In Novy Urengoi, Gazprom chooses the mayor and runs the local TV station, which is called Gazprom TV. When I flew there in 2005, I was told by a burly policewoman at the airport that my Russian visa was not enough. To enter, I needed a special invitation supplied by Gazprom officials in the town.

As she filed my passport in a safe and got distracted by new arrivals, I wandered into town anyway. In the language of the local reindeer-herding Nenets (close cousins of the Selkup), Urengoi means 'rotten, godforsaken place'. I could see what they meant. The wind howled among the bare apartment blocks. There were huge areas of sandy wasteland, where dogs roamed, followed by men with vodka-red faces in leather jackets and waving mobile phones. Women in high heels and fur coats clambered in and out of yellow Gazprom minibuses as fast as they could, to avoid the wind destroying their elaborate hair-dos. The way into the half-built hotel was over duckboards. The heating was off and the corridors smelled of paint.

Novy Urengoi provides a third of Europe's gas. The only foreigners in the place were German gas people, looking out for their nation's heating. If Gazprom turned off the taps here, Europe would get mighty cold in winter. And with new supplies soon coming from Krasnoselkup, Gazprom has big plans to replace Britain's diminishing North Sea reserves with Siberian gas. At the time of writing, Gazprom had already bought one British gas-supply company, Pennine Natural Gas. And there were press reports that it wanted to take over Centrica, the owner of British Gas, the country's leading distributor.

Eventually they came to get me. A young spook and his interpreter had been detailed to round me up and take me back to the airport. They worked for Gazprom, of course. The spook wore an open double-breasted suit of cheap cloth to display his importance. I explained that I had come to see some scientists from Tomsk. He wondered how I knew that the scientists were not mafia, and would not kidnap me. I wondered how I knew he was not mafia, because he had certainly kidnapped me.

The airport departure lounge was full of overcoated construction workers returning home after a week-long shift in the 'rotten, god-forsaken place'. The walls were covered with pictures of Nenets, their camps and their reindeer – celebrating a world that gas had destroyed.

21

My Electricity: Old King Coal Lives on at Drax

I wanted to know where my electricity came from. It proved a hard question to answer. My electricity comes, via a local supply company, from the National Grid, which in turn gets it from generating companies that run power stations. But electricity is not a commodity like any other. It doesn't come in packets that I can track. It is an electrical current, maintained by the constant whirring of turbines at power stations all over the country – and one or two in France as well – and distributed by the National Grid.

Only the very biggest users can answer the question fully, because they need dedicated lines from power stations. So Rio Tinto's giant aluminium smelter on Anglesey gets its power largely from the Wylfa nuclear power plant close by, and will probably shut when the power plant closes in 2010. Likewise the huge surges of power required to run Europe's nuclear-fusion research reactor at Culham in Oxfordshire come down a high-tension cable from Didcot power station.

So who supplies the National Grid? There are three main types of power sources: nuclear, coal and gas. The diminishing band of nuclear power stations were mostly built more than thirty years ago, usually in remote spots round the coast, in case anything went wrong. Many of them are far past their design lives and cannot be kept going much longer. Their fuel is uranium, mostly from Australia and Canada. Inside the power station's reactor, the metal is bombarded with neutrons to create heat that makes steam that drives turbines that generate about a fifth of our electricity.

It's clever stuff. Six grams of uranium fuel generate as much electricity as a tonne of coal. My household benefits from the irradiation of nearly 4 grams of uranium a year. The technology is rather old hat now. But the risks of getting it wrong are fearsome, as Chernobyl showed. And we don't yet have any final resting place for the spent fuel, which is extremely radioactive. Currently it is stored in giant swimming pools at the power stations and occasionally goes by train, in high-tech and hopefully impregnable flasks, to Sellafield in Cumbria for storage. The government wants to build more nuclear power stations, but promises it won't do so until it has figured out what to do with this accumulated waste. We have heard that before.

Since the 1960s, Britain has been awash with cheap natural gas from beneath the North Sea. At first we used all of it to heat homes and run factories. Then it became a fuel in power stations, too, as the coal mines were shut. But now North Sea gas is running out. Increasingly, our gas is coming from abroad, in refrigerated tankers from Algeria and Qatar. Within a decade Britain may be importing 90 per cent of its gas. Ten large gas-storage projects are currently being developed to receive those imports. But meanwhile, international gas prices are rising. As a result of all this, greenhouse-unfriendly coal, once written off as yesterday's fuel, is making an unexpected comeback. Energy company E.on is pressing hard to build a new coal plant at Kingsnorth in Kent.

In 2006, the contribution of gas burning to our electricity supply shrank to about a quarter, while coal returned to the number-one spot, with a 40 per cent market share. The remaining 15 per cent or so is either imported from France (an extra dose of nuclear fuel) or is from renewables like wind and, predominantly, Scottish hydroelectricity. But for my footprint, the trail to follow is coal.

Anyone travelling north from London to Newcastle and Edinburgh will see the three giant power plants on the flat lowlands around the River Trent. They call this Megawatt Valley. It is among the most concentrated sources of electricity generation on Earth – and of greenhouse gas emissions. The three plants are named after the villages they invaded: Eggborough, Ferrybridge and Drax. They were built by the Central Electricity Generating Board back in the 1960s and 1970s to burn coal from a planned new coalfield at nearby Selby.

Drax was the last of the trio, completed in 1974. It is Western Europe's largest power station, with a capacity of 4,000 megawatts, so large that the company running it does nothing else. Drax produces 8 per cent of our electricity. Its turbine hall is a quarter of a mile long and it has twelve cooling towers. Its 250-metre chimney was once Western Europe's biggest single source of acid rain. They cleaned that up by fitting 'scrubbers' between 1988 and 1996, to absorb the sulphur emissions from the burning coal. This was Britain's initially grudging contribution to a continent-wide effort to take the acid out of Europe's rain. It was worth it. Since then, the fish have been returning to Scandinavian lakes.

But greenhouse gases? There are as yet no scrubbers to remove the carbon dioxide. Some 22 million tonnes of CO_2 go up Drax's infamous chimney each year. That is as much carbon dioxide as comes from a quarter of Britain's cars. And it is more than all the planes leaving Heathrow airport produce in a year. Drax emits more carbon dioxide than Sweden.

Under the EU emissions-trading scheme, which set levels on emissions for large industrial plants from 2008, Drax is allowed 9.6 million tonnes of CO_2 emissions, less than half what it actually intends to emit. The chief executive at Drax, Dorothy Thompson, plans to make up the difference by buying permits from companies with spare, including from Centrica, the owner of British Gas. Centrica has spares because it can't sell as much gas to power stations as it would like to – partly because Drax is undercutting it. It's a funny old world.

One day, Drax may capture the carbon dioxide from its smoke-stacks – and perhaps liquefy and bury it in the empty oil and gas wells beneath the North Sea. But Thompson is cool. 'An interesting concept' is as far as she will go. Fair enough, since the technology is still distant. Most studies say it is $20 billion and two decades from commercial application. Instead, she says she hopes to convert Drax to replacing 10 per cent of its coal with rapeseed, willow cop-pice and elephant grass grown by local farmers. That's the hope. But in 2006, Drax actually cut its biofuels use by 90 per cent, because coal was cheaper. Who said King Coal had been dethroned?

This kind of short-term ultra-commercial approach does not win friends. In the summer of 2006, demonstrators camped outside Drax to protest against its emissions. They wanted to turn Drax into a Greenham Common of the carbon age, and shut the place down. In that they failed. But they will return. I might join them next time.

One thing perplexed me. Drax burns 30,000 tonnes of coal a day. But Margaret Thatcher shut down the Selby coalfield that was intended to supply it, so where does it get its coal? Half, it turns out, comes from British open-cast mining operations. The other 4 million tonnes come from abroad. For all its claimed green creden-tials, Britain is today the world's fourth-largest coal importer – shipping in 47 million tonnes in 2006, double the figure in 2000. Megawatt Valley takes most of the 12 million tonnes entering through the Humberside ports of Grimsby and Immingham. Drax is among a group of power companies pushing to invest in port capacity so it can import more.

While we fret about the wisdom of importing Siberian gas in future, one of the more curious legacies of the Thatcher era is that the biggest source of Britain's coal imports today is Russia. Most of it comes from beyond the Ural mountains, from Kuznetsk in south-west Siberia. Dug from deep mines of the kind long since closed in Britain, it travels overland for no less than 4,000 kilometres, starting on the Trans-Siberian Railway and then taking branch lines across European Russia all the way to the Baltic coast. From there, it goes by ship to Immingham, and then returns to rail for the last hop up Megawatt Valley to Drax and its fellows.

Kuznetsk seems a very distant place indeed. And it is. The journey is only possible because the Russian government provides huge subsidies for its mines and railways. Yet, bizarrely, as I checked one day for more information on those mines on the BBC website, I discovered that less than two hours before, its Moscow reporter had filed a story about a Yorkshireman who lived only a couple of miles from Drax. He had just been named as one of more than 100 people killed by a methane explosion in one of Kuznetsk's biggest mines, at Ulyanovskaya. It was the worst Russian mine accident in a decade. With tragic irony, Ian Robertson was working with a British consultancy firm to improve safety systems in the mine. They got the job after twenty miners died in another methane explosion down the same pit two years before. Suddenly Kuznetsk seemed rather closer, and its link to Drax rather more poignant.

Coal used to be regarded as too expensive to move very far. It was burned close to where it was mined. It was also owned by state enterprises and earmarked for keeping the home fires burning. No more. Coal has become a global commodity, and the big mining conglomerates have taken control. The largest, BHP Billiton, operates coal mines in Colombia and South Africa, Australia and New Mexico and Alaska. The other two kings of coal are Anglo American and the Swiss company Glencore.

These Big Three supply most of the rest of the coal that Britain imports. Thanks to them, South Africa is the world's third-largest coal producer and second-largest coal exporter, after Australia. Britain is among South Africa's biggest coal customers, taking 13 million tonnes a year. Almost all of it is mined in the Drakensberg mountains and exported from the Richards Bay coal terminal on the west coast north of Durban. It exports around 70 million tonnes of coal a year, a figure that will probably have risen to 91 million tonnes by the time you read this. People talk about global oil production reaching a peak. Hooray. But coal production shows no sign of peaking. And that is very bad news for the climate.

22

Wheels and Wings: Busting the Myths of Green Travel

Not having a car (sorry to shock you, but in London that is possible), I travel a lot by train. As much as I can. You see much more: especially the backs of places, which are much more interesting than the fronts that you see from the road. And the train is much more civilized. Better than a plane, because it is city centre to city centre. And better than a car because the ride is smoother and more reliable and somebody else drives you. Going to Scotland for instance, on a sleeper. Or Paris or Brussels on the Eurostar. Train is a great way to go to Venice: rolling across the causeway at dawn is the height of luxury. And I have always assumed that it is greener.

But just how 'green' is train travel? In 2007, several train companies were making some pretty determined claims for the environmental high ground. First out of the sidings was Virgin Trains. It claimed that its new Pendolino tilting trains to Glasgow used '78 per cent less carbon dioxide' than domestic flights, and 65 per cent less than cars. Then Eurostar claimed to emit 'ten times less CO_2 than flying' on its routes from London to Paris and Brussels. All these numbers made me suspicious. Why such precise figures? Do they add up?

Both Virgin and Eurostar reckon that short-haul aircraft emit around 150 grams per passenger-kilometre. Virgin put car emissions at 180 grams per person-kilometre with a typical occupancy of 1.2 people. Virgin reckon that when travelling half full, its Pendolinos clock up 27 grams; while Eurostar claims to average 11 grams on the journey to Paris and 18 grams to Brussels. Clearly, these numbers depend entirely on how full the respective trains and planes are. A couple of days before seeing Virgin's ad for the first time I had been on one of its Pendolinos, which was largely empty all the way to Manchester. By contrast, most planes travel full these days. So it was possible that my emissions on that journey were greater than if I had travelled in a full plane. And why, come to think of it, was Eurostar's claim so much better than Virgin's? Could it really emit less than half as much as a Virgin train?

I enjoy a statistical scrap, so I went exploring. I solved Eurostar's superiority quickly enough. It was buried in the small print of the company's website. The figures, it said, 'are based on actual passenger numbers, exact distances, actual aircraft types [all very reassuring] and the mix of electricity sources used by Eurostar trains.' Cracked it. In France, where the trains spend most of their time, most of the electricity comes from nuclear power stations. They don't produce carbon dioxide. Eurostar couldn't quite bring itself to say 'our trains are greener because they run on nuclear power', but that is what it meant.

That left Virgin. Two things emerged here. First, the new Pendolinos do much better than some other trains. Such as Virgin's own workhorse, the Voyager train, which, it agrees, produces nearly three times as much carbon dioxide per passenger-kilometre on a similar loading: 74 grams compared to 27 grams. So my actual emissions for a given journey clearly depend a lot on what train I ride on, as well as how full it is. For instance, if I caught a Voyager train that was less than about a quarter full (and I've been on those), I would emit more carbon dioxide per passenger-kilometre than a typical averagely full short-haul flight.

Here is another thought. I have happily been assuming that my carbon footprint for taking the overnight sleeper train to Edinburgh is less than if I flew. But sleeper cars have just sixteen berths. Typically, they carry fewer people than a quarter-full regular carriage. So I fear it would have been better to fly. Oh, well.

That is an exceptional case, I agree. But green as it may generally be in comparison to air travel, the railway is using ever more energy. Most of the electric lines into London from the south coast are currently having their voltage upgraded so they can take modern trains. These use more energy because they accelerate faster, have energy-guzzling kit like air conditioning and automatic doors, and are heavier because they have crash-resistant super-structure and other adornments like double glazing. Some recent new commuter electric trains have engines with twice the power per seat of older engines.

Network Rail admits that when all this was planned nobody thought about the greenhouse-gas implications. Its 2006 corporate responsibility report says it is talking to rail operators about what to do to reduce emissions. It suggests lighter rolling stock. Maybe, but most new trains are heavier than the old rolling stock. Some weigh as much per passenger seat as a Land Rover Discovery.

Network Rail also wants to encourage 'regenerative braking'. This is a way of slowing the train by using the engine rather than a conventional brake, which wastes energy in the form of heat. Instead, the motor will return the power to the supply system for use by another train. On commuter lines, this could reduce electricity use by as much as 20 per cent. Scandalously, according to the government, the motors on 60 per cent of electric trains can already do this, but it requires a change of operating methods, and only 15 per cent do it in practice. The railway industry clearly has a long way to go before it can justify its green slogan.

The trouble is that fuel costs are a relatively small part of the total cost of running the railway, so many companies don't care. It turns out, too, that Network Rail, which provides the electricity for trains, does not meter them individually. The costs are pooled among the companies operating on a line, so individual companies lack a direct incentive to cut emissions.

Rail should be an efficient means of transport compared to road, for the simple reason that there is much less friction between a steel wheel and track than between rubber tyres and the road. So it is often assumed that trains are better than all forms of road travel. But not so. Express coaches emit about a quarter less carbon dioxide than trains. An express coach carrying twenty passengers emits 37 grams per passenger-kilometre, compared to 50 grams for an average train averagely loaded. Coaches are the greenest way to travel. At the time of writing I haven't seen any big posters advertising this fact. But they can't be long delayed.

By contrast, buses may not be so good. They are more likely to run with most of their seats empty, and they are constantly stopping and starting to pick up passengers. Even so, it's a shock to discover they often produce more than 100 grams per passenger-kilometre. Green campaigners push for more rural buses to break the stranglehold of the car outside towns. I stand by that. And I use them. But the problem is that large numbers of buses are driving around substantially empty. Where I use such empty rural buses – on Stagecoach routes in West Sussex – the main problem seems to be that they are ludicrously expensive. Only the rich (and pensioners with their passes) can afford them. As a result, it is often literally true that emissions would be less if everyone got a taxi. And – whisper it quietly – sometimes the dreadful 4x4 could be the green option. Indeed, there are days when Sussex buses of my acquaintance are burning up more fuel per passenger-kilometre than a jumbo jet on the way to Hong Kong.

Which brings me to Heathrow. Britain has the dubious distinction of having two of the world's largest single sources of carbon dioxide emissions to the atmosphere. One is Drax, Europe's largest power station, as we saw in Chapter 21. The other is Heathrow, the world's busiest international airport. At its four (shortly to be five) terminals, more fuel is loaded on to more long-haul aircraft than anywhere else on Earth. At take-off, as much as a third of the weight of these aircraft is in the fuel tanks. Passengers are rarely aware of how much combustible material they are sitting beside. But they got a hint in December 2005, when a fuel depot at Buncefield in Hertfordshire exploded. The blast has been called the biggest ever peacetime explosion in Europe, and was heard 160 kilometres away. Black smoke was tracked as far as Spain.

Buncefield is one of three giant oil stores that keep Heathrow going. It is a staging post on pipelines from oil refineries on Merseyside and the Humber estuary. At any one time, Buncefield stores up to 270 million litres of fuel. It supplies Heathrow with 7 million litres a day, a third of the airport's daily demand. Another pipeline brings fuel from the Fawley oil refinery on Southampton Water in Hampshire; a third comes in from another depot at Walton-on-Thames in Surrey.

These huge volumes of fuel converge on Heathrow like the tributaries of a giant river. Yet they end not in an ocean but in hundreds of aircraft fuel tanks. Aircraft at Heathrow load up 7,300 million litres a year. Then they take off and burn it across the skies of the world. In the process, they release more than 18 million tonnes of carbon dioxide. Thus the 65 million passengers using Heathrow each year typically emit around a quarter-tonne of carbon dioxide during each flight.

The total emissions from aircraft leaving British airports represent about 6 per cent of British carbon dioxide emissions. When other emissions from those aircraft engines are included, the aircraft are responsible for around 12 per cent of the warming effect of British emissions of greenhouse gases. But you won't read that in the official statistics, because aircraft emissions are excluded from the Kyoto Protocol. So they don't formally have to be declared. Why so? Because, when the protocol was being negotiated in Japan back in 1997, nobody could agree on who should be responsible for aircraft emissions. Should it be the country from which the plane departed? Or the country where it arrived? Or the country where the airline was based? Or maybe it should be shared out among the nationalities of the passengers? You can see the difficulty, but it is a scandal from which Britain, as a major global hub for flights, benefits greatly.

Greenhouse gas emissions are only part of the 'footprint' of Heathrow, of course. There is the land, too. Heathrow began in the 1930s as a private aerodrome on land sold by the vicar of Harmondsworth. He has a lot to answer for, you might say. The aerodrome grew as a wartime base for air crews scrambling into the skies to defend London during the Battle of Britain. And after that, it just grew and grew. Almost every time an airport expansion is planned for London, Heathrow emerges as the least worst option. It still has only two runways, but more and more terminals and more and more flights are packed in. Terminal 5 will be finished in late 2008 and already they are talking about Terminal 6. In its way, that is a huge virtue. In crowded Britain, land matters. I can't help but admire the sheer efficiency of how Heathrow uses the space it has.

Sitting one day at the small municipal airport outside Bournemouth, I decided to compare it with Heathrow. I was waiting to fly to Pisa for a conference on the science of measuring ecological footprints, so I found several layers of irony in my task. Bournemouth airport was once known as Hurn airport and was a wartime base for supplying the French Resistance. Afterwards, until Heathrow opened, it was Britain's main international airport, the imperial hub from which the first service from Britain to Australia took off. Now it specializes in budget flights, with about a dozen departures a day and 300,000 passengers a year.

Heathrow occupies less than four times the land area of Hurn, and yet it sees off more than 200 times as many passengers. Heathrow passengers, me included, complain a lot about the congestion. But, per passenger departure, Heathrow is fifty times more efficient in its use of land than Hurn. Not only that: Hurn was built by concreting over part of one of Britain's premier patches of heathland. So, if we have to have airports, Hurn's land footprint is grotesquely large for what it does, while Heathrow's footprint is miraculously small. There are other good things about Heathrow. You can reach it readily by public transport, whereas they shut the old Hurn railway station years ago. And the last bus from Bournemouth left three hours before my early-evening flight to Pisa.

But Heathrow's efficiency in the use of land, and its economy in having only two runways, comes at a high price for those who live under its flight paths. I am not too amused to be woken fairly regularly, especially in summer, by planes flying in from the Far East. They start at about 4.30 in the morning. The problem is that both of Heathrow's runways run east to west, ensuring maximum possible noise over the maximum number of people. The area where the noise exceeds the official nuisance threshold of 63 decibels is 19 kilometres across and 3.5 kilometres wide, covering some of the most heavily populated parts of west and south London. Peter Hall, Britain's most distinguished town planner and a fan of airports in general, calls Heathrow 'one of the country's truly great planning catastrophes'. Perhaps he lives under the flight path, too.

I have taken a few detours in this chapter. Casting Heathrow as a green airport was a bit of a stretch. So was coming up with occasions when it might be better to take the 4x4 than the bus. I don't apologize for this because I do think it is important to think through these issues carefully. The answers are not always obvious. But I'd like to end up with the truisms about the environmental footprint of travel. Planes are still bad. There is as yet no such thing as a green plane, though everyone from Boeing to Richard Branson will try hard to persuade us differently. Cars are still bad, the wrong way to make most journeys when there is a feasible alternative. Only planes make them look good. We should still mostly take the train and the bus and the coach, or get on our bikes.

23

London: My Part in the Metabolism of a Capital City

I live in London. I use its services. It sustains me and 7 million others. The city is like a living organism that consumes materials and spews out waste. And I am like a single cell within that organism. I have my own small world, but depend on the city for my food and transport, water and waste-disposal systems, power and gas and so on. And I hope I contribute something to it as well. So if I want to judge my 'footprint', I need to recognize my part in the city and the place I have in its metabolism.

This idea of the city having a metabolism comes from the ecologist Herbert Girardet. In a famous investigation, completed in 1994, he tried to quantify the main inputs and outputs of London. He found that the city's inhabitants consume almost 40 million tonnes of construction materials, 2.4 million tonnes of food, 2.2 million tonnes of paper, 2.1 million tonnes of plastic, 0.4 million tonnes of glass and 1.2 million tonnes of metals. On top of that the city's vehicles and power stations gobble up 20 million tonnes of fossil fuels, while we humans consume (either by breathing in or by burning) 40 million tonnes of oxygen, and drink, shower and flush a billion tonnes of water.

On the other side of the equation, he calculated that London's wastes comprise more than 60 million tonnes of carbon dioxide and other air pollutants, nearly 8 million tonnes of sewage, 12 million tonnes of demolition and industrial waste and 4 million tonnes of household waste. Now inputs and outputs don't balance out in Herbie's metabolic calculation, partly because the city is doing more building than demolition, but mainly because there isn't full accounting for the water. The main elements are there, however.

Where do I fit in? Broadly, I imagine I take my share of food and paper and plastic (about a third of a tonne a year for each of them) and metals (about a fifth of a tonne, not including the rucksack). I breathe and drink and flush the toilet with the rest. I don't pour any cement personally. And my house has not seen much since it was built a century ago. But we all contribute to the city's footprint through the urban infrastructure we use. We take a share of the materials that build the roads and bridges that we, and the goods we buy, travel. We take our share too of the tunnels and pipes and reservoirs that our water and sewage pass through, and the sea walls that protect us from rising tides. Not to mention the power stations and factories and runways and car parks and ports and – well, the list is pretty much endless.

Cement is essential to any modern city. It is made by heating limestone and clay to very high temperatures in a kiln. The process releases large amounts of carbon dioxide – about a tonne of CO_2 for every tonne of cement. What share of the new construction should I take? Rather a lot, I fear. I am not a driver, so I might imagine my share of the roads is small. I'd very much like to deny that I had any hand in the M25 motorway ringing the capital. But even if I rarely go on it myself, I'd guess most of the things I buy in London's shops have orbited round it before trailing into town for delivery to the shops I go to.

Even as the planes fly overhead and wake me in the morning, I have to admit to being a serial user of Heathrow airport. So I must take my share of the half a million tonnes of concrete and 8,000 tonnes of steel that are going into building its fifth terminal. Likewise, several times in a typical year I buy into the ribbon of concrete, cable and metal that stretches across Kent to take the Eurostar trains to Paris and Brussels.

Somewhere beneath my feet in south London runs the city's water ring-main. I have never seen it, but I rely on its 80 kilometres of concrete pipes, all large enough to drive a car through, to keep my taps running. And I cannot escape the fact that my water bills will probably soon be contributing to the construction of the billion-pound Abingdon reservoir, which is intended to supply London with water by 2020. It will be only a few hundred metres from the coal-burning Didcot power station, the M4 motorway and the Great Western Railway – all infrastructure that helps keep me warm and mobile.

What other services contribute to my footprint? A few hundred yards from my house is Wandsworth Prison. Formerly the Surrey House of Correction, it is Europe's largest prison, the famous compulsory digs for everyone from Oscar Wilde to Ronnie Biggs and the scene of 135 executions (the old execution room is now a tearoom for prison officers, who drink harder stuff in my nearest pub, The County Arms). I trust that I will never be a resident there, but politicians tell me its services to the community help keep me and my stuff safe. Likewise, I have to be reassured by the presence of all the defence establishments that block my routes (and my views) on country walks, and the hideous Spook House (more properly the headquarters of the Secret Intelligence Service, or MI6) that spooks me two train stops away in Vauxhall.

I have greater personal experience of, and sympathy for, the operation of St George's Hospital in Tooting, and the schools my children attended. All part of our urban fabric, my city's metabolism. Estimating the ecological footprint that the government creates on my behalf would be a book in itself. But for the record, the Carbon Trust says public services emit about 11 per cent of Britain's total carbon dioxide emissions, with more than a third of that from schools and local government services, and almost a sixth from hospitals. Frankly, I don't believe its tiny numbers for the Ministry of Defence. The real numbers must be an official secret, or maybe they are just ignored because they are excluded from the Kyoto Protocol.

A lot of research has been done recently into carbon footprints. It is only part of our total footprint, of course. But the figures are interesting. The Carbon Trust, for instance, shows that half of all Britain's carbon dioxide emissions come from the 'built environment', and a quarter from our homes. That phrase is rather a catch-all. It includes not just the construction and maintenance of buildings, but also heating and lighting them, running their phone lines and computers, and most of the things that we do in buildings, like cooking and bathing and turning on the TV. One estimate reckons that just 10 per cent of a typical building's lifetime carbon dioxide emissions comes from construction, while 85 per cent comes from use and 5 per cent from eventual demolition. The source for that is the cement company Lafarge, which I guess has an interest in lowering the construction element. But for my 100-year-old house, it could be right, though I am hoping to avoid the demolition element.

So I set out to monitor how my house and I match up here. What is the energy throughput? First I looked at my utility bills. In the past year, my household got through 3,100 kilowatt hours of electricity and 25,800 kilowatt hours of natural gas, which have a combined CO_2 footprint of 6.2 tonnes. Divided among three people, that is just over 2 tonnes each.

Meanwhile, I filled in a footprint calculator put online by the WWF. That disclosed that in my personal life, my carbon footprint is below the UK average at nearly 8 tonnes of carbon dioxide a year, including a contribution for the services government provides. But then I added in my professional life. Some people say I shouldn't do that. But I am freelance and by and large I can choose where I travel and how. Anyhow, it didn't look so good. See Chapter 29 on carbon offsets for what happened when I tried to calculate my horrible carbon footprint for travelling to write this book.

But really I knew the problems. I fly. A lot. And when I am at home, I live in a one-house urban heat island. I imagine if we took one of those thermal-imaging pictures of our house in winter, it would be glowing red-hot from all the escaping heat. The checklist is embarrassing. No cavity insulation in the house walls, though admittedly that is hard to do when there are no cavities. Old and thin loft insulation, which we should fix. And several rooms without curtains.

The house is still full of energy-guzzling tungsten-filament light bulbs that I am bad about turning off (though I gather in winter they are rather efficient at warming the house). My computer is on sixteen hours a day, making it the biggest electricity user, getting through between 500 and 1,000 kilowatt hours in a year and responsible for between 200 and 400 kilograms of CO_2 a year.

The fridge is none too efficient, even when we remember to defrost it. That must be the number-two electricity user. Because we've never got round to buying a microwave, we stick baking potatoes in the oven for an hour, which is a real energy nonsense. We toast bread under the grill, which is both slower and takes five times as much energy as using a toaster. What else? We bathe rather than shower. That is not only bad for water consumption, it also probably makes the moment I run my thrice-weekly bath the biggest single energy-guzzling moment in the house.

So what's the good news? Well, we keep the thermostat fairly low (about 18 degrees) and only run the heating for parts of the day. We don't leave the TV on standby (well, not often). Nor do we have a plasma TV, which would use four times as much power as our old cathode-ray-tube model. We don't have a tumble drier (which is the biggest energy user in most houses that have one). Instead we have a carbon-neutral washing line and several clothes horses – though these do have a downside: drying clothes cools the house. We don't have a dishwasher either, but some studies say that modern energy-efficient machines use less hot water that the average sloppy manual washer-up. And we were almost right not to get double glazing. Apparently it takes many years of use to recoup the energy expended in making the aluminium frames.

Any other basic tips? Often it is better to wait till things wear out before replacing them, even if the new machines claim to be more energy-efficient. Assemble a full load before running things like washing and washing-up machines. Laptops use *much* less energy than PCs, because they are designed that way.

In ten years' time, the government wants all homes to be 'zero-carbon', with no net carbon dioxide emissions from heating, lighting or electrical appliances. I'm not clear how that is going to happen in practice, but I evidently have a long way to go. I deliberately tried not to change my lifestyle while writing this book. But now it's done, I will be reading carefully what I am sure is the best book on how to live a low-carbon life. It is by Chris Goodall and it is called just that: *How to Live a Low-Carbon Life*. I recommend it.

One in a Billion: *Greg, the Gold Man*

With his shirt open to reveal some chunky jewellery, and chain-smoking in the final weeks when such a thing was allowed in public, Greg Valerio had the air of an old colonial gone to seed, or even of a chancer in the mining industry. But then, he is not the most orthodox of characters. For behind the raffish exterior is a man often called the world's first ethical jeweller. Actually, so far as I can tell, he is the world's only ethical jeweller.

Expelled as 'uneducatable' by his local school in Chichester in Sussex, Greg became a Christian and headed off to Africa to teach. He began to fund his travel by selling African jewellery to his friends, and then set up in business. Ethical business. 'I decided that instead of standing round complaining about what was going on, the best way of developing my ideas about ethical trading was to get into the business and provide a market for it.' So now he is back in Chichester, selling ethical gold over the counter and on-line from his modest shop, called Cred, near the station. Beauty without cruelty, he calls it. I'd be fascinated to know what his old headmaster calls it.

It was all very well being an ethical jeweller, but first he needed supplies of ethical jewellery. Eventually Greg found a Colombian activist called Catalina Cock. Working in the South American jungle, she had noticed that small communities on the edge of the rainforest were renting their territories to gold-mining companies, who wrecked the land and left it unfit for agriculture. She encouraged the communities to take up mining themselves instead, and to adopt less toxic methods, so that the land could be returned to farming and the rivers to fishing. Catalina set up Green Gold, and together she and Greg founded the Association for Responsible Mining. 'I am the responsible jeweller; Catalina is the responsible miner,' Greg says.

Green Gold operates in one of the places in the world you might least expect to deliver 'ethical' anything. Its headquarters are in Medellín in Colombia, hotbed of the drug barons, and the gold is mined in the Choco region, near the country's remote, rebellious northern border with Panama. But the 1,000 or so miners panning the local rivers deliver about 4 kilograms of gold a month, enough for 400 rings. The next step, Greg and Catalina agree, is to get formal fairtrade certification. 'We hope to get that before the end of 2008,' Greg says. The main hold-up could be providing safe passage for the fairtrade inspectors to go there.

But Greg is on to something big. On the back of the film *Blood Diamond*, the ethical-jewellery business is set to take off. His model is the Body Shop ethical franchise chain established by the late Anita Roddick just down the road in Littlehampton. And he is as ambitious. 'We want three hundred outlets by 2009,' he said. 'But all this depends on being able to get sufficient certified supplies.' He is lining up more gold miners' groups from Bolivia, Peru and several African countries, along with silver miners from the Philippines and diamond prospectors from Tanzania – and who knows, one day from the cauldron of blood diamonds, Sierra Leone, too.

Greg won't be alone, of course. 'I can see large mining companies like Rio Tinto, and large retailers like Tiffany's, moving in to the fairtrade jewellery business, promising fair prices for artisan miners,' he says. 'If they follow the rules, that's OK.' But he intends to apply tougher rules for the kinds of suppliers he works with. 'It's not just about prices. It's about communities and the environment. We will stick to working with cooperatives that make commitments about their methods of mining,' he says. 'That is what we regard as the truly ethical business, and we think many of our customers will agree. I'm a social entrepreneur, if you like. I may make some money along the way, but we will stay true to our values.'

Greg is also determined to keep oversight of his entire supply chain – the casters and refiners and manufacturers as well as the miners. He doesn't want any scandals. 'We buy raw gold from the miners. We use a commercial refiner based in the UK, which runs distinct batches for us so there is no contamination with other metal. Then we send the gold with our own designs to the casters, who alloy it to eighteen carat. The jewellery is then finished in our own workshops.'

Walk into most jewellers today and ask where their gold comes from and they will look blank. As Greg puts it, 'A couple could set out to choose a wedding ring – a symbol of love, trust, integrity and purity – and end up with a piece of metal tied to exploitation, oppression, poverty and environmental damage.' By going to Greg's, they buy gold they can feel good about, and get a certificate giving its origin in a specific community mine. 'Our end game is to make it culturally unacceptable to buy jewellery without some sort of certification.'

Part Six

Downstream

24

My Rubbish: Down the River and Across the World

My waste goes downstream. Sometimes a long way.

Once, I interviewed a woman who literally produced no bin waste at all. She recycled or reused everything. She didn't even possess a dustbin. I'm still not sure how she did it. The average Briton produces more than half a tonne of household waste a year and only sends a quarter of that for recycling. Someone worked out that Britain's refuse vehicles complete more than 10,000 rounds on our streets every working day. Every Wednesday morning one of them comes to empty my bin. It takes the contents a mile or so downhill from my house, past B&Q and McDonald's and Homebase and a Travel Inn to the Western Riverside Transfer Station, close to where the River Wandle joins the Thames. One morning I followed.

The transfer station is a whopper, as tall as a church tower and with a central aisle – where the refuse trucks drive and dump their contents down twelve chutes into containers – that is longer than Canterbury Cathedral's. No wonder that Lynne Cure from Cory, the company that runs it, calls it a 'cathedral of rubbish'. It has loomed on my skyline for years but I had never been inside. It takes the contents of getting on for a million bins from four London boroughs, delivered by relays of trucks driving up a ramp one at a time, at the command of a green light. The trucks are almost lost inside, as they lift up their rears and dump their 12-tonne loads. My Wandsworth truck emptied my rubbish down chute number 6.

The transfer station has always been controversial in Wandsworth. When it was first proposed twenty-five years ago, there were protests and I remember we were promised it would only be around for a few years. Nothing permanent. Lynne says that was never true. And Cory now has a contract to handle waste there till 2032. Rubbish is a bad neighbour. And like most bad neighbours, it is hard to dislodge.

We left the cathedral and went round to the river side of the operation, where the chutes empty into containers. Out there, even the containers looked small. A huge crane picked up the container with my rubbish and lifted it on to a barge floating at the dockside. Each container holds 12.5 tonnes of rubbish. Each barge can take thirty containers. So that is 375 tonnes. And the tug that will take us downstream, the *Regain*, was lining up to pull three of them. Some days it takes four. With three journeys a day, they can take up to 4,500 tonnes of rubbish in a day. From just four boroughs. It makes you almost proud to be a Londoner – a citizen of the capital of trash, a worshipper at the cathedral of rubbish. We hopped aboard the *Regain*, waited for the tide to turn and we were off. Me and my rubbish – and that of a few tens of thousands of other people – heading downstream. Always downstream.

The *Regain* wasn't pulling all the rubbish my household had produced that week. There was also the recycling collected in orange sacks the same day as the bins were emptied. Sometimes I put out two sacks and feel almost more virtuous than if I put out one. The small council truck we saw crossing Wandsworth Bridge as we headed downstream could have contained my two sacks. It was also headed downstream. The council website says that its recycling is 'sent directly to reprocessors for recycling into new products'. Up to a point, as we shall see later.

On board the *Regain*, we made a steady 4 knots. Before we were under Wandsworth Bridge the cook had offered us ham, eggs and chips, which we ate in front of a centrefold of a model with her legs apart. Being Thames lightermen, as these truckers of the river are called, is a time-honoured trade. It takes longer to learn the tricks of the river than it takes to learn 'the Knowledge' to be a black-cab driver. Or it did. New EU rules now allow lightermen trained on the Rhine and Danube to ply the Thames with just six months' preparation. This is not appreciated down on the tideway. Not least because the Rhine bargemen might rumble that, strictly speaking, these tugs might not need a crew of five (Captain Geoff plus the bloke who steers, two ropemen and the cook).

Soon we were past the shell of Battersea Power Station, the flash flats of Chelsea Harbour, Spook House in Vauxhall, the Houses of Parliament in Westminster, St Paul's and Tower Bridge. There is no better way of seeing the sights of London than by cruising down the river, even if you have several hundred tonnes of putrefying rubbish on your tail. Soon we took our precious cargo past Canary Wharf, through the Thames Barrier and past the jetties of Tate & Lyle, where the bulk carrier the *Buse Stevens* was tied up. Our barges still had a way to go, but they stayed overnight just downstream of the Barrier. Our two ropemen finally earned their egg and chips, leaping from the tug on to a pontoon and securing the cargo for the night.

I haven't yet mentioned my third waste stream, which was also coming downriver. My sewage. London's geography used to be full of references to its crude waste disposal systems. The capital's foremost biographer, Peter Ackroyd, records Pissing Alley and Dunghill Lane, Midden Lane and Shiteburn Lane. Until little more than a century ago, the city was full of night-soil men, scooping up its ordure and removing it in the dead of night.

Dickens gave one waste tip pride of place in *Our Mutual Friend*. But most waste never reached anything so formal. Filth was everywhere. The city's trades included bone-pickers and rag-gatherers, cigarette-pickers and sweeps and dredgermen and mudlarks – all engaged in the ancient rites of recycling the city's discarded rubbish. After the water closet was invented, more of the city's effluent went down the sewers, where freelance scavengers known as toshers were soon lifting manhole covers and sliding down the pipes to see what they could find.

The sewers emptied into the river, and by the mid-nineteenth century, the stench on the Thames was so bad that Parliament hung sheets soaked with chlorine across its windows to ward off the worst. When such measures ceased to staunch the stench, they paid an engineer called Joseph Bazalgette to construct two giant sewers along either bank of the Thames to take the capital's excrement downstream. The Victoria and Albert Embankments are built on top of them. The sewers mostly contain what you would expect. But there are also pharmaceuticals and other small toxic things that seem easiest to get rid of by flushing. Then there is paper. A lot of it. Each one of us apparently uses more than 11,000 sheets, or 13 kilograms, a year. That's thirty sheets a day. (No, I don't either. But that's the official figure.) For 7 million Londoners, that is 90,000 tonnes of paper down the toilet a year, or a million trees.

Bazalgette's north-bank sewer ends at Beckton in east London, the largest sewage-treatment works in Europe. My sewage, making its way along the south bank beneath Southwark Cathedral and the Globe Theatre, ends up at the only marginally smaller Crossness, just downstream of the mooring point for the Cory barges. Read Thames Water's PR and it sounds a rural idyll. It is surrounded by one of the last areas of grazing marshlands in London. There are nesting sand martins, reed beds, a bat cave and even cycle access. But this is also where some 700 million litres of sewage is treated every day, enough to fill the Albert Hall seven times over.

The sewage is filtered to remove large items, then mixed with bacteria that eat up organic matter, and allowed to settle. The liquid is discharged into the Thames estuary. And the solids are left to dry to a thick sludge. Londoners like me individually produce around 20 kilos of sewage sludge a year, or 60 grams a day. One-third of the sludge is burned in two east London incinerators. The other two-thirds is sold to farmers as a cheap fertilizer. Yes, the night-soil men are still in business, only now wearing Thames Water overalls.

Downstream from Crossness, we reached Crayford Marshes, home of a 'materials recovery facility' used by Wandsworth and many other London boroughs to handle their domestic recycling. Here a company called Grosvenor sorts 400,000 tonnes of miscellaneous recycled paper, cans, glass, wood and plastic a year. Somewhere among it all were my orange sacks. The sorting begins at a spinning drum with holes in the walls. As it spins, bottles and cans tumble out, while paper and card stay inside. Then the rubbish goes along conveyors where magnets hook out ferrous cans and jets of air remove light plastic bottles.

The Grosvenor plant, and others like it, do the jobs we are too lazy to do, separating our recyclables into different streams. It even divides up paper so that the newsprint recyclers don't get landed with cardboard and Yellow Pages and pink *Financial Times* that would muck up their processes. A lot of London waste does get recycled, mine included. But what surprised me was how and where – and that many of the claims being made for what happens to our recycling are simply untrue.

Take glass. It makes up around a quarter of our household recyclables. Until fairly recently, we were all asked to divide up our glass by colour. Then it could all go off to be turned into new glass of the same colour. But now nobody asks us to separate glass by colour any more. The notice on the bins accepting mixed-colour glass outside my local supermarket declares that recycling one glass bottle or jar saves the energy 'to power a TV for 20 minutes'. Well it might if it were turned into new glass, but it isn't. Instead my old bottles go to Day Aggregates in Brentford, west London, where they are ground up and mixed with the 3 million tonnes of construction materials the company delivers across south-east England each year.

There is a certain logic. Glass started out as sand and now ends up as, in effect, a substitute for sand. But is turning rubbish into aggregate really recycling? Now that local councils have targets for recycling, this is an issue over which lawyers as much as waste technologists are fighting. And I am not too happy with my recycled glass going to make new roads. I expect many greens would be similarly upset.

My aluminium cans go to Novelis on Merseyside and my steel cans to AMG Resources, which strips the tin coating off for sale as tin ingots, and adds the steel to the huge international trade in general metal scrap that is eventually smelted and turned into new goods. It might go to the steel works of Bangladesh, for instance; scrap metal is Britain's biggest export to that country.

Britain produces 3 million tonnes of plastic waste a year, most of which ends up in landfill. But we are getting better at handing plastic on for recycling, especially plastic bottles made of PET (polyethylene terephthalate) and HDPE (high-density poly-ethylene), and there is a ready international market. Grosvenor says its PET makes fleeces and car upholstery and its HDPE often resurfaces as drainpipes. For now, roughly half our plastic bottles returned for recycling are sold to China.

Ray Georgeson at the government-funded Waste and Resources Action Programme (WRAP) says a British plastics-recycling business could be kick-started if plastic-bottle makers would agree to accept 25 per cent recycled feedstock. But they won't. It's not cost-effective, they say. The going rate for old plastic bottles is about £120 a tonne, which is about half a penny per bottle and more than twice what British recyclers say they can afford to pay because of the high wages they have to pay.

Recycling of plastic seems to make sense in energy terms, even if it is done in China. Georgeson says that every tonne of plastic waste that is recycled prevents the emissions of about 2 tonnes of carbon dioxide in making new. Certainly the case for recycling British plastics looks more robust than that for recycling paper, right now.

Britons send more than 7 million tonnes of paper a year for recycling. We have a simple faith that this is a good idea. The notice on my local recycling bin says with disarming simplicity: 'Each tonne of paper recycled saves an average of 15 trees.' But the closer you look, the harder it is to be sure. The biggest market for used newspapers and magazines is the Aylesford paper mill in Kent. Grosvenor also sends my cardboard and 'mixed paper waste' to the Smurfit Mill in Kent, another giant of the industry. And my old office paper goes to M-Real's plant for making the Evolve brand of new office paper.

Told that way, it sounds as if virtually all my waste paper is recycled in Britain. But nationally, almost 4 million tonnes of waste paper is exported, and the amount recycled at home is declining as paper mills close, even though the amount we collect for recycling is soaring. For companies like Grosvenor, the pressure has been on to sort and find homes for all this lovingly collected material. And things have been going wrong.

Poor old Grosvenor. At the end of 2005, the BBC discovered a containerload of paper waste from London boroughs on a dockside in Jakarta, Indonesia. Inside were private letters bunged in bins months before by the citizens of Islington. There could have been my bank statements and credit-card slips in there too, for all I know. The reporters brought some of the letters home and popped round to ask what their previous owners thought about Islington's recycling practices.

The fact of our paper waste being exported is not exactly news. What was odd was the route taken by this particular cargo, as eventually tracked down by the council. The 450 tonnes of waste paper went in twenty containers from Grosvenor's Crayford plant by truck to a 'materials processing' plant in Münster, Germany. But the company rejected the containers in January 2005 because it said they contained too much 'contamination'. So Grosvenor found another buyer, a mysterious 'reprocessing company' on the other side of the world in Jakarta. In early February, Grosvenor consigned the containers via Rotterdam. Then there is a long gap till June. By this time, the mysterious Jakarta company had equally mysteriously gone out of business. The BBC wondered aloud whether the company had ever existed, since the address on the shipping documents was a closed-down Japanese restaurant. At any rate, the consignment was left sitting on Tanjung Priok dock.

After the BBC got a tip-off and went filming, the containerloads were hurriedly sold for a third time, to a company in Malaysia. After turning up at the Malaysian port of Port Kelang in August, they appear to have been sold one more time, before finally reaching a bona fide recycling plant in the capital Kuala Lumpur in October, where the contents were eventually turned to pulp around the end of the year and sold to local paper mills. It probably turned up eventually in the *New Straits Times*.

The entire journey from London to Kuala Lumpur took eleven months, and involved a host of changes in ownership and legal jurisdictions. The paper seems to have been 'sorted' at least three times. The journey was not typical, but it was symptomatic of a dysfunctional industry. And it formed part of a perceived pattern at Grosvenor that led the Environment Agency into a series of investigations, culminating in a conviction in April 2007, when Grosvenor pleaded guilty to the export of the equivalent of ninety lorryloads, almost 4,000 tonnes, of unsorted household waste found in containers opened during a crackdown on the dockside at Rotterdam. The paperwork said the containers were full of 'mixed card and paper' destined for recycling in China. In fact, according to the Dutch authorities who impounded them, they also contained plastic packaging, batteries, drink cans, old clothes, carrier bags and wood.

Europe bans the export of waste, but positively encourages the export of material for recycling. Unfortunately the boundary between the two is often blurred. Grosvenor said the contamination wouldn't stop the paper and card from being recycled. But the Rotterdam authorities and the Environment Agency disagreed, and Grosvenor pleaded guilty.

Even as the Islington papers were en route from Rotterdam to Jakarta, the head of waste management at DEFRA, the government department responsible for overseeing the recycling business, had sent out a circular to local councils warning of widespread 'illegal exports of municipal waste'. After some spot checks, the Environment Agency concluded that half the containers leaving Britain labelled as carrying waste paper for recycling abroad contained no such thing. Grosvenor seems only to have been unlucky in being found out. But I'd be surprised if the scandal didn't accelerate its takeover in late 2007 by another waste company, Viridor.

Every year, Britain consumes 12 million tonnes of paper and board, which requires 150 million trees. To grow that amount of timber each year would take a forest the size of Wales. So, on the face of it, the argument for recycling our paper and card is irrefutable. And it is hard to argue with the sheer scale of the operation carried out just down the road from the Grosvenor plant in the Kent village of Aylesford. Here on the River Medway, a traditional British centre of paper making, is Europe's largest paper-recycling mill. It is entirely devoted to manufacturing newsprint for our daily papers – from old newspapers and magazines, including mine.

Aylesford receives one in five of all the newspapers and magazines recycled in Britain. Some 30,000 truckloads of paper come through the gates each year. That's more than 70 million newspapers, the product of more than 5 million trees. The paper is soaked in water to make pulp, treated with soap and solvents to remove ink, and then screened, spun and further treated to remove staples, plastics, glue and grit. Cleaned-up pulp is finally re-formed into paper on colossal machines that turn out a constant stream of newsprint 9 metres wide at a speed of 100 kilometres an hour. Almost one in every twenty newspapers in Europe is made from newsprint from this one plant. On average, they say, the complete cycle from mill to printing press, newsagent, breakfast table, recycling bin and back to the mill takes about fourteen days. The biggest leakage in the closing of the loop is freesheets, most of which end up in municipal bins or picked up by the people cleaning buses and trains. Mostly those end up in landfill.

But despite the Aylesford plant's obvious success, some are questioning whether the routine recycling of newspapers is environmentally the best option. I first came across this a decade ago when I wrote a cover article for *New Scientist* titled 'Burn This'. It suggested that so much energy was being used carting waste paper round the country for recycling that it would be better to incinerate it. One study in rural Norfolk found that cars travelled 270 kilometres in journeys to local recycling points for every tonne of paper waste posted into the collecting bins. And even once the paper reaches the bins, it probably has a long journey to Aylesford. On the other hand, incinerators are usually more local, so the energy for trucking waste paper to the incinerator is much less than trucking it to a paper mill. Mills create new paper, but incinerators can create large amounts of energy.

Of course if you burn the old paper, you have to make new. And it still takes more energy to make virgin paper than to recycle old paper. So recycling is still better. Or it would be, except that most of our virgin paper comes from Scandinavian mills, where they get their energy from burning wood chips that are constantly being re-grown in the forest. The mills are effectively carbon-neutral. Take that into account, says Matthew Leach of Imperial College, London, and making virgin paper consumes roughly half as much energy as recycling old paper. So burning is best. Sacrilege? Maybe, and other studies have reached different conclusions. But it is certainly interesting.

I know that lots of people hate incinerators, fearing dioxins coming out of the chimneys. My reading is that a lot of old municipal incinerators did indeed emit toxic nasties, including dioxins, and there is some evidence of cancer clusters around some of them. But modern plant is much cleaner. And, if they also generate 'green' electricity from my waste, then I am in favour of them. It looks like that will soon happen. Cory has won permission to build a £100-million new waste incinerator at Belvedere in Bexley to handle much of London's waste, including mine, after 2011. It will take 600,000 tonnes of rubbish a year and generate enough electricity to power 70,000 homes.

But for now, my waste goes on downstream, beyond Bexley, to the splendidly named Mucking. Just beyond Tilbury Docks, it is the latest in a long string of huge landfills created for London on the Essex marshes. Mucking is the underbelly of our throwaway society. It takes a fifth of London's waste, and is one of Europe's largest landfills. It has a perimeter fence 6 kilometres long. The waste has filled the old gravel pits and is now forming a rising mount in the marshes. Pipes capture from the site large amounts of methane, which is used to generate electricity on the site. The power plant's capacity is 23 megawatts, a third of the capacity of the Belvedere incinerator that will replace Mucking.

Beyond Mucking is the North Sea. Much of my recycling material still has a long journey to go on. Every week ships pass here taking my 'recyclables' to docksides in Indonesia or China or India, or wherever shadowy brokers in Rotterdam or Dubai or Hong Kong or Singapore choose to direct them. Some of it may get recycled one day. I will return to that in a later chapter.

But what of my third waste stream – my sewage? I last saw this at Crossness, where the solid was sold to farmers and the liquid was deemed clean enough to discharge into the outer reaches of the Thames estuary. Thanks to a mixture of European directives and public outrage there has been a major effort in recent years to clean up our rivers, estuaries and beaches. Things aren't perfect, but from a public-health perspective, they are a lot better. But here is an unexpected problem. Nature finds our rivers and estuaries and coastal waters just too clean.

On my journey down the Thames, where did I see most wildlife? It was at outfalls of sewage and drainage water, where birds gathered. Birds also followed the waste barges, collected at the Mucking landfill site and pecked at the litter-strewn 'strandlines' along the water's edge, where rubbish washed up. The birds don't want the sewage or the garbage so much as the other creatures that thrive on it. And worms, the estuary's famous cockles and other invertebrate species all like our garbage.

John Pethick, Britain's leading coastal geographer, first pointed this out to me. As we have tidied up our fields, conserved soil on the land and concreted over our urban areas, rivers have become starved of natural organic matter from soils and rotting vegetation. For a long time that natural organic matter was replaced by the huge amounts of sewage effluent we put into the rivers. Too much untreated sewage killed the river, of course. But partially treated sewage effluent, especially when discharged into estuaries and bays, often acted as a convenient fertilizer for river plants and sustained their ecosystems. 'Where treated sewage is still discharged, it is often about the only source of nutrients left in our rivers,' says John. 'And when that disappears, wildlife suffers.'

Mark Rehfish at the British Trust for Ornithology agrees. 'We have seen dramatic declines in wader birds round our shores. The loss of sewage discharges is a major factor.' Twenty thousand wader birds disappeared from Liverpool Bay after a sewage outfall on the Mersey estuary shut in the 1980s. One of Western Europe's largest populations of knots disappeared when they cleaned up the sewage from Cleethorpes. New sewage works in north-east England had a similar effect on birds theoretically protected by a European directive on wild birds. Arguably that makes the sewage works, required under one EU law, illegal under another. The Thames estuary too has been starved of nutrients.

It is a startling discovery. Cleanliness is not necessarily an ecological virtue. Often it is a vice. The same applies to our obsession with cleaning beaches. Wildlife suffers both from the cleaning up of outfalls and the removal of flotsam and jetsam by local councils keen to pick up Blue Flags and other awards for their cleanliness. The sanitizing of Britain's beaches is becoming a major ecological catastrophe, says Paul Llewellyn, a biologist from the University of Swansea, who has been on the case for years.

As I write this, the latest beach survey from the Marine Conservation Society lands on my desk. Every September, the society organizes hundreds of environmentalists to walk the beaches of Britain and pick up rubbish. But these sanitized beaches are environmental deserts. It may seem an odd suggestion, but leave some rubbish behind, please. Nature needs it.

I have to own up to something here. In some small part, the national obsession to keep our beaches clean is my fault. Back in 1981, as a young journalist, I wrote a cover feature for *New Scientist* on how filthy Britain's beaches had become, how bathing waters were full of dangerous bacteria from sewage outfalls, and how the government of the day was cynically manipulating a new EU directive on dirty beaches to avoid its obligations to clean them up. Every national newspaper took up the story – especially because it was published on the day the schools broke up for the summer. The scandal rumbled through Brussels, and Britain was forced to embark on a clean-up. Someone in Whitehall later said my article had cost the government a billion pounds.

I don't regret that. When I was a young child in the 1950s, hundreds of children died in a polio epidemic partly spread by swimming in sewage-laden bathing water. The story of one man whose son had died in just that way fuelled the anger in my article.

But footprints are strange things. And mine, in the sands of Britain's beaches, has proved rather unexpected.

25

Trade Not Aid: Joining the Great Global Jumble Sale

The Milonge brothers were on a roll. They came to pick me up at my hotel in downtown Dar es Salaam, eager to show off their business selling the Western world's cast-off clothes. In Tanzania, they call old shorts and shirts and skirts and socks *mitumba*, meaning a bale. That's how they come, in bales unloaded from containers at the Dar dockside just down the road.

The delivery of *mitumba* to Tanzania started as charity, but now it is big business. *Mitumba* is the biggest export to Tanzania from both Europe and North America. The European Union alone exports more than 10,000 tonnes, valued at about 1 euro, or 60 pence, a kilogram. And Geoffrey Milonge and his brother Boniface are proud of what it has done for them since they came to Dar from their village out in the bush ten years ago. We piled into the big car, and I couldn't help noticing their big rings, big stomachs and, to be fair, big smiles too. The brothers were generous and keen to do business.

On average, each of us buys around 35 kilograms of textiles a year. We eventually throw about 30 kilograms of that into landfills and hand over about 5 kilograms to charities such as Scope,

Oxfam and the Salvation Army. We probably don't think much more about it, beyond having a vague sense that the clothes are probably given to someone who needs them. So after putting a bag of old clothes into the Scope bin in Wandsworth, I set out to discover what happened to it.

Scope told me that the contents of the charity's recycling bins are emptied weekly by contractors and trucked to a depot in Croydon. There, the clothes sit for a while in a big pile, until smaller vans turn up and collect bundles of stock that are taken to individual shops. I knew from a friend who works in one of the shops that there are not enough UK buyers for even the relatively small amounts of old jumble that people like me put in the bins. I do my bit. My friend brings me near-new, top-brand shirts that have been clogging up the racks in Scope shops in south London because nobody wants to buy them, even for a few pence. But with the high streets full of cheap clothes, I seem to be in a small minority.

So plenty of unsold stock is left 'out the back', as Scope's recycling manager Nick Wilks put it, for recollection, this time by rag merchants. They sort the clothes again, and decide what they can sell where. It could be resale to people in Eastern Europe or Africa or for industrial rags.

This struck me as a rather convoluted and wasteful distribution system, in some cases involving clothes being driven across the country several times. But I had stumbled on a sizeable trade, a modern version of the old rag-and-bone merchants immortalized in the sitcom *Steptoe and Son*. One of the firms that buys from Scope, J. M. P. Wilcox of Bilston in the West Midlands, handles 500 tonnes of old textiles a week, and fills seven or eight containers for export. Wilcox advertises bales in forty-five categories, ranging from ties and net curtains to men's zipper jackets and women's bras.

I contacted a few of Scope's regular buyers. One trader, Lynne Wright, who runs a company called Wastesavers in the seaside resort of Skegness, got in touch. She had for several years been shipping containerloads of old skirts, blouses and much else to a man called Kazim Remtulla, whose splendidly named Mohammed Unique Company is based in Dubai. Not that the people of Dubai wanted the clothes. They were en route to Africa, mostly to Africa's largest *mitumba* markets in the streets of Dar es Salaam.

Kazim had recently pulled out of his arrangement with Lynne. The weak dollar meant he could do better buying from the US, she said. But Lynne had a new customer, a *mitumba* trader in Dar who had been buying from Kazim and wanted to do his own trading. And that is how I came across the Milonge brothers. Geoffrey responded to my email within hours. To be honest, his poor English had led him to think that I might be planning to sell him some bales of good-quality British *mitumba*. He pointed at my shirt. 'We'd sell that for four thousand shillings [about £1.50].' But even when he learned I was only a journalist, he kept up the bonhomie. Great guy. Good businessman.

We were in the car in seconds and heading downtown. The brothers told me they were excited about receiving their first consignment direct from abroad. They were cutting out the *wahindi* – their name for the Asian middlemen who had ruled their lives so far. Lynne's container had 500 bales, each weighing 45 kilos. It was still at sea, probably somewhere in the Suez Canal, but it would be arriving in Dar port within a week.

Soon we were in the heart of the Kariakoo district of Dar, a big central trading area. The brothers had a corner shop at the junction of Kongo and Mhonda Streets. It was full of men and women picking through the piles of old clothes. Showman that he was, Geoffrey had his knife out within seconds. He had just bought a new bale from the port, dispatched by another UK supplier. The label said LMB London – which turned out to be Lawrence M. Barry & Co. of London E16. LMB too handles textile hand-me-downs from Scope. The bale contained 240 men's shirts, for which the brothers had paid 200,000 shillings. At £80, that was double the usual price for British *mitumba*. It worked out at 32 pence a shirt. But men's shirts are the most popular line in Dar, and

Geoffrey reckoned there was a gold mine here. What would they sell for? I watched.

It was a lucky dip. There was a Paul Smith shirt in there; it sold quickly for 7,000 shillings, or £2.80 – a mark-up of more than 800 per cent. The female buyer said she planned it as a present for her lover. An almost new brown Marks & Spencer shirt went for 5,000 shillings to a middle-aged man. A Next shirt and another from Burton would sell for nearly as much, Geoffrey reckoned. Several customers told me they were looking for fashionable labels, even though they would cost more. In Dar as much as in Oxford Street, labels sell.

Geoffrey expected overall to make a 20 per cent profit, but it depended on how lucky they were with the bales. A good bale might fetch more than a million shillings and yield 500 per cent. 'The best quality is from the UK,' he told me. 'English clothes are much less worn. The US is good too, but their clothes are rather large. The Germans wear their clothes too much.' You learn a lot about a nation from its *mitumba*.

The next morning the brothers had the car at the hotel again. We went to some of their market stalls out in the suburbs. At the Mukumbusho market, there was a huge pile of American clothes all for sale at 500 shillings. A John Henry red dress caught my eye. Another pile of trousers retailed at 1,500 shillings. Here were some brown cords very like the ones I was wearing. Made in Mexico. There were Land's End jeans made in Malaysia, Cherokee chinos from Hong Kong and Mauritius, as well as Bonjour bags from the Dominican Republic and Haggar and St John's Bay trousers from Mexico.

The brothers sold fifty bales a month from this stall alone. 'It's all American at present, because that's what the *wahindi* are buying. But Americans are so big, we have lots of clothes left over,' said the guy running the stall. Geoffrey could have worn his stock OK, but his thinner compatriots would have been swamped by many of the mega-girth jeans and belly-stretched shirts I saw on display. But Lynne's container was at sea. All would change soon.

Next was the Urafiki market. Three-quarters of Dar's food is traded here. All around are cafés and photo studios, grocery stores and furniture emporia, butchers' and beauty salons. And the Milonge brothers had one of the best pitches. They sold more variety here. I saw branded American leather hiking boots for 40,000 shillings; Adidas soccer boots for 15,000; Reebok pumps for 5,000; women's business suits and second-hand Korean schoolbags for 2,000; and Canadian baseball caps for 1,500. Bras were popular at 2,000; slips at 1,500.

Here I also found some new clothes on sale. They were mostly end-of-line stock from US budget stores. Some still had their final dollars-and-cents price tags on. I saw some Gap Oxford-weave shirts, made in Indonesia, and Van Heusen shirts made in Thailand, both with Thrift Store sale stickers for $0.95, but on sale here for 2,500 shillings. That was almost $2. So these clothes were being sold in Dar at more than their final knock-down price in Denver or Des Moines.

The *mitumba* trade shows how Africa has changed. When Tanzania became independent in 1961, one of the first acts of the first president, Julius Nyerere, was to ban imports of used clothes. Apart from disliking the heavy symbolism of wearing colonial cast-offs, he wanted to build up a domestic textiles industry. Sadly, the new industry, backed initially by state subsidies, attempted to ape Western tailors rather than providing cheap and cheerful clothing for the masses. Result: millions of men wearing ill-fitting suits and women in dowdy skirts and blouses.

As Africa got poorer and trade globalized, the indigenous textiles companies collapsed and *mitumba* started to creep in again. First, it came through the back door, smuggled from Mozambique and Kenya. Then Western charities started handing out old clothes for free. But demand was so great that soon they were charging, to raise money for other projects. And then the business got handed over to the *wahindi* and other entrepreneurs. The charities restricted their activities to collecting the clothing back in Europe and North America.

Some people in rich countries are surprised that clothes they donate to charities end up being sold to poor people for a profit. But this is 'trade not aid', and the Milonge brothers are doing very nicely, thank you. In her book *The Travels of a T-shirt in the Global Economy*, the American economist Pietra Rivoli said the *mitumba* business was the nearest thing to a free market in the heavily subsidized and quota-controlled cotton industry. That may not be a virtue in itself. But supply does meet demand in the markets of Dar. At least a third of Africans dress in our old clothes, and in Tanzania the figure rises to 80 per cent. As many visitors have commented, Tanzanians do seem to be much better dressed than they used to be.

26

Beyond the Grave: A New Life for Joe's Old Phone

Our household survived without a mobile phone for a long time. Even as a journalist, I resisted. The first arrived when our son Joe bought a bog-standard Nokia in 2003. Always on the look-out for a bargain, he paid £10 at Carphone Warehouse. It did the job. Or it did until – and there is no sensible way of writing this chapter without sharing the family tragedy with you – until his death in 2005. In fact it did the worst job of all. After Joe collapsed while out jogging at university, the nurse at Leeds Infirmary found 'MUM' in the memory and used it to tell us the news. Anyhow, this is the story of that phone.

Along with the toothbrush, the mobile phone is about the most ubiquitous piece of personal equipment on the planet today. No invention has ever spread round the world to so many people so fast. Twenty new users are connected every second. Some time in 2006, the 2 billionth phone went live. By the time you read this, there will be one for every three people on the planet. Even in the poorest countries, mobile phones are everywhere. In 2006, in Tanzania, where average income is just $560 a head, I saw more signs advertising top-up cards from local phone companies like

Vodacom and Celtel than billboards for Coca-Cola. Every village store, every roadside shack seemed to be selling them. And millions of Tanzanians were buying. The cheapest top-up cost the equivalent of about 10 pence, enough for a 45-second call.

Joe's purchase plugged him into the modern world of global commerce like no other commodity can. Nokia is a Finnish company, which began life 140 years ago making paper, before getting into rubber and finally electronics. Today it is the largest supplier of mobile phones in the world, with more than a third of the market. Nokia and subcontractors like the Taiwanese company Foxconn assemble more than two phones every second in each of nineteen factories spread round the world. Nokia says it has a strict policy of not revealing which factory individual phones come from. But it is most likely Joe's came from China, which makes roughly half the world's phones; and probably from Foxconn's plant in Shenzhen, the manufacturing boomtown in southern China, which employs 70,000 people.

But these factories are just the end of a manufacturing web similar to that making computers. Every Nokia phone contains some 400 different components. Each year, Nokia and its subcontractors assemble an estimated 100 billion resistors, capacitors, motherboards, display screens, keypad buttons, batteries, covers and other parts. The Shenzhen plant feeds off dozens of local component manufacturers, like Delta, which employs 20,000 young workers in nearby Dongguan and is the world's largest manufacturer of adaptors and capacitors for computers and mobile phones. And Hua Tong in nearby Huizhou, which makes Nokia's circuit boards. Like Foxconn, both are Taiwanese companies.

Shenzhen is a city literally made by mobile phones. Twenty-five years ago it was a fishing village surrounded by rice paddy. Today it is an urban sprawl of 12 million people – twice the size of Hong Kong – and stretches for 100 kilometres along the east bank of the Pearl River to Dongguan. I met a man who had been resident for eighteen years in Shenzhen. He claimed he knew nobody who had been there longer. I certainly felt, and quite possibly was, the oldest person in the city.

But this is no bargain-basement metropolis. The city's gleaming new central business district has five-star hotels, a stock exchange, concert hall, huge exhibition centre – and a profusion of Starbucks. This is the new China. Not just the workshop of the world, but increasingly a consumer capital too. They say that as many mobile phones are sold in the stores of Shenzhen as are manufactured in its factories. I can believe it. At one store I saw, at a rough estimate, 10,000 phones on display. The aisles were packed with buyers – not just for Western brands like Nokia, but for would-be Chinese global brands like CETCs, from the state-owned China Electronics Technology Group Corporation. Many people were also buying parts and having phones custom-built on the premises.

Companies don't make phones, of course; people do. And Foxconn and the other mobile-phone manufacturers in southern China employ hundreds of thousands of young women migrant workers. Communist social control and capitalist money have combined here to extraordinary effect, creating the modern work-shop of the world – as dominant in its influence as Britain once was at the start of the Industrial Revolution 200 years ago. Somewhere about 2003, the delicate fingers of a young woman called Hua or Lee or Ling probably put together Joe's phone and shoved it in a box for dispatch to Clapham Junction.

Behind the component suppliers lies another vast industry, mining and refining the metals and other materials that go into the components. The phone is a miniature smorgasbord of metals and other ingredients. Many are toxic, and accumulate in the food chain. They can damage the human nervous and reproductive systems, cause cancer and damage our genes. An individual phone won't do this, but as the ingredients accumulate in the environment, they may. Nokia has won praise from Greenpeace for cutting the use of some of the nasties in its new handsets. But older phones, like Joe's, still contain them.

About half the weight of a typical mobile phone is the casing, which is made of moulded plastic with a little added iron and aluminium. The plastic contains phthalates. These are 'gender-bending' chemicals that are used to soften the plastic, making PVC flexible, for instance, and also create the 'jelly rubber' in sex toys, I am told. High doses of phthalates damage hormonal systems. They shrink testes – which sounds a bit of a turn-off for a sex toy. Another quarter of the phone's weight is wiring and the circuit board. These are mostly made of copper but also contain magnesium, tin solder, and small amounts of gold, as well as arsenic, chromium and beryllium, which can produce toxic dust during manufacture and recycling. The circuit board also probably contains brominated flame retardants, which prevent your phone bursting into flames, but may produce dioxins if the phone is one day incinerated. The phone screen is made of glass and ceramics. Then there are cobalt, lithium and carbon in the battery, silver in the keyboard and tantalum in the capacitors.

A typical mobile phone today weighs only around 75 grams, but taking its many ingredients from the Earth requires the mining of 30 kilograms of rock. In addition, manufacturing the chips requires several hundred litres of water, and the energy that probably comes from burning several tens of kilograms of fossil fuels. And making the batteries and keeping them charged through a phone's typical two-year life raises the weight of a phone's overall rucksack to about 75 kilograms – a thousand times the weight you carry in your pocket. Not including the water.

But what of the phone's footprint in human lives? A year or so before Joe's Nokia rolled off the production line in Shenzhen, the papers were full of stories about a mysterious substance called coltan that was essential to mobile phones. It was mined under inhuman conditions from the forests of central Africa, in the midst of a vicious civil war that had killed up to 4 million people. In pursuit of the footprint of Joe's phone, I decided to investigate.

Coltan turns out to be an African nickname for a bunch of

minerals, usually found together, that contain two elements, columbium and tantalum. Tantalum is what the fuss was really about. Even rich Westerners only get through about 2 grams of the stuff in a year, but tantalum is literally essential to the modern mobile phone. The hard, dark grey metal has an exceptionally high melting point (almost 3,000°C) and is extremely resistant to corrosion and chemical attack. It can be pulled and pushed and squeezed to make tiny wires and sheets and tubes. And, most handily of all, it can be made to store and release an electrical charge.

Tantalum was first used as the filament in light bulbs, till it was replaced by tungsten. Then, a bit over half a century ago, the military started using it to make capacitors in radar receivers and missile-guidance systems. Capacitors are the tiny components of electrical circuits that store and release electrical charge. For a long time, most of the world's tantalum was mined in Western Australia by a company with the improbable name of Sons of Gwalia, and sold to Cabot, a US refiner, before being stockpiled by the US military, which regarded it as a strategic metal. Another refiner was H. C. Starck in Germany, a subsidiary of the industrial giant Bayer.

Tantalum has found other uses. It turns up in heart pacemakers and insulin injectors and automatic-braking systems in cars. But the big boom came with rising demand for portable electronic devices like laptop computers, PlayStations, digital cameras and, most of all, mobile phones. You can make capacitors with ceramics or aluminium. But tantalum is more compact and operates at a low voltage. So batteries last longer. Without it, mobile phones would still be the size of bricks and need recharging every fifteen minutes. And the smarter the phone, the greater the number of tantalum capacitors. A phone with a camera and video functions requires more than twenty.

Today more than half the world's tantalum goes into making more than 20 billion capacitors every year – over three for every person on the planet. The world's biggest tantalum-capacitor manufacturer is Kemet Electronics in the US, which has a long-term supply agreement with Cabot. But when the mobile-phone business took off, other tantalum refineries and capacitor manufacturers set up in Japan, Taiwan, China and elsewhere in Asia. In 2004, Kemet opened a new manufacturing plant in Suzhou, the Chinese computer-manufacturing centre west of Shanghai (see Chapter 15). Another maker is Guangdong Kexin in Shenzhen. Most likely one of these supplied the capacitors in Joe's phone.

As the world got hooked on mobile phones, tantalum demand soared. Speculators cashed in and tantalum prices rose fivefold in just a few months, to more than $1,000 a kilo. The rush was on to find new supplies. The first to be exploited were the coltan reserves in eastern Congo. By some estimates, the provinces of Kivu and Ituri contain 80 per cent of the world's tantalum reserves. Mining it is easy: you make a clearing in the forest, dig a pit and ship out the dull grey rock just beneath the surface. In those provinces some unsavoury rebel military leaders were already conducting a vicious civil war. When coltan prices soared, they realized they could make fortunes out of the ore and use it to raise cash for arms, or simply to fill their Swiss bank accounts.

The warlords overran some legitimate mines, while others remained open in circumstances that raised eyebrows. They also pressganged child soldiers and prisoners to mine the coltan and ship it off to brokers, who were often little more than gun-runners paid in coltan. The UN Security Council began an investigation. It found that for several years, one or more Western mining companies were extracting coltan from eastern Congo under the protection of a rebel army. Much of this material, it is claimed, ended up with specialist companies like Starck.

The UN also reported that foreign armies invading from neighbouring Uganda and Rwanda organized shipments. Top dog was Rwandan Brigadier-General James Kabarebe, who for a while made $20 million a month working with a mystery woman, dubbed Madame Coltan, who warehoused coltan at her cigarette factory in the eastern Congolese town of Bukavu. And the UN study uncovered an alleged coltan trail to Eagle Wings Resources International, a subsidiary of an Ohio-based company called Trinitech International, in which companies 'obtained their own mining sites and conscripted their own workers to exploit the sites under severe conditions.' Eagle Wings, it claimed, had 'close ties with the Rwandan regime' and flew its coltan to Starck as well as to metallurgical plants in Kazakhstan and China. Starck has repeatedly denied obtaining coltan from central Africa and says it took steps to ensure that it did not do so. And the Chinese plant denied doing business with 'any individual or any entity that represents somebody or some entity in the DRC.' The investigating panel, while noting these denials in its report, claimed to possess information to the contrary.

This is the unsavoury story of how mobile phones got made. Amnesty International says that coltan 'paid for a war within a war that claimed hundreds of thousands of civilian lives and subjected millions of others to a humanitarian catastrophe.' But, despite the UN investigation, nobody has been called to account. And the efforts of the phone makers at the time to clean up their supply chain were, to say the least, half-hearted. Companies like Nokia and Motorola say they first learned about the trade out of Congo in early 2001 and asked their suppliers to avoid purchasing tantalum from there. But the fact is that for a while the Congo was the main source of the world's coltan, and much of the world's coltan went into mobile phones. As the Americans say: go figure. I'd be very surprised if there wasn't Congolese tantalum in Joe's phone.

Coltan prices eased in 2002 and the Congolese civil war subsided soon after. But the warlords are still in business – mining coltan and making trouble in the jungles. The two are undoubtedly linked. And since then another vital resource tied to mobile phones has come under their control. Rising global demand for tin – driven in part by new rules banning lead solder in phone capacitors – has triggered a rush for rich Congolese reserves of cassiterite, an ore containing tin oxide. The same soldiers, and the same illicit supply channels through Rwanda, are involved.

Joe didn't use his phone for long. Most mobiles are discarded within two years – that's 15 million every year in Britain alone. The value of an individual metal in an individual phone is probably only a few pence. That's why most phones end up in the local landfill. But collectively this is crazy. All that copper and silver and gold and tantalum wasted. All that arsenic and antimony and lead and other toxins leaching into the ground. So, deciding what to do with Joe's old phone, I pondered the alternatives.

Recycling seemed the obvious bet. The new European directive on electronic waste, charmingly called the WEEE directive, is big on ensuring that the materials get recycled, but much of this seems to be carried out illegally and dangerously in China and India. In any case, why not prolong the life of the phone itself? Find someone else who wants it.

The mobile-phone industry has begun take-back schemes. In the UK, Fonebak claimed to have processed 6 million phones by the end of 2006, of which around two-thirds were reused and a third sent for recycling. But I read an independent study which said that many of the recycled phones from such schemes end up being exported to untraceable companies. I wanted to be certain where Joe's phone went. I suggested to Nokia that they might like to help me track the final destination of a phone sent to them for refurbishment. Helsinki seemed keen, but their London office stopped returning my emails. Perhaps they got bored.

Then I spotted a sign in a shop in Sussex promising to collect old phones and send them for resale in Africa. Their agent, Phones For Africa, turned out to be a small enterprise, collecting around sixty phones a month and run by a photographer in Dar es Salaam, the capital of Tanzania. Paul Joynson-Hicks was the nephew of the chairman of the shop, called Cookshop. I already had a trip to East Africa planned. And everyone along the line seemed keen to help me hand on Joe's phone in person to a new owner.

Everything worked like clockwork. Paul was a bit vague about how the phone got to Dar. Import duty is a bit of an issue, I gathered. But two months later, on a hot and dusty Saturday afternoon, I found myself standing at a tiny kiosk in a litter-strewn slum street in inner-city Dar, briefly reacquainted with Joe's phone. Eventually, my buyer showed up. And that was when I had a surprise. Ally got out his cash and handed over 40,000 Tanzanian shillings. That was the equivalent of £17. But, two years before, Joe had bought the phone new for only £10. Paul smiled when I asked about this later. 'That's the going rate here,' he said. 'Actually I marked the price down a bit to make sure you got a sale.' He said the locals like slightly bashed reconditioned phones because they know they are not counterfeit – unlike some on sale in shops down the street.

I didn't quibble. The deal was done. Ally, a student of similar age to Joe, was unaware of how market forces had played out in his case. But he said the phone was cheap. And he was happy to be the second of four adult brothers to get a phone. His father, a preacher, had given him the money. Then, he headed off for evening prayers at the local mosque.

So my buyer was happy. And, in the end, my qualms about the price were mollified by the discovery of what happened to the money raised by the sale. The next night, Paul took me to a workshop behind his studio on the city's outskirts. It was dark because the power was out. In the gloom, he called over Justin. It took a while. Justin had no legs, only a couple of stumps. But he did have a blowtorch. Justin, it turned out, was one of a team of twenty-five polio victims that Paul had recruited over a couple of years, mostly from a nearby traffic island favoured by beggars.

The profits from selling phones like Joe's went into training them as welders, and buying equipment. Paul – a gangling, amiable guy able to win over industrialists as well as beggars – obtained scrap metal and surplus stock from local traders, and the team was turning out a constant stream of rather fetching metal sculptures that sold in local art stores, on the internet and through direct commissions.

Wildlife sculptures are the big sellers. The Wonder Welders catalogue (check it at www.wonderwelders.org) includes dragon-flies and gazelles, crabs and turtles, rabbits and giraffes, crocodiles and chameleons, antelopes and aardvarks. Once, the welders made a life-size metal rhino to a detailed spec drawn up by a zoologist. More modestly, I brought home a small warthog made of nails, a spring, a couple of links from a bicycle chain and some copper wire for its bushy tail. It is sitting on my desk as I type this – a strange swap for Joe's phone.

The Wonder Welders are doing such good business that Paul and his workshop manager Ellie have diversified. Paul introduced me to disabled women boiling up paper waste to make new specialist paper for photo albums, wedding invitations and novelty cards. They sometimes incorporate scraps of metal, too. The next 14 February, my wife received a pretty Valentine's card featuring two flamingos decked out with the metal from a Castle beer can. The workshop makes soap, too. And glass-blowing is next.

In the back streets of Dar this hive of activity was hugely impressive. There is clearly a limited market for Wonder Welders, though I would guess that dozens of African cities could sustain similar enterprises. But the imagination and creativity and energy that has gone into this scheme shows what potential there can be for recycling our discarded gadgets, and how unexpectedly wide the benefits can be. Wonder welders, indeed.

At any rate, I was happy with the outcome of my decision to find a new life for Joe's old phone, and I know that Joe would have been just as pleased. A student got a reconditioned phone at less than Dar shop prices. Polio victims are getting off the streets and into creative jobs that are the envy of their fully limbed mates. Some of Dar's growing piles of scrap metal get recycled. And I get to smile at that warthog. I flew out of Dar feeling that my footprint was, for once, positive.

27

Unexpected Heroes: The Queen of Trash and Other Chinese Titans of Recycling

Cheng Shengchan is an ebullient self-made man with curious habits, like rolling his trousers above his knees while making tea for his guests in his office. He runs what has a reasonable claim to be the greenest, most socially inclusive and 'sustainable' paper mill in the world. And the much-derided paper recyclers of Britain can claim a significant part in his success. Here is his checklist of achievement. It is enough to make any European executive in charge of corporate social responsibility green with envy. 'My mill runs entirely on waste paper,' he told me as he served tea. 'It is fuelled entirely on biofuels; its labour force is made up of the disabled; and not a drop of effluent leaves the site.'

Cheng took over the loss-making CXXR United Paper Mill, outside the southern Chinese city of Xiamen, when the state decided to shut it down in 1994. He was a manager back then, though he says now that he had no control, no supplies of raw materials and few markets. But he was confident he could make a go of it, and bought a 50 per cent stake. With the state a sleeping partner, he has run it as his own business ever since. And business is good. After he had introduced me to his son, who he hopes will one day take over the plant, we headed into the yard. Truckloads of waste paper from local factories were arriving constantly. It accumulated so fast that the mounds of waste almost engulfed the staff as they shovelled it on to conveyors for mixing with water to boil up into a pulp.

Cheng said he uses no chlorine or other chemicals. The pulp just gets a dose of palm oil to help it solidify, before being pressed into giant sheets of thick brown paper that are rolled up and sold to be made into laminated boxes. Meanwhile, the waste water squeezed from the new, drying paper is constantly recycled. I saw a fair amount of evidence of that. But his settling ponds did create a sludge that must have been cleaned out from time to time. Still, there were no streams of noxious effluent running into local rivers. And there was no ambiguity about how Cheng fuelled the factory boiler. Coal was a thing of the past. Now he burned rice husks, bought from a local food factory. Cheng said the husks cost him less than half as much as the coal he used to burn. And since the husks would have otherwise been left to rot and release their carbon into the air, this was a genuine carbon-neutral biofuel.

Cheng was jovial and candid. He employed handicapped staff because it brought tax benefits, he said. 'We qualify as a welfare company. It is easy work for them, so there are no problems.' The staff seemed to agree. But I wasn't sure about the health and safety ethic. Where were the guard rails, and the masks to filter the dust? But this was China and the place seemed fun. One woman worker darted this way and that among the piles of paper to avoid being photographed. Another male worker pulled a handle to drop a big roll of paper at my feet with a loud thump – just to make me jump.

The waste card was coming in from local drinks- and food-packaging plants. But besides this local waste, Cheng said he bought containerloads of European waste paper imported at Xiamen docks by a big local trading conglomerate called Xiamen C&D. He took several thousand tonnes each year, most of it from Britain. Xiamen C&D failed to identify the UK source for me. But its local rival, BCEL, was more helpful. It provided me with a list of all the foreign companies with approval to supply China with paper waste for recycling. In a list of several hundred, only ten British companies made the cut. It seems that ill-sorted paper waste from the UK has been a well-recognized problem in China. Customs officials tightened up on the flows in 2004 to make sure there was not too much 'contamination' of the valuable raw materials for recycling with general garbage.

Cheng manufactures 35,000 tonnes of paper a year. And his biggest customer is Top Victory Electronics, a Taiwanese company with a factory 200 kilometres up the coast that makes liquid crystal display screens for TVs. So, in the wonderful world of globalized recycling, the boxes made from paper waste exported from Britain to his mill probably come back to Britain on the next available container from Xiamen harbour.

It is amazing how much waste gets recycled in China. Earlier in the day I had visited an old garage in the heart of Xiamen where local street sweepers and cleaners brought card, cans, old plastic bags, and glass and PET bottles scavenged from their daily rounds to a man called Mr Fu. He paid surprisingly good money: 2 pence for a glass bottle and about 1.5 pence per aluminium can, which is slightly more than the going rate at Latchford Lock in Britain. Some street cleaners made half their income this way, he said. He got occasional supplies of imported European mixed waste, but it was badly sorted, so there was a lot of material he could not recycle and had to dump. Same old story.

Fu made a good profit. As I watched a rat scuttle away from behind a big cardboard box that once contained a Sanyo TV, Fu said he bought used PET bottles for 4,000 RMB (about £270) a tonne and sold them on at 7,000 RMB a tonne. That is roughly half the price that the local Coca-Cola plant paid for new PET, I later discovered. His turnover for buying and selling all his trash was 3,000 RMB (about £200) a day. He said there were 500 other traders like him spread around a city of maybe a couple of million inhabitants. It sounded as if remarkably little recycleable material escaped these freelance collectors.

After seeing Fu, I visited a large junkyard entirely devoted to plastic waste: drums and bottles, toys and flipflops, baskets and hoses, bits of cars and old phones. Mr Wong said he sent out his truck to people like Fu, and brought back about 3 tonnes of plastic a day, for which he paid maybe 15,000 RMB. He seemed to have more than he could cope with. There was about three months' stock in the yard ready to be cut up and shredded and sent off for reuse somewhere. But business was good. The nice BMW parked in a corner of the yard was his.

All this was technologically primitive, but evidence of a well-developed industry for sorting, handling and ultimately recycling a wide range of materials that in Europe would be unlikely to find a home other than a landfill. And it flourished wherever there was waste – in Chinese cities, or where containerloads docked from Europe. Wong said imports of waste plastic didn't reach him, because they were snapped up by people nearer the port in Xiamen. But elsewhere I heard of vast amounts of plastic waste being imported from Britain to Hong Kong and shipped on barges up the Pearl River delta to recyclers around the industrial cities of Dongguan and Shenzhen. There, whole villages specialize in specific types of plastic waste, like PET bottles or plastic bags made of LDPE (low-density polyethylene). We in Britain occasionally get press reports of Tesco's bags billowing through the back streets of southern China. I am sure it happens, and it may not be an edifying spectacle. But it is a fact that most of the plastic sent to China does get recycled, often at the very factories that made the stuff in the first place.

The trade in rubbish sounds bizarre, but from the Chinese end it makes eminent economic sense. With so many containers going back to China empty, after delivering goods to the UK, it costs just £100 to hire a 40-footer to ship waste for recycling from London to Shanghai. That is a tenth of the price of the journey the other way. The problem is that it is cheaper to send waste to China for recycling than to pay landfill charges in Britain. So the temptation is to cut corners and send unsorted rubbish. But make no mistake, this is big business, and one the Chinese are keen to encourage.

So yes, we are sometimes sending rubbish to China. But it beats me why people imagine the Chinese would buy our rubbish in order to put it into a landfill. The truth is that they buy it because, in a country with a desperate shortage of raw materials of all sorts, anything that can be recycled is valuable and will be sorted and turned into new products. China needs and uses most of the estimated 2 million tonnes of 'rubbish' exported there from Britain each year. If there is waste that does get dumped, it is because British suppliers are falling down on the job of sorting the waste properly prior to dispatch. Once in China, paper and card become the packaging around more products heading back to Europe on the next container. Plastic will often be made into low-grade products like plastic drums and chairs and toys, or new bags. PET and glass bottles get turned right back into new PET and glass bottles.

China has a 'queen of trash'. Her name is Cheung Yan, and hers is an amazing story, now quite famous in China. Cheung's parents worked in textile factories, and after her father was jailed in the Cultural Revolution she signed up for the sweatshops as well, supporting her mother and seven siblings. Then she got a job in a small paper mill and worked her way up, opening her own recycling business in Hong Kong in 1985.

A decade on, she spotted a chance to expand when China banned logging after big floods in the Yangtze River in 1998, and faced a chronic paper shortage as a result. She and her husband went to the US and drove round in an old mini-van, begging garbage dumps to sign deals for shipping their waste paper to China. It worked a dream. And today that business, called Nine Dragons, has become probably the largest paper-recycling business on the planet, buying more than 6 million tonnes of waste paper a year, mostly shipped by container from Los Angeles and Rotterdam.

The imported waste goes direct from Chinese ports aboard a fleet of 500 trucks to her huge mills at Dongguan in the south and Taicang, near Suzhou on the Yangtze delta. Each is close to the main exporting zones for Chinese manufactured goods. Millions of the 'Made in China' boxes being shipped to Europe and North America these days are made of corrugated cardboard that comes out of Cheung's giant paper-recycling plants. In late 2006, Cheung was declared mainland China's richest person, man or woman, and is probably the richest self-made woman in the world. By the time this book is out she hopes to have surged ahead of paper giants like Weyerhauser and Smurfit to become the world's biggest manufacturer of packaging.

Nine Dragons is leading a huge global surge within the paper industry towards recycling. The industry is close to a milestone where more than half of all the paper and board produced worldwide comes from recycled material. Chinese entrepreneurs, it could reasonably be said, are leading the way to a future in which the 'loop is closed' on major materials flows, and recycling becomes the norm. There may be doubts about whether paper recycling in Britain is better than incineration for power, but in most countries there can be little doubt that recycling is the green option for paper waste.

The Chinese recycling industry sounds too good to be true, and of course it is. Not everybody in the recycling business is like Cheung. My swift reality check came just down the road from Cheng's CXXR United Paper Mill outside Xiamen. I dropped in unannounced at Xiamen Yixiang Metal Products, where they recycle aluminium offcuts from local can makers to turn them into new ingots of aluminium. We stumbled on a primeval plant. I watched as men in slippers and without any protective gear worked twelve-hour shifts, dunking lumps of waste metal into cast-iron pots suspended in an open kiln beneath the factory floor.

The metal was heated to 700°C, when the aluminium melted, and then slipper-men scooped up the molten metal in an open, long-handled ladle and walked it across the floor to pour it into open moulds.

We walked around for half an hour, unsupervised, watching the men at their dangerous work, sweltering in the heat of the kiln and breathing in the acrid fumes. Then the boss, Mr Liao, showed up and invited us into his office. He could recycle up to 8 tonnes of aluminium a day here, he said. Since the moulds contained 6.7 kilograms, that was more than 1,000 hand-pourings of molten aluminium a day. Liao used to import foreign cans, but the Customs people had stopped it, he said. None the less, he was part of the global aluminium economy. He bought his aluminium at 17 RMB per kilogram (about £1.10), and sold it at 21 RMB, in line with the international price on the London Metals Exchange.

I was about to ask him about the lax health and safety conditions at the plant when he began complaining that regulations in China were too tough and his boss was thinking of moving to the Philippines. And it turned out he was proud of working conditions at his Dickensian plant. He brought out of a back room the framed certificate, dated 2005, of his accreditation with ISO 9001, a reward for good documentation of working practices. Our jaws dropped. 'That must have cost a good lunch,' said my companions later. Sure. This is China.

28

E-waste: What to Do with that Old Computer

I have a slight phobia about getting rid of old computers. It's not that I've left anything embarrassing on the hard drive; it's just an uncertainty about what to do with them. I left an old Amstrad in a house I emptied before moving fifteen years ago. And I have four computers in my current loft. I presume landfill is not a good idea. About two-thirds of the heavy metals in landfills these days come from electronic waste like computers and mobile phones. At my local waste transfer station in Wandsworth, they often put computers and monitors to one side. But what then? Sale to Dubai waste brokers for shipment to India, China and African recycling centres such as Lagos in Nigeria? I don't fancy that, even in the name of recycling.

Around a million old TVs and computer monitors are exported from Britain to developing countries every year. The precise legality of such exports seems to depend on the declared motive for shipment. Disposal is banned, but reuse, repair and recycling are generally OK. But of course what it says on the paperwork may be rather different from what actually happens in some distant country when no officials are watching. It was the reality in practice that I wanted to know about. And that took me to Mandoli, an ancient Indian village now being consumed by the sprawling metropolis of Delhi. Mandoli is one of the charnel houses of the computing world, where the printed circuit boards in discarded computers end up.

Mandoli was clogged with trucks and ox carts and dirt. We drove to an area of wasteland, probably a former quarry, known locally as Gadda, meaning 'the ditch'. That had it pretty well. The 'ditch' stretched for several miles towards the haze of Delhi. A huge sewer pipe from the city ran down it, and not far away was a narrow but persistent stream of nasty black fluid from a fly-by-night operation dying denim jeans for a city garment factory. Then we came across a smouldering pile of black metallic-looking ash with a nasty acrid stench. And further on was an area with a rudimentary network of alleys and brick walls about head high. It looked as if someone had decided there was no need to finish the construction of buildings. Open-air workshops would do just as well.

The alleys crunched under our feet. They were covered in bits of old yellow and green computer circuit board. We opened a gate and entered one of the workshops. 'No, there are no circuit boards here,' said a youth squatting on one of the half-built walls. When I pointed out a pile of them right by his wall, he shrugged. 'We wash them to get the copper,' he said. How? 'In acid.'

And there was ten-year-old Rajesh doing just that. He was dunking circuit boards into an old blue oil drum that contained acid. The drum was almost as tall as him; he was on tiptoe to complete the task. The boards would stay in the hot acid for several hours, he said. During that time the thin layers of laminated copper within the boards would be released.

Rajesh had thick rubber gloves. They were a bit big for him. But so long as he kept them on, they protected his hands. But as he leaned over the edge of the drum, he splashed his thin trousers and torn Adidas T-shirt. He had no goggles or mask, nor were there any lying around. The whole process was perfunctory, hazardous and wasteful. There was a pool of discarded acid in the dust. Sometimes, they said, they poured the spent acid into the open sewer by the road.

Rajesh had come here with his brothers a couple of months before, from the poor Indian state of Bihar. Bihar is notorious for supplying gangs of labourers to work on India's booming construction sites, doing the hard labour on farms and – as here – the nasty dangerous work that nobody else, even in India, will do. Rajesh wasn't the youngest person working here. His little brother, who looked about six years old, darted among the drums behind him. He only seemed to be doing odd-jobs. But he was coughing. In the oppressive heat of the day, the acrid yellow-green fumes from the drums were trapped behind the brick walls. I too was coughing after five minutes in the place.

'When new workers come here, they suffer giddiness and headaches from the fumes,' admitted the older, shaggy-haired brother of the other two. 'But at the end of the day we have a strong drink and we are OK,' he laughed. 'We Indians are strong. And it is better than having no job. Before this I was unemployed in Bihar.' His name was Rakish. 'I'm fourteen years old, I think,' he said. He looked old before his time.

Next Ajay showed up. He was twenty-five and in charge of the seven-person workshop. He worked directly for the owner, but wouldn't say who that was, only that 'he lives in Delhi'. Ajay said he went to the local market to buy sacks of waste circuit boards. Usually, they had already been stripped of capacitors and other valuables, so they were cheap. A bag containing a kilo of boards cost between 5 and 10 rupees, or less than 15 pence. Once dunked in the acid for a few hours and scraped clean, they could yield several hundred grams of a red sludge containing copper, which he sold for around 300 rupees a kilo.

Copper prices had quadrupled in just five years. And though he was hardly in a position to drive a hard bargain, Ajay knew it was a seller's market. He sold to traders, but I guessed the eventual market was two works manufacturing copper wire, both within a couple of miles of the village. The leftover plastic boards could also sometimes be sold. Otherwise, Ajay said, they just dumped them in a ditch, or set fire to them. Ajay's unit processed 15 or 20 kilos of circuit boards a day, he said. So that might provide an income of a few hundred rupees. Ajay had to buy the acid, of course. And he paid the workers 50 rupees a day, a bit over a dollar, for the privilege of wrecking their lungs.

It was a meagre business. But this unit, which measured about 10 metres square, was one of perhaps twenty clustered round the alleys of Gadda. There were maybe 100 workers, including other children, all engaged in the same activity. Each had a manager, like Ajay, who worked for an absent owner. The workshops were full of bags containing old circuit boards, stamped with household names from the computer industry. One board I picked up at random was from Invensys, the British-based computer-systems company. Intriguingly, some bags contained bits of unused boards, bright and clean but broken into pieces. They appeared to be off-cuts from manufacturing.

I went to Mandoli with Priti Mahesh, a researcher at Toxics Link, an environment group based in Delhi. She mentioned that she had seen boxes of broken pristine circuit boards all labelled from Akasaka Electronics based in Mumbai, and from Samsung, for whom Akasaka made circuit boards. The companies involved had done nothing wrong, but it appeared that some waste-disposal sub-contractor in Mumbai had sold the broken circuit boards at the market in Mandoli.

Tests on the environment around the workshops have found heavy metals in the soil, caused by a mixture of ash from the fires, fallout from the toxic fumes and residues in the spent acid poured on to the ground. Yet nobody working there was concerned. I spotted one vacant plot right next to a copper-recovery unit where someone was growing vegetables. The leaves would certainly have been heavily laced with toxins.

Most people in the units were temporary workers, but I met Javed, who had been in the business for ten years. In his blue pullover with a 'Duke' logo, he was better dressed than most. Javed denied the business was dangerous. 'Some people get burned when the acid is splashed but we don't get major injuries,' he said. 'They have rubber boots and gloves and masks.' I only ever saw gloves; and some units didn't have them.

The delivery of circuit boards seemed quite organized. Trucks come to the Mandoli village market once or twice a month, Javed said. 'In the early days, we had TV and radio circuit boards. The computer boards only started turning up in the market about five years ago.' That was interesting. It seemed Mandoli started receiving the boards only after the Indian government passed laws making it illegal to import electrical waste of this sort. Presumably, a black market developed in place of the legal trade – and ten-year-old children got roped in to do the dirty work. Graft was clearly endemic. 'The local police come and harass us all the time, so we have to pay them,' said Javed. But the public spotlight on places like this was growing. A year before, police shut down a similar copper recycling operation in Silampur after some media reports. He reckoned big recycling firms would take over eventually.

But for now, these small backyard workshops form a significant part of a much larger industry. Ravi Agarwal, director of Toxics Link, described for me how that industry worked in India. He estimates that two-thirds of the e-waste in Delhi's scrapyards is imported. E-waste comes from South-east Asia, Europe and the US, frequently after being traded by brokers from Dubai. That city has a long tradition of smuggling goods to India, and ways and means of getting past Customs controls at Indian ports. A generation ago it was gold. Now the government bans imports of e-waste, and the Dubai traders are neck-high in that business.

The containers arrive at ports on the west coast, such as Mumbai and Kandla. An estimated 1,000 truckloads of electronic waste come up the crowded highway from Mumbai to Okhla in the south of Delhi each year. Scrap dealers in Okhla auction off the waste, which may turn up later in Muslim neighbourhoods on the outskirts of Delhi, such as Silampur and Mayapuri and Turkmangate, that specialize in dismantling computers and other e-waste. Perhaps 1,000 PCs make this journey every day.

In Silampur, marketers who once traded in fruit and vegetables and rice now set to work dismantling e-waste. As we toured the district, it was often hard to tell if the businesses were computer-repair shops or recyclers. Monitors and their casings, the chips and capacitors and gold-plated pins and solder from the circuit boards, the stripped motherboards, the keyboards, disk drives, mice and other components all have their disposal routes, and their own specialists adept in the dark arts of low-tech, high-risk materials recovery, with hammers and screwdrivers and pliers and acid.

Circuit boards alone may go to several specialists. One to take the chips, another to remove gold and silver, another to melt off the solder, and finally to the copper collectors. Mandoli is pretty much the end of the line. Meanwhile, cables and transistors are stripped of their copper by burning and boiling. In Shastri Park in east Delhi, they smash up old monitors and dismantle printer cartridges, creating clouds of toner dust, some of which is collected and sold on. Plastic PC casing often ends up in another Delhi suburb, Mundaka, which houses Asia's largest market for waste plastic.

Delhi is not the only place round the world where these activities are carried out. The suburb of Sher Shah in Karachi, Pakistan's main port, is another. One study in Lagos found 500 containers of e-waste, with perhaps 100,000 old PCs inside, arriving at the port each month. A cluster of villages known collectively as Guiyu, near Santou in southern China, has become notorious for its crude recycling of e-waste, partly because, being in a formerly rural area, the activities are much more visible than when spread across a large urban area like Delhi.

In high-wage economies, e-waste has always been regarded as a liability to be disposed of as cheaply as possible. But in low-wage economies, where people will work for virtually nothing and in poor conditions, e-waste is a resource. It can be profitably mined for tiny amounts of valuable raw materials. This is recycling: closing the loop. We should all be in favour. But in places like Mandoli, the human cost is too high. The air is rich in mercury and dioxins; the drinking water is tainted with toxic metals. The children are scarred or worse by acid, their lungs blackened and diseased by fumes; and an air of exploitation and graft permeates the wider society.

How responsible should we feel for what happens there? Britain alone produces more than a million tonnes of electronic waste a year. That's the weight of 2,400 jumbo jets – and includes some 50,000 tonnes of scrap circuit boards. Half a million old and warranty-returned TVs and 100,000 video-recorders and 120,000 computers are exported. Brokers pay £15 for old TVs, whether or not they are working.

There are hundreds of traders exporting British e-waste. Many of them are not based in the UK, and often do not even declare their addresses, say industry insiders. You reach them by mobile phone or via websites. A report for the Environment Agency says they 'do not seem keen to divulge information about the destination or fate of equipment and will only discuss the equipment they want and what they are prepared to pay'.

In 2007, the UK enacted new European laws, the WEEE directive, to increase recycling of computers and other electronic waste. The WEEE directive requires that 'recovery' rates for e-waste – that is the proportion not going to landfill – should rise from 15 per cent today to at least 75 per cent. But where will all this end up? In purpose-built facilities in Europe? Or in the Dickensian workshops of Delhi or Lagos? In theory, the retailers and manufacturers are responsible for what happens to their products. They have to take back old products and find them a safe disposal route. The paperwork is all checked and the ultimate fate of the material ensured.

Really? How scrupulous can we expect them to be? Who is physically opening the containers destined for Singapore or Mumbai or Dubai or Shenzhen? Who is judging whether the contents are capable of being safely recycled and sold in a distant land, where labour is cheap and pockets empty? Untangling the paperwork will be hard enough, let alone deciding if any of it is truthful. The WEEE directive looks increasingly like a bogus-recycler's charter. Certainly in India they say the directive is increasing the number of shipments they receive. That may be good if the recycling is genuine and safe. Bad if it all ends up in Mandoli.

This was all very depressing. Surely there was some way I could dispose of my computer with a clear conscience. I went first to Billingham on Teeside, to what is advertised as 'Britain's largest electronics recycling plant'. Owned by the Wincanton trucking group, it promises to handle up to 10 tonnes of e-waste an hour – 75,000 tonnes a year. Millions of consumers and many retailers will be entrusting their e-waste to this facility as the WEEE directive comes into force.

Standing in the warehouse, I saw a sample of the wares already coming to Billingham. There were bagless vacuum cleaners, Compaq computer mice, Gameboy control consoles, miscellaneous keyboards and old BT phones. On other days it could be washing machines and vending machines, lawn mowers and TVs, medical equipment and electric toothbrushes, toasters and vacuum cleaners. Much of this material was unsold stock from shops, in unopened boxes, and sometimes included entire pallets of single items. There were piles of boxed-up Bush VCRs, unsold even when knocked down to £24.95. This was stuff going for recycling before it had been used once. What a waste.

A conveyor belt of computers disappeared into a large hopper.

Inside, two heavy chains whipped round at high speed and broke up the equipment. Out came mangled, fist-sized pieces of e-waste. A dozen or so staff in overalls picked through these gobbets of our cyber-economy and put them in the right bins, marked for batteries, cables, PC boards, copper and iron components, stainless steel, aluminium and so on.

I had expected to see real recycling going on. Instead it seemed to be the British equivalent of Silampur, where they dismantle the e-waste and pass it on. 'Basically we just separate the toxic stuff from the recyclable stuff,' said general manager Chris Wilson. 'What we do could be done by men with screwdrivers. But we'd need about two hundred people, rather than ten people.' The only real difference is that in India it is cost-effective to use people; in Billingham chains work out cheaper.

Out at the back the different waste streams were assembled for dispatch. A lot of metals go to Liverpool-based European Metal Recycling (EMR), the biggest scrap-metal merchants in Europe. EMR in turn sells it on to Corus, formerly British Steel, or to steel works abroad. Most circuit boards, with their chips intact, go to high-tech metals recovery plants such as the Boliden refinery on the edge of the Arctic Circle in northern Sweden. But many refineries already cherry-pick the boards with the most valuable metals, like gold, silver and lead. They don't want the rest, which is why they go to India and China right now.

Batteries are recycled in Britain. Cathode-ray tubes used to be recycled to make new tubes. But now everyone wants plasma and LCD screens, so that route is gone. There is a growing cathode-ray-tube mountain. Old copper cable goes through a high-tech version of the Mandoli operation, with PVC stripped off prior to making new cable. Plastics go to China.

That's the theory. But in practice the waste goes through a chain of brokers. And already much e-waste goes east. I was left worried by how the directive was being implemented. Chris thought it was the Environment Agency's job to regulate the brokers. But at the agency they say the onus is on the exporter. So who were the brokers, I asked. Maybe I could check them out myself. 'We use a number of brokers,' said Chris. 'We just look for the best deal on the day. We won't name them because of commercial confidentiality.' Oh, boy.

A big problem is that the WEEE directive is all about the environment and does not have any specific health and safety requirements. Recycling is recycling is recycling, whether at high-tech Boliden or low-tech Mandoli. When licensing brokers, the Environment Agency can't insist on socio-economic conditions. Chris couldn't guarantee that his broken bits of old computer motherboards wouldn't end up in Mandoli. His only thought was that Billingham's relatively 'clean' waste streams could usually command high prices, which made the dodgier waste practices unlikely. I wasn't sure of the logic of that. It might prevent the majority of the waste being dumped. But that doesn't happen much anyway. And an Indian copper-smelting company would still buy a containerload of old circuit boards, and still send them down to Mandoli for the Rajesh treatment, if that was the cheapest option. Arguably, high prices in Billingham, by squeezing margins, made the attractions of cheap recycling in Mandoli greater, not less.

We probably have to accept that micro-managing recycling in distant countries is not possible. And perhaps not desirable either. Countries like China and India need raw materials to maintain their fast-growing industrial sectors. Increasingly, that is coming from the recycling of products previously sold to the rich nations. As Chris said, 'We cannot say for sure that WEEE won't stimulate poor recycling conditions in India and other places. It may. But at the end of the day, if they don't recycle, then that would stimulate more primary-materials production – more mining and refining of ores – which would have its own health and safety downside, its own social problems and its own victims.'

So what should I do with my old computers? My first inclination is to leave them sitting in the loft. They may not be giving up their precious metals to anyone for recycling, but at least they are doing no harm either. But surely there must be a better way. Finally, I found it.

A couple of months after visiting Delhi I went to a workshop in Nairobi where they take in containerloads of old computers from Europe and North America. But rather than breaking them up, they refurbish them and ship them out to secondary schools. The scheme is the brainchild of social entrepreneur Tom Musili, who had seen something similar going on in Canada and thought he could bring it to Africa.

Tom began refurbishing computers from a bench in a spare room at a local school in 2003. Computers for Schools Kenya now has a small staff, and is busy setting up a network of regional centres to handle the increasing numbers of old computers it is being offered, both from Kenyan corporations and from around the world.

Containerloads of computers arrive regularly at Mombasa port on the coast and come to Nairobi by train. The day I was there, Tom's livewire coordinator Norman Makinga had received a consignment from the University of Bradford in the UK and was tracking the progress of another containerload from Britain. 'We get an average of one container, that's about four hundred and fifty machines, each month. So we are handling about twenty machines a day.' The operation is straightforward and efficient. Incoming machines are coded, cleaned and checked over. About a fifth of them don't work or don't meet the specs. They are cannibalized for parts for the rest. With the rest, the memory is wiped and new software installed. A deal with Microsoft means there is no charge.

Norman's team pack up computers in batches of twenty, ensuring one machine between two pupils in classes that typically have forty children. Before Tom came along, most schools in Kenya, even large secondary schools, had no computers. By late 2006, Tom had supplied some 300 Kenyan schools with more than 7,000 computers, and there were another 850 schools on the waiting list.

There isn't much storage space in the workshop, so typically computers are on their way to schools within four days. I looked at the schedule pinned up on the wall. It was a rare day when some school somewhere in Kenya did not get a new computer lab. Computers go to the most remote areas of the country, where the constraint is not broadband access (forget it; there isn't any) but electricity. At the end of my visit, Norman was just shoe-horning one last keyboard into an old Ford van with forty-five computers destined for three schools in Garissa, a poor, dusty, rebellious town close to the border with Somalia.

A small party gathered to see off the driver on a four-day journey. The roads out there are bad and the equipment could get damaged, so Norman had taken the sensitive hard drives out of the machines and protected them in bubble-wrap. 'We'll put them on the front seat,' he said. It was the last leg in the long journey those computers had made from Bradford in England.

What is the lifetime for these refurbished computers? 'We reckon that a decent branded computer has a lifetime of around ten years,' said Norman. 'So we won't take computers more than six years old.' Sorry, but they don't take Apples.

Every day, four or five machines don't make the grade. Where do they go? Norman took me to a second workshop. 'We recycle virtually everything here. But we work hard to make sure there is no bad practice.' In the yard there were piles of mice and keyboards and casings both metal and plastic, and motherboards, and wires and hard drives – even boxes of screws. I got him to take me in detail through the story of what happens to those piles. If I was going to give one of my computers to CSK, I didn't want its motherboard to end up dunked into an acid tub by a ten-year-old street kid.

There is a market for almost everything, he said. Hard disks sell for 30 shillings each (about 20 pence), aluminium casings for 50 shillings a kilo and copper wire for 60 shillings. Metal casings get turned into guttering. Aluminium is recycled in Nairobi, but hard plastic goes to China. 'We even take the metal balls out of the mice and they go for recycling, too, mainly for their lead.' He handed batteries over to recyclers. 'But we have to keep a close check, because some of them will just pour the acid they don't need into ditches.' Hmm.

Upstairs, he had a big collection of monitors in store. Some he would sell to a college for students to cannibalize. 'We sometimes let artisans have the monitors to build cheap TVs round them, and sell them in the local Jua Kali market,' said Norman. 'But the circuit boards are the most difficult thing.' He had a buyer, who wanted a containerload at a time. That would take six years and Norman wasn't sure where they would end up even then. Delhi, maybe?

Norman clearly works hard to find a safe home for the detritus from his computer refurbishments. It is not perfect. I would imagine that things do fall into the wrong hands. But is this a good, valuable business – a worthy end for my computer? I think so.

Around half of CSK's computers come from Britain via a London-based charity call Computer Aid International. CAI is the world's largest not-for-profit provider of computers for developing countries. Its donors range from British Airways and Mitsubishi to Christian Aid and a bloke who lives down the road from me. Its boss and founder Tony Roberts has fought continued scepticism in the environment community about the morality of shipping old computers to developing countries.

Some say the risks of them ending up somewhere like Mandoli are too high. But he says we should see the potential good that can be done as well. In mid-2008, shortly after the organization's tenth anniversary, it also celebrated its 100,000th delivery. Three-quarters so far have ended up in Africa, where Kenya takes the most. When we spoke, he was trying to set up a new computer lab in Kibera, the huge slum on the outskirts of Nairobi.

The potential of CSK to take the world's computers may be limited. But Tony believes there is huge potential to set up similar enterprises round the world. Most discarded computers have several years of active life left in them. And now that more and more computer owners are having to think about where their old kit ends up, the potential is growing fast.

Tony had offered to pick up one of my old computers and rush it out to Nairobi so I could see it being refurbished by Norman's team. It was a nice idea, but they would have had to put it on a plane rather than in one of the regular container shipments. Could I really justify those air miles? I thought not and turned that idea down. Anyway, I wanted to see the operation first. Now that I have, I am convinced. I can't think of a better place to send my computer.

Part Seven

The Footprint Doctors

29

Carbon Offsets: Green Fraud or Painless Panacea?

It was a night for partying. Fireworks fizzed across the Brisbane sky as half of the city's inhabitants celebrated their annual festival along the banks of the River Brisbane. Then came a deafening roar. An F-111 of the Australian air force swooped over the revellers, leaving behind a stream of flame hot enough to feel below. I instinctively ducked down. Within a second the plane was gone, and cheers went up as the DJ announced the completion of the highlight of the evening, a 'dump and burn'.

The aircraft had dumped the contents of its fuel tanks into the sky over the city and ignited it. Later, in the local paper, the festival organizer announced that 300 trees had been planted outside the city to soak up the estimated 68 tonnes of greenhouse gases released by the F-111. Here we had a new paradigm for our age: dump, burn and offset. I will keep an eye on those trees. There was a big drought going on in Queensland. Probably the worst for 1,000 years. So I wonder if the trees will survive to soak up their allotted CO_2? I reckon that, as one of the half-million spectators that night, about 150 grams of that offset is my responsibility.

The Brisbane tree planting formed one small part of one of the fastest-growing businesses in the world, the sale of promises to remove carbon dioxide from the atmosphere. Some see offsetting as the ultimate, painless and guilt-free solution to global warming. I am tempted to think the same. I am feeling guilty about my large carbon footprint from travelling round the world for this book. I too dump and burn. Can I offset my travels with a clear conscience? I decided to explore the world of carbon offsets.

There are two kinds of offsets: the official and the unofficial, or voluntary, offsets. The official ones help organizations meet their targets under the Kyoto Protocol. Corporations can get round limits on their carbon dioxide emissions by investing in offset projects. Plant trees that soak up a tonne of CO_2 and your emissions permit rises by a tonne. These projects have their detractors, but they are at least controlled by tight rules and a complex bureaucracy aimed at preventing fraud.

In the voluntary sector, individuals like me, or corporations without formal targets who are keen to be green, can pay one of a growing army of charitable and profit-making bodies to organize offsets. This freelance business is separate from Kyoto and keeps bureaucracy to a minimum. This is one reason why its offsets typically cost only half as much.

Though still smaller than the Kyoto offsets, sales of voluntary offsets grew from 3 million tonnes of CO_2 in 2004 to somewhere between 20 and 50 million tonnes in 2006. I counted more than sixty organizations that would sell me offsets, mostly online. More are being started all the time. You can go online, calculate your emissions from flying on holiday, running your car or running your life, and cleanse your environmental sins as quickly as you can give them your credit-card details. So can corporations, for whom voluntary offsets are great PR. And cheap. Prices range from £13 to as little as £3 per tonne of CO_2 offset.

British Airways offsets with the Oxford-based Climate Care, for instance. And the HSBC Bank, which purchased 170,000 tonnes of emissions offsets in 2006, subsequently claimed to be 'the world's first carbon-neutral bank'. Sky TV claims offsets have helped it to become 'the first major media company in the world to become carbon neutral.' Some corporations also offer their own customers the chance to assuage guilt about buying their products by signing up to offsets through their own websites. BP's 'targetneutral' scheme assures its customers that 'it is now possible to drive in neutral', for a modest fee.

But nobody really knows what they are buying. A study by offsets expert Mark Trexler for the New England environment group Clean Air – Cool Planet concluded that 'There are no widely accepted standards as to what qualifies as an "offset" . . . almost anyone can offer to sell you almost anything and claim that this purchase will make you carbon neutral.' Many offset marketers provide little information about where the money you give them is being spent, or even what criteria they use to select suitable projects. Nor do most make clear what time-scale their offsets work over. Trees don't grow overnight, after all.

Take this tale, tracked down by my *New Scientist* colleague Rob Edwards. Under its previous name of Future Forests, the CarbonNeutral Company sold offset 'investments' in trees on the Orbost estate in the remote north-west of the Isle of Skye in Scotland. Lovely spot; really romantic. Investors included the Rolling Stones, the car maker Volvo, travellers with the adventure holiday company Crystal and thousands of rock fans attending the Glastonbury festival. The Stones helped make their 2003 UK tour 'carbon neutral' by persuading more than 2,000 fans to pay £8.50 each 'to plant trees at Orbost'. Crystal said offsetters would 'get a tree planted'. Volvo has claimed that its investment will be 'creating woodlands in Orbost'.

None of this is strictly true. As Rob discovered, not one additional tree was planted as a result of these investments. The idea that the Stones' tour had been made carbon neutral was an illusion. Read the small print and you discover that would-be offsetters did not pay to plant trees, but rather to purchase 'carbon sequestration rights' in the forest. That is, they bought the right to claim that they had captured the carbon. But in fact most of the trees were already in the ground. Nearly 130,000 saplings were planted during the winter of 2002–03, while the Stones were still rehearsing. And all the money for planting was already committed by Highlands and Islands Enterprise, the government agency that owns the estate. Rob quoted the forest manager Kevin Sutton saying that Future Forests' purchase of the carbon rights for £34,275 made no difference.

The would-be offsetters paid £10 (including VAT) per tree. But Future Forests bought the 'sequestratian rights' for just 54 pence per tree. Now all NGOs have overheads to cover. And the Orbost forest offset scheme was one of Future Forests' first. But, even so. The forest managers were not unhappy since the cash was 'extra money for something we hadn't really thought of.' It improved cash flow, they said, and paid to refurbish a path. But it did not plant trees. CarbonNeutral has declined several opportunities to rebut these charges. I ruled out CarbonNeutral as a potential offset provider, but pressed on.

I thought I would start by finding out about offsetting my flight to the River*festival* in Brisbane, and went online to check what was on offer. I picked several companies and asked their websites how much carbon they thought I emitted during that economy-class return flight. That should be easy, I thought. Well, no. The online calculators produced figures ranging from CarbonNeutral's 1.8 tonnes, through 5.4 tonnes with the Oxford-based Climate Care to a staggering 12.5 tonnes with the German offsetters Atmosfair. That is a sevenfold difference.

To be fair, the discrepancies partly reflect a real scientific debate. Aircraft emissions are complex. The CO_2 emissions are easy to calculate: burning one tonne of aircraft fuel produces 3.15 tonnes of CO_2. But aircraft also emit nitrogen oxides and water vapour. The water vapour can make contrails that form heat-trapping bands of cirrus clouds. The nitrogen oxides create ozone, a greenhouse gas, which may sometimes itself destroy methane, another greenhouse gas. All these reactions vary with temperature, altitude and even whether it is day or night.

To make matters even more complicated, the various gases last in the atmosphere for different amounts of time. Water vapour sticks around for only a few hours; a lot of CO_2 stays in the air for centuries. So calculating the actual warming effect of aircraft emissions depends on what period of time you are interested in. If I only care about warming over the next few years, the figure will be higher than if my perspective is for centuries hence. I am sorry to complicate matters so. But when we are being sold offset packages like cans of beans, it is wise to know a bit about what's in the tin.

Most scientists agree that the CO_2 emissions from an aircraft flight need to be multiplied by some figure to give a reasonable estimate of the warming effect of all the emissions. The UN's Intergovernmental Panel on Climate Change says the best estimate, based on a 100-year time horizon, is that the warming effect of emissions from aircraft is 2.7 times the effect of CO_2 alone. Atmosfair multiplies CO_2 emissions by three, Climate Care multiplies by two and CarbonNeutral simply calculates CO_2 with no allowance for other gases.

That explains some of the discrepancy between the calculators for my Brisbane trip, but not all of it. So I dug deeper. It turns out that each company takes its own view of exactly what share of the aircraft emissions that, sitting in seat 36K, I should be responsible for. Most assume the plane is 80 per cent full and ask me to pay my bit towards the empty seats. I can see the logic of that, though it doesn't seem quite fair. Climate Care says I am responsible only for my own seat. It says that most long-haul flights travel at full payload. If there are fewer passengers than normal, they put on extra freight.

I had to accept that there was no 'right' answer to the number of tonnes of CO_2 I should pay for. The next step was to discover how much I should pay. But here again, different companies offered very different prices. Atmosfair charged £13 to offset a tonne of CO_2, while Climate Care and CarbonNeutral both charged around £7.50. When I combined the different calculations of emissions and offset prices, the cost of offsetting my flight to Brisbane ranged from £165 with Atmosfair and £40 with Climate Care to a bargain £13.30 with CarbonNeutral. I began to wonder if I was being taken for a ride by Atmosfair, and whether CarbonNeutral wasn't the Ryanair of offsets.

So what do I get for my money? In truth, we can never know at the time of purchase whether our offset investment will buy a good environmental return. Offset companies don't stress the point, but some projects deliver their promised returns only over time – sometimes many decades. So we are effectively taking a punt on offset futures. Take tree plantations, which have absorbed most of the offset money spent so far, and which cover an estimated 40,000 square kilometres. Brisbane's F-111 released its emissions into the night air in less than a second. But the trees intended to offset that release will reabsorb the gas only gradually, over about three decades. If all goes well.

Even successfully nurtured trees that grow to be tall sticks of carbon do not live for ever. What happens when they die? In theory, all the offset timber could be turned into antique furniture, and live a long and useful life. But sooner or later, those trees will yield up their carbon to the air, as the timber, or products like paper, burn or rot. Most offset companies promise to maintain their forests for ninety-nine years. After that – and assuming that the company or its successor still exists – they regard their obligation as discharged.

There is a superficial logic to this. Those ninety-nine years are roughly equivalent to the amount of time that an average molecule of CO_2 released into the air will last before it is reabsorbed by the oceans or soils or vegetation; so the trees will hold on to the CO_2 for the time that it would have been in the air. Job done. I accepted this idea for some time. Then the truth finally dawned on me. What offset forests are actually doing is simply postponing emissions. CO_2 absorbed by offset forests will be emitted in about 2100, rather than today.

This is, to say the least, problematic. It is, of course, just possible that by the twenty-second century the concentration of CO_2 in the atmosphere will be lower than today, or that we will have learned not to care. In which case this time-shift will have been useful. Maybe the plantations will have morphed into natural forests and planted their own successor saplings to take up more CO_2 as the pioneer trees die. More likely, I suspect, the offset CO_2 will be released back into an atmosphere already choked with the gas. It will give an extra push to global warming at a time when the climate may be at its most vulnerable. Future generations may not thank us for this. If one of the central tenets of good environmental practice is not to impose new burdens on future generations, then offset forests fail that test.

There are other concerns about forest offset schemes. They may dry out soils or release methane. Either could negate the gains from storing CO_2. Outside the tropics, where trees grow fastest, the dark canopy of the forest may heat the air more than its growing timber can offset the warming. And large forest projects also have a nasty habit of creating social conflicts by turning poor people off their ancestral land.

Don't get me wrong. There are plenty of good reasons for plant-ing forests. Social and environmental. But they have to work in their own terms. Not as carbon offsets. Many offset companies are getting out of the trees business. They say the burden of long-term monitoring and verification, and the potential for disputes, are just too great. So what are the alternatives? Some offsetters promise to invest in capturing non-CO_2 greenhouse gas emissions like methane as they leak out of landfills or the slurry pits of South American farms.

For most offset companies, the alternative to planting trees is to invest in green energy projects in developing countries. Projects like wind turbines and solar panels, more efficient cooking stoves and energy-efficient light bulbs. 'Funding energy projects is intuitively better than forests because it stops pollution, rather than soaking it up later, and you are contributing to a wider move away from fossil fuels,' says Climate Care's Mike Buick. I agree. The schemes also double as development projects, helping poor rural communities rather than, as too often with forest offsets, stealing their land.

But these projects raise a whole new set of dilemmas. Most critical is the question of 'additionality'. In other words, has the project really changed what people would have done anyway without the intervention? And if so, by how much? If my money goes to putting energy-efficient light bulbs into schools in Kazakhstan, or cleaner cooking stoves into homes in Honduras, how do I know that the stoves and light bulbs would not have been installed without my intervention? And if I am buying offsets by the tonne, I need to know how much timber or coal or electricity the beneficiaries would have burned in the absence of the project.

The trouble is that nobody can be sure about the future. Even apparently copper-bottomed 'additionality' can spring a leak. In 2005, Climate Care funded the distribution of free energy-efficient light bulbs in a Cape Town slum, and sold the offset emissions to its customers back in the UK. But only months later, the South African power company Eskom responded to electricity blackouts with an energy-saving programme that involved distributing similar energy-efficient bulbs in the same township. In fact, the job was partly done by the same sub-contractor. So, as it turned out, there was no 'additionality' for the Climate Care project.

Many people – including corporations trying to sell their green credentials – want to fund projects closer to home. But here the logic of additionality becomes even more difficult. The question is: can you claim additionality if you are only helping people do what they are already legally required to do? You would think not. And yet most offset schemes in countries with Kyoto targets do precisely that. CarbonNeutral funds wind farms in New Zealand. The Woodland Trust in Britain funds tree planting with offset sales. And there are plenty of others. Sue Welland, founder of CarbonNeutral, told me her forest projects meet Kyoto Protocol criteria, and so are quite legitimate. But if the countries where these projects take place have Kyoto targets, then these projects – or others with similar benefits – would have had to be carried out regardless of the offsetters' intervention. So where is the additionality? I can't see it.

The same problem, incidentally, would arise if I decided to buy electricity on some of the 'green tariffs' offered to environmentally concerned customers. There are already government requirements for power companies to use renewable electricity. None of the majors have yet achieved them. So I would just be subsidizing power companies' efforts to meet those legal targets.

Hardliners say that offset projects can never be a substitute for cutting emissions. For them, 'dump, burn and offset' is the worst possible outcome. Of course, so far as the climate is concerned, a tonne of CO_2 kept out of the atmosphere is equally beneficial however it is done. But the act of buying an offset implies a certainty about achieving that end which mostly we do not have. None of this, I think, says that offset projects are in themselves bad. But they don't quite do what it says on the tin.

Is buying an offset better than not buying? For me, despite the horror stories, the answer is usually yes. But only if you can be fairly sure where the money is going. You may have guessed from some of the foregoing that I reckon the best in the market, as of 2007, is Climate Care. And I am not alone. Trexler's study does not deliver a league table. But read the appendices and tables, and it is clear that Climate Care comes out top. But in 2008 Climate Care was bought by JP Morgan. Will it retain its ethical approach now it is in the hands of a Wall Street investment bank? Some doubt it.

What about my footprint from publishing this book? It is an inescapable question, and one I have thought about for some time. Clearly the production of the book itself is not entirely in my hands. But I do think my UK publisher has taken some steps to 'green' its publishing. All its black-and-white hardbacks and most of its paperbacks are now printed on paper approved by the Forest Stewardship Council, the leading certifier of sustainably produced timber. That is, timber produced without trashing the forest. Some greens grumble about how rigorous the Council is in applying its rules. But I think this alliance of the timber trade and mainstream environment groups like WWF has a generally good track record in outlawing forest destruction and promoting replanting. So I am pleased this book carries the FSC logo.

The book has – barring any last-minute change of plan – been printed on paper made from Russian FSC-certified wood at the Anjala mill in Finland, which is owned by the local paper-giant Stora Enso. From there, the paper is shipped to Tilbury docks and then driven to Suffolk, and finally hits the presses about 140 kilometres from London in the small town of Bungay, courtesy of the printing company Clays.

What's the carbon footprint? Some products now come with labels announcing the amount of carbon emitted during their production. Books have not got that far yet. Figures supplied by Anjala suggest that manufacturing the paper for a typical book produces an amount of carbon dioxide that is something like two-thirds of the weight of the book itself – so around 300 grams for the volume you have in your hands.

On top of that there is the work of the publisher. The UK arm of the publishing giant Random House, of which Eden Project Books is one imprint of many, reckons that its corporate footprint from handling about 80 million books and running its offices amounts to nearly 7,000 tonnes a year of CO_2, or something like another 85 grams per copy. Sadly, I don't have a figure for the retail end of the business, but I guess it might be at least as much again, giving a total carbon footprint for producing the book in your hand of almost half a kilogram of CO_2, slightly more than I expect it weighs.

But I think my most direct personal responsibility is for the footprint from researching the book – my travels. Since I have no idea how many copies of the book will ultimately be printed or sold, I cannot say now what the research footprint of each individual book will be. But, unless the book sells more than 40,000 copies, it looks as if the research footprint will be at least as great as the footprint from printing and publishing it. I must say, that has come as a surprise to me.

During the year I was researching this book more or less full-time, I estimate that I flew about 180,000 kilometres. That means, by Climate Care's calculations, that I was responsible for the emission of 22.5 tonnes of CO_2. I hope it was worth it to bring you this story. I accept some of you may think not. At any event, on 29 August 2007, I paid the Climate Care Trust £168.75 in the hope that its projects will ultimately offset those emissions. It felt odd, handing over cash without receiving goods in return, only an emailed certificate. And I should probably have felt even more uneasy if I did not slightly know several of the people involved at the Trust. Even so, they should be assured that I shall be following their progress with care.

30

Too Few Planets: Scary Science in Siena

There is a science of measuring the 'ecological footprint' of individuals. It is not just about carbon, though that is part of it. The aim is to come up with a figure for the amount of land that each of us needs to support our lifestyles. And, by adding those all up, and factoring in activities organized on our behalf, like schools, hospitals and the military, we can get a sense of whether we are over-using the planet's resources. This science is the basis for those slightly bizarre claims that appear in the media from time to time that we are using the resources of 1.2 planets and will need two planets to live on by 2050. As a science journalist, I am wary of such claims. What exactly do they mean? But as a human being living on one planet, I can relate to them. And, since we are not in a position to move half our population to Mars, I find them rather worrying.

So I decided to join a group of scientists behind the ecological footprint who were holding a meeting in Siena, one of my favourite Italian cities, with its central *campo*, lovely orange brick and idyllic surrounding hilltop towns and villages. But the town also has a small ecological footprint because of its low car use and because it

314

gets most of its electricity from clean geothermal energy. 'We don't have cities like this in the US,' said the conference organizer Mathis Wackernagel – who learned at the knee of the inventor of the footprint concept, William Rees of the University of British Columbia in Vancouver. 'The people of Siena have an ecological footprint only a third that of an American of similar wealth. It shows we can have wonderful lives and a small footprint.' To underline the point, the conference was held in an old hospital whose thick stone walls kept us cool in the height of a Mediterranean summer, without air conditioning. To get there, I flew, and took taxis at either end. This was shaming when several other delegates had minimized their footprints by making a forty-hour journey by train from York.

But to the footprint science. Planet Earth has a surface area of 41 billion hectares. Mathis calculates that if you take out the ice caps and deserts and largely unproductive deep oceans, you are left with about 11.3 billion hectares of croplands, pastures, wetlands, built-up areas, forests and coastal fishing grounds – or something like 1.8 hectares for each of us. That is almost two soccer pitches. Unfortunately, by his calculation, the average citizen of the world consumes the output of 2.2 hectares. Humanity's footprint over-shot what the planet can sustain some time back in the 1980s.

The Earth is a natural system that regenerates many resources. But it now takes the Earth almost fifteen months to regenerate what we use up in twelve months. We are harvesting trees faster than they can regrow; taking nutrients from soils faster than they can be replenished; depleting fish stocks faster than they can restock; and emitting carbon dioxide into the air faster than nature can reabsorb it. 'Humanity is living off its ecological credit card,' Mathis said. 'Overshoot will ultimately liquidate the planet's ecological assets.'

It is a persuasive story. And the Siena conference was great for scary statistics. One square metre of office space has an ecological footprint of 2,800 square metres. To run the world today requires the electricity you would get from burning the entire contents of one giant oil supertanker every minute. But the more you look at footprint analysis, the more of a shaky first draft it looks. How exactly did Mathis come up with his numbers? Scientists can make a reasonable stab at the land required to feed us and to provide wood for timber and paper. But how do we measure the amount of ocean required for our fish? Or how much land is needed to provide us with water, which generally flows in rivers or is buried underground? And how do you measure the footprint of air pollution?

The biggest element in the global footprint calculation, currently making up about half of the total, is carbon dioxide emissions. In the standard methodology, this is the amount of land you would have to plant with trees to soak up the carbon from those emissions. That is reckoned at about a fifth of a hectare for every tonne of CO_2. Of course nature is not doing that sufficiently; the gas is actually accumulating in the atmosphere, gradually warming us up. So the footprint is rather theoretical – a crude surrogate for real ecological impacts.

Footprint analysis falls down in other ways, too. Most land has multiple functions, so that forests and soils can both produce crops and soak up CO_2, for instance, while the rocks beneath may store water and be mined. And the current methodology assumes that it takes as much land to grow a tonne of grain or some other crop, wherever you are in the world. It says nothing about eco-efficiency, or even about 'closing the loop' by recycling materials. No credit is given to countries or cities or even individuals who do things better. So your calculated ecological footprint from eating vegetables is the same whether you grow food in your back garden or import it from Africa on a plane. Applied strictly, footprint analysis could almost be an incentive *not* to become more eco-efficient.

I don't want to be too negative. The great virtue of footprint analysis is that it breaks out of national boundaries. It looks at your global footprint, regardless of where that may fall. And what emerges from this unique perspective is how rich countries live off the resources of others, culling their cotton and cocoa and corn as if there were no ecological consequences. At the Siena meeting, Gorn Dige of the European Environment Agency pointed out that Europe is grabbing ever more of other people's environment. However 'green' Europeans may feel, 'Europe's share of the world's resources is rising even as our share of the world's population is falling.'

By Mathis's calculation, Europe's global footprint is currently 4.7 hectares per person, roughly twice its productive land area. Europeans are not the top consumers, however. Above them, Australians and Canadians require between 7 and 8 hectares each, and Americans 9.7 hectares. Meanwhile at the lower end, the Chinese require around 2 hectares, and Indians 0.7 hectares.

One interpretation of all this is that if we all lived like Indians, we would be well within the planet's capacity. But some people want to do the calculations a different way. They suggest that countries with larger land areas should be able to use more of the planet's resources, because they have greater indigenous biological resources. Geoff Hammond of the University of Bath argues that countries with ecological footprints that are less than their national ecological resources, or 'bio-capacities', should be regarded as the good guys.

Looked at this way, Europeans are still bad guys, with densely populated Britain very bad indeed, using almost four times as much biologically productive land as it has within its borders. And Japan is even worse, overshooting its bio-capacity sevenfold. But the 20 million Australians and 30 million Canadians are in ecological credit. Their large individual ecological footprints are compensated for by their even larger land areas.

By this measure, the Indians, a billion people crammed into an area little bigger than Kazakhstan, are running a small ecological deficit. So they are not a model of ecological rectitude, after all. And Bangladeshis, who individually have among the world's smallest ecological footprints, are deemed bad guys because they overshoot their country's meagre bio-capacity by about 80 per cent. In fact, they overshoot by about the same margin as the US, which has twenty times the human footprint of Bangladesh, but also twenty times the bio-capacity. Can this be a fair reflection of the ecological burden that the two nations place on the planet? It is the same as saying it is OK for me to live in the lap of luxury provided I have a country estate. It is hard to believe so.

Several organizations at the Siena conference had developed their own calculators for measuring personal footprints. Later, I road-tested some of them. Because they try to analyse lifestyles as the basis of a few indicators, and do it in contrasting ways, the results are far from uniform. One calculator didn't allow me the possibility of not driving a car, so I just had to tick the lowest mileage option. Two other calculators did not allow me to own up to any of my air travel. None of them allowed me to declare my very high level of air travel over the previous year. My calculated footprint varied from 4 to 13 hectares. But my actual footprint must be way above even the top estimate.

One thing shocked me as I boarded my easyJet flight home from Siena. Mathis and the conference organizers had not estimated the ecological footprint of the event itself. Even big corporate conferences often do that kind of thing these days. Why hadn't the kings of the footprint footprinted themselves? Mathis said he was interested in 'systems' changes and not personal footprints. I don't really know what he meant by that. I think we have to be held personally accountable before anyone takes the 'systems' seriously.

One in a Billion:
Paul, the African Laird

Paul van Vlissingen was almost certainly the richest man I have ever met. The Dutch industrialist, chairman of the SHV group, was a billionaire, head of the ninth generation of a family that has built ships and steam engines, and now owns Calor Gas and runs the biggest supermarket chains in both Indonesia and Venezuela. He owned a castle near Utrecht, had married a *Guardian* journalist, wanted to introduce wolves to his Scottish estate and, for an encore, had cornered the market in privatized national parks across Africa.

They called him the laird of Africa. But was he the saviour of Africa or a land-grabbing latter-day imperialist with dangerous delusions about the nobility of nature red in tooth and claw? I went to see him at his castle in the summer of 2005, more or less at his summons after I had questioned his motives in print. 'Every Dutch journalist knows they can call me even in the bush, and I will answer their questions. But you didn't,' he said. Fair enough. So I went. He must already have known he was dying of cancer. He didn't let on, but I had the sense of a man nearing the end of his life and wanting to set the record straight. Only a few months later, he announced that he had turned down chemotherapy in order to die a quicker death.

The African adventure 'started with a conversation with Nelson Mandela, when he was president of South Africa,' Paul said. 'We got into a discussion about why ecology was not high on the priority list of his government. He said he had other things to do first to help the poor, but I said the poorest people in Africa lived in the remotest areas, where his programmes on education and water and housing weren't working. Government gets less effective the further you get from cities. But if you focus on those very remote areas with national parks, you can help both wildlife and the poorest people.' Paul said government-run parks in Africa were a disaster, but private management could work.

Mandela bought the idea. Paul's first park, Marakele, had been collapsing when he took it over in 2003, but two years later it was one of South Africa's three most visited parks. Professional management was the key, he said. That and local consent. 'The people living in the park have to know there is something better to do with a zebra than eat it. That they can benefit by protecting it.'

After the South African success, governments were queuing up to hire his expertise – and his money. He had parks in Zambia and Ethiopia and plans in Malawi, Sudan and elsewhere. We touched on my earlier criticism. The Ethiopian government had controversially moved a lot of tribal people out of a park shortly before Paul's park managers took over. He was equivocal. It was up to the government, he said. The people were squatters. The government had intended to get rid of them anyway. He had refused to take over until the relocation was completed.

I wasn't convinced by this, but I was seduced by his wider enthusiasm. 'The traditional way with parks in Africa is that park rangers and policemen beat up everybody who they think is poaching. We have a different way. We reward not-poaching. Revenue from tourism funds development projects to compensate when hunting is stopped. We say the park rangers have to visit the villages and offer to help, to be a friend of the community, not an enemy. The park rangers have radios that can bring in doctors when people get sick. In Liuwa, our park in

Zambia, there used to be sixty or eighty murders a year over various disputes. The first year we got that down to twenty-six, and the next year to two.'

I found in him a curious mixture of an old-fashioned romantic about African wildlife and a modern professional when combining development with wildlife protection. He meant it. He was putting in huge amounts of his own money – more than £10 million in the year before his death – to get the parks up and running, while insisting that they would have to pay their way eventually.

He was calling in favours, too. He got money from the World Bank and the US State Department. What was their interest in running African parks exactly? I never quite got to the bottom of that. But he denied the charge of neo-colonialism. 'I want to protect the culture of Africa. I think parks can give African people a new respect. But you cannot freeze cultures and economic situations in Africa when everyone else on the planet has cars and TVs and education and hospitals.'

There was a deep patrician sense of obligation about all this. He told me he thought his family had a debt to repay to nature and society. 'We were instrumental in killing the Rhine,' he volunteered. 'We had the largest transport fleet on the river in the nineteenth century, and we re-engineered the river to take out the curves. It made it more productive for us, but it also killed the salmon, and today the flooding problems are much worse because the water flows downstream much faster. I'm sure my ancestors never realized that one day we would have to put huge sums of money back into the system to create new areas for the river to flood – areas that existed naturally before they eradicated them.' But he was forgiving. 'Nobody can see the problems future generations will face. We always have to solve the problems that we confront in our own generation.'

In his final years, Paul heard the call of the wild in Scotland, where he bought Letterewe, the country's largest foreign-owned estate. Scotland used to have wolves and lynx, and he thought they should be returned. 'Scotland has ratified treaties promising to bring back extinct wildlife. I helped bring back the white-tailed eagle to Scotland. Why not the wolf?' He never saw it happen. I find that sad. But local opposition was strong, and even he could not imagine a reintroduction without local support. It would be a fitting tribute to his influence if his wish were fulfilled. But I rather doubt it will happen.

With a Scottish estate, a Dutch castle, all those African parks, not to mention a chunk of English downland famous for its orchids, which did he like most? 'The best for me is sitting under a thorn tree in Africa,' he said. 'We have spoiled so much of Europe. Have you noticed how we rarely see the Milky Way here? There is too much light pollution. When I'm in Africa I see it every night. What is economic development when you can't see the stars?' Well, I think he did see the stars. And good for him.

Part Eight

My Species and Saving the Planet

31

Close Shave: Why We Are All the Children of Toba

It was the night the human race almost died. A night colder than any known for a million years – a night that lasted a thousand years. And when it ended, *Homo sapiens*, the newest hominid on the planet and already its most accomplished globetrotter, was reduced to maybe 2,000 people, scattered around campfires in East Africa. That's fewer members of our species left alive than died on 9/11; fewer than live in the prison down the road from me – or the village where I grew up.

We could all have been wiped out on the sunless plains. And then who would have inherited the Earth? Those hairy, low-brow Neanderthals in their caves across Europe? Or the dwarf 'hobbits', whose remains were recently unearthed on an Indonesian island? Or even the founding fathers of humanity, *Homo erectus*? In the event, it was *Homo sapiens*, the naked apes, who swept all before us, and ultimately eliminated our rivals. And some believe that the long, dark night was the making of us. That it was then that we discovered our soul. That we emerged in the dawn as artists and religious people; as fashion victims and technologists and conquerors.

What happened that night? It was 73,000 years ago, and a great carbuncle on the Earth's surface exploded. Mount Toba, a volcano on the Indonesian island of Sumatra, erupted. Toba is right on a geological faultline known as the Sunda Arc, the most volatile region of the Earth's crust. We have heard from the Arc more recently. The Boxing Day tsunami of 2004, which killed a quarter of a million people, began with an earthquake along the Arc. The island of Krakatoa exploded here too in 1883. But that was nothing compared to the day Mount Toba erupted.

Molten rock from deep inside the Earth had been welling up inside Toba for more than half a million years. Slowly the pressure built and the geological pus accumulated, lifting the mountain ever higher. Until one day it gave way. It is hard to imagine the scale of what happened. Geologists believe it was the largest volcanic eruption on the planet during the past 25 million years. Toba ejected into the upper atmosphere an estimated 800 cubic kilometres of fine ash – 4,000 times more tiny bits of shattered mountain than came out of Mount St Helens in 1980, and fifty times more than Krakatoa managed. In the wake of the ash came 3,000 cubic kilometres of lava, gushing from the hole created in the Earth's crust by the explosion – enough to fill 200 Grand Canyons. Last but not least, 10 billion tonnes of sulphur particles, and 100 billion tonnes of water vapour gushed out, combining in the stratosphere to make sulphuric acid.

Today, Toba's ground zero is a massive scar called Lake Toba, 100 kilometres long and 30 kilometres wide. It has largely filled with the rainwater. But in the middle is a large island – the first sign of the next accumulation of volcanic material. A few tens of thousands of years from now, it will cause the next mega-eruption. Toba could yet be the end of us. And it is little more than luck that we are here to contemplate the matter.

The heaviest debris fell to Earth soonest. Within hours it was raining so much rock on Malaysia that a layer of ash formed as high as a three-storey house. And 3,000 kilometres away in India, geologists have measured Toba debris 6 metres thick in places. But much of the debris stayed in the air and blotted out the sun across most of the planet, creating an instant 'volcanic winter'. Temperatures fell by many degrees Celsius and stayed there. In eastern Canada, on the other side of the planet, temperatures seem to have fallen by 10 or 15 degrees.

The man who has pieced together this story of global disaster is Stanley Ambrose, an anthropologist at the University of Illinois. His best guess is that the most intense phase of the volcanic winter persisted for about six years, and that a sulphurous smog and dust storms kept temperatures cool for some decades longer. But that wasn't the end. The smog lasted long enough for the cold to trigger growth in the ice caps. Ice and snow are white and reflect the sun's heat. So, even after the smog had cleared, the planet stayed cold. The Earth had begun a brief but intense ice age, which lasted about 1,000 years. The loss of vegetation caused massive soil erosion. Dust storms raged round the world. Planet Earth would have been an extremely inhospitable place.

Not all researchers, it should be said, agree with all this. But Toba undoubtedly exploded in the way Ambrose describes. And the evidence that this created a cataclysmic global event is strong. We know from Greenland ice cores that there was a massive burst of acid rain, also that there were widespread global dust storms and armadas of icebergs infesting the North Pacific. The millennium after Toba was probably the coldest in the last million years. And, critically for the four hominid species inhabiting the Earth at the time, it happened literally overnight. No time to prepare; no time to move to somewhere warmer, or even lay in a store of food. On the day before Toba erupted, hominids were quite well established on at least three continents. On the day after, the very survival of these species was under threat.

Who were they? There was *Homo erectus*, who had left Africa and walked the plains of Asia almost 2 million years before. He had seen out more than a dozen ice ages. There were the hunched and hairy Neanderthals, in caves from Europe to Siberia. And *Homo floresiensis*, the tiny people dubbed hobbits, on the Indonesian island of Flores, just east of Toba. And there was *Homo sapiens*, the newest and nakedest species, who had emerged out of Africa about 70,000 years before Toba.

On the day Toba blew, these tribes of hominid hunters and gatherers would have been confronted by a world in which temperatures plunged, hot volcanic ash rained down, the plants were dead and animals were dying all around. The first hours were the worst. As Michael Rampino, an earth scientist at New York University, puts it: 'Breathing in volcanic ash is like breathing in tiny needles. It combines with the moisture in your lungs to make a kind of cement that pops the blood vessels. Basically you choke to death.'

For those that survived, the next problem was food. Once the carrion was gone, hominids were in trouble. Stone tools for cutting and gouging and killing were useless without anything to cut, gouge or kill. Many died where they stood. Possibly nobody from any human species survived in large parts of Asia. The Neanderthals from the north probably did best. They lived furthest from the volcano and, being short, stocky, barrel-chested and hairy, were best adapted to survive in cold climates. The hobbits, though small in number, may have survived through living just upwind of Toba, missing the worst of the initial debris as the volcano exploded. Likewise, *Homo erectus* lived on.

But the interesting case is *Homo sapiens*. The naked ape evolved in Africa during the long warm era before Toba, but had spread widely through the Middle East and Europe, and probably also around the shores of the Indian Ocean. *Homo sapiens* hated the cold. Being naked was an adaptation to help him hunt on the hot plains of tropical Africa. Now it left him vulnerable. All the archaeological evidence is that most *Homo sapiens* died hungry and shivering in the days after Toba exploded. Some survived – we know because we are here. But probably not many.

Genetics experts have long been perplexed about why the

near-7 billion of us, though superficially different and composed of a number of races, are genetically almost identical. Spookily so. This is partly because we all evolved from a single individual – dubbed mitochondrial Eve after her genetic identifier – who lived about 160,000 years ago, probably in Ethiopia. But DNA analysis shows that there must have been another, much later, date when we were reduced to a small group of individuals. And even before they heard of Toba, the experts had dated that genetic bottleneck at around 70,000 years ago. Ambrose was the man who first proposed that Toba created the bottleneck from which our ancestors emerged to rule the world. And he hypothesized that the survivors from this global catastrophe found refuge in a few isolated hide-aways in equatorial Africa.

Northern Tanzania is a good bet for our crucial refuge, says Ambrose. It may have been our ancestral home. Certainly, caves there have been occupied by *Homo sapiens* for most of the last 100,000 years. And the mountains to the east, including Mount Kilimanjaro, the highest in Africa, would have shielded anyone in their lee from the first ash clouds.

For forty or so generations, *Homo sapiens* hung in there. Perhaps as one group; more likely as a series of tiny isolated tribes. What saw us through? At that time we were not markedly different from our fellow hominids. Before Toba you would have been hard-pressed to identify *Homo sapiens* as obviously superior to the Neanderthals, for instance. Both species had fire, maybe primitive language, probably wore rudimentary clothing and ritually buried their dead. We may have interbred at times. But the initial disastrous decline of *Homo sapiens* after Toba might suggest that we were an inferior species, less able to adapt than our rivals. That must have been how it looked at the time. But it is not how things turned out in the longer run. Why?

Ambrose argues that something changed in us during the long Toba winter. We evolved, not genetically but culturally and perhaps psychologically. We became very different from our cousins – and much more adept at making our way in the world. Like some prolonged version of the Biblical stories of tortured souls spending forty days and forty nights in the wilderness, we seem to have emerged transformed. In our case, it took forty generations. Ambrose reckons that the harsh conditions 'selected strongly for an unprecedented degree of social cooperation.' We united in adversity.

Paradoxically, our near-extinction in a suddenly hostile environment forced us to cooperate in larger groups than before. And that change seems to have become embedded in a new culture. The cowboys and misfits and loners perished. Only the smartest and most socially organized survived. By drawing together round the campfires during that long, dark volcanic night, we both survived till the dawn and turned ourselves into people who could adapt to the changing environment around us. Before Toba, we looked different to Neanderthals but acted much the same as they did. Afterwards, we acted very differently. As the climate began to improve and our numbers grew, small foraging groups became larger societies that retained the new skills of cooperation, and prospered as a result.

We had other attributes. We were sociable, witty, cultured, musical, superstitious, belligerent, adaptable and innovative. By the fires in our caves, we developed art. Not just hunting scenes, but abstract and beautiful designs – signifying abstract and aesthetic thoughts. Soon we were using new tools to make small sculptures, inspired perhaps by our new aesthetic sensibilities. We learned to make and play musical instruments – which is both technologically clever and artistically unambiguous. We became recognizably the people we like to believe we are today.

Critics of Ambrose's hypothesis say there is evidence of *Homo sapiens* developing new sensibilities before Toba. For instance, ancient shell beads, painted with red ochre and dated at 80,000 years old, have recently been found in Moroccan caves. This suggests an artistic and aesthetic life. Chris Stringer, the human origins expert at London's Natural History Museum, says humans displayed 'widespread symbolic behaviour' before Toba. Maybe so. But Ambrose's case is that the Toba winter acted as a crucible which allowed, indeed demanded, that these attributes be developed. It created a cultural 'big bang' in which disparate useful traits came together to forge a new set of sensibilities. It was the makeover that was the making of us.

His narrative fits the facts. The remains of *Homo sapiens* in the Rift Valley of Ethiopia, Kenya and Tanzania and elsewhere reveal that our technological and social innovation was much faster after the dark millennium. The old skill of making stone tools, which all hominids (and even some chimpanzees) had practised for millions of years, moved on by leaps and bounds. Soon after 70,000 years ago, the first microliths appeared. These are small flakes and blades that are highly specialized for different jobs and made from antlers and bones and ivory as well as stone.

Ambrose says we developed these specialized tools because we were learning how to plan and anticipate tasks. And after Toba, our new tribes, with their newly acquired social skills, swapped objects and tools and ideas much more freely than their suspicious predecessors. Systems of exchange speeded up the spread of new ideas. No other hominids did this, it seems. Invention and exchange also allowed us to adapt to changing climate and other problems much faster. We came to be much more in charge of our destiny. We were for the first time proficient networkers, even the first globalizers. Modern man was on his way.

As the climatic impact of Toba abated, the new-look, super-adaptive *Homo sapiens* fanned out, pushing back our rivals and reclaiming former territories. Some groups headed back east, round the shores of India to the islands of Indonesia, where they would have become reacquainted with previous colonists, *Homo erectus* and the mysterious hobbits. But they pressed on, arriving in Australia as early as 60,000 years ago.

Other groups went north, through the Middle East into Central

Asia. From there, one branch followed what later became the silk road to northern China and Siberia, where they may have domesticated dogs to help them hunt the local mammoths. Another branch went west into Europe, probably reaching the British Isles, the very edge of the known world, around 30,000 years ago. Footprints found on the shore of an ancient lake in Mexico suggest that by around then *Homo sapiens* also became the first hominid to reach the New World.

This colonization was partly a resumption of our wanderlust prior to Toba. But there was more to it. For, as we went, the planet was again sliding into a new ice age – this time caused by celestial forces rather than a volcano. But far from suffering in the cold, the naked ape seems to have thrived. Even during the coldest period of the ice age, around 20,000 years ago, we continued to make headway. This is extraordinary. Our physical attributes, ideal for Africa, remained apparently hopeless for colder regions. *Homo sapiens* should have been in a bad way. The Neanderthals, already long-established residents outside the tropics and physically suited to the cold, should have seen us off.

And yet it was just then that the Neanderthals appear to have breathed their last, while *Homo sapiens* swept on. It is still disputed why Neanderthals disappeared. One theory, that they might have simply merged with *Homo sapiens* through interbreeding, now seems unlikely. More likely, we used our new social attributes to make the most of our survival skills. And, as resources diminished, we may have used our new prowess with technology to wage war on the Neanderthals. There is no direct evidence for this, though everything we know about ourselves today suggests it is all too likely.

In any event, the Neanderthals met their end. And they were not alone. By the time the ice age ended about 10,000 years ago, all our cousins were gone. *Homo erectus* (last heard of in Java), the Neanderthals and even the hobbits were gone. Only *Homo sapiens*, the upstart from Africa, the naked ape in a cold climate, had survived. And in increasingly large numbers. The few thousand, at best, who survived Toba had grown to an estimated 10 million by the time the ice sheets retreated. Our time had come. The children of Toba had inherited the Earth.

What does this mean? Why tell this story in this book? Well, because it seems to me to define who we are as a species. We all want to know where we came from and what made us as we are. Toba and its aftermath seems to tell a story about us, about who each one of us is, and why we act as we do. It also offers some other lessons. About how, whatever our fears about man-made environmental change, we are all ultimately at the whim of the great uncontrollable forces of nature. But also about how we were forged in a crucible of adversity – climatic adversity – in which we learned to adapt, not just technologically but in our social and cultural behaviour.

What does this mean for our present predicament? Our planet is certainly in trouble, and us with it. More than 6 billion of us cannot fail to leave a dangerously large imprint. We consume 40 per cent of all the plant growth on the planet, a third of the marine life and half of the available freshwater. We have halved the geographical extent of most natural ecosystems, from wetlands to rainforests to grasslands. Our pollution has tripled the amount of nitrogen that nature has to process each year, and doubled the amount of sulphur. We have added more than a third to atmospheric levels of carbon dioxide, the planet's thermostat. We are running down her resources, like soil and clean water, as certainly as if we were running up a credit-card bill. The planet's very life-support systems are under threat.

I want to put faith in the children of Toba, with their survival genes. These are traits that may stand us in good stead as we face our own modern, man-made environmental crisis. The story of Toba suggests that, as a species, we are very vulnerable to climate change. But also that we are capable of reinventing ourselves to make it through. Once a survivor, always a survivor.

32

Good News from Africa: Why We *Can* Feed the World

It must be true. We've been told it so many times. The over-farmed and over-grazed soils of Africa, especially on the fringes of the Sahara, are losing their fertility and eroding away. As the population grows, poor farmers are mining the last goodness from their land. Their animals graze the grasslands away to nothing and the desert sands move in. Environmentalists say it; development economists say it; politicians say it; soil scientists say it.

'An area the size of Somalia has become desert over the past 50 years. The same fate now threatens more than one-third of the African continent,' according to the UN Food and Agriculture Organization. 'The main cause is mismanagement of the land.' Its sister body, the UN Environment Programme (UNEP), claims that 900 million Africans face starvation as their soils crumble away. UNEP masterminded a UN Desertification Convention in 1996 in an effort to reverse the trend.

But out in the shimmering heat of arid Africa, where tens of millions of farmers scratch a living from the soil, new research suggests that this apocalyptic vision is little more than a mirage. Farmers are finding ways to grow more without destroying their soils. Farm yields are often up, not down. Soils are often getting better, not worse. Fast-growing populations continue to be fed. In places, the desert sands are even retreating. Indeed, for most places at most times, the whole notion of desertification makes no sense.

This rosy picture is not always true, of course. Droughts can still be devastating. And the case of Darfur, the blighted western province of Sudan, is evidence of the combined effects of dry weather, fragile soils and civil war. But consider, on the other side of the equation, the dusty desert margins of northern Nigeria around the ancient caravan city of Kano. Here, population density has soared to levels similar to Belgium, and some 85 per cent of the land is now cultivated. Rainfall is declining, thanks to government incompetence the availability of chemical fertilizer has fallen by 80 per cent, and only the richest farmers can afford high-yielding grain varieties or irrigation. The poor make do with small scraps of sandy soils. Surely these fields should be turning to dust as yields plummet, hunger spreads and refugees head for the cities?

But that's not what I saw when agricultural scientist B. B. Singh, who heads the Kano office of the International Institute of Tropical Agriculture, drove me through the area. The dusty roadsides between the closely spaced villages were busy with fruit and vegetable stalls and behind them the fields were already green with bushes laden with the first black-eyed peas of summer.

We visited Ado, a farmer who tended a 2-hectare plot on the outskirts of Badume village, 50 kilometres north-west of Kano. Ado was exultant. The previous year, he had harvested just two bags of peas from his plot. This year, he got seven bags for the same effort. He had a good sorghum harvest too. Ado took me behind the high mud walls of his compound to an inner sanctum where the reasons for his new-found success were bleating. He used to let his sheep roam free. Now he had half a dozen tethered here, munching away at straw left over from his fields and creating a large pile of manure to fertilize the next crop.

Sheep manure is transforming Ado's life. 'Now I can send my

three children to school,' he said. 'The boys will become farmers, but I want my daughter to become a doctor.' His neighbour Galadima was doing the same thing on his 6 hectares. 'Crops grow much better with manure,' he told me. 'I don't use chemical fertilizer at all now.' His two wives and eighteen children came running out of the house and lined up for a family photo. They all looked well fed.

Singh's researchers confirm Ado's interpretation. But there's another reason for Ado's success, he said. The black-eyed peas are leguminous crops that fix nitrogen from the air and deposit it in the soil. It is the manure plus the legumes that have made Ado's soils so productive. And the same formula is common in the region around Kano, says Frances Harris, a soil scientist at Kingston University in Surrey. 'The zone is supporting intensive cultivation without suffering from land degradation. The key is the integration of crops and livestock, because it enhances nutrient cycling.' Legumes and manure put back what the grain crops take out.

As a result, the Kano region, though arid, is the most agriculturally productive part of Nigeria. Yields of sorghum, millet, cowpeas and groundnuts are increasing despite reduced rainfall. All this in a region where many experts believe only expensive irrigation systems can produce worthwhile crops. Back in his small office in a back street of Kano, Singh is adamantly optimistic. 'Even less than three hundred millimetres of rain is enough for good crops. We can double yields here easily and improve the environment at the same time. And we can do it all over Africa.'

Harris makes another point – far from being a liability, the high local population densities around Kano are essential to this form of intensive rain-fed farming. In a land where tractors are rare, people provide the labour to tend fields, feed animals and spread manure. The old environmental shibboleth that rising populations trigger soil abuse and desertification is being turned on its head here. As is the idea that livestock are an environmental curse. Far from it. More people and more livestock mean the land can be looked after better.

All this would be a mere curiosity if the Kano story was a

one-off. But similar stories are emerging from all along the Sahara's edge, from Niger and Senegal, Burkina Faso and Kenya. A region that a generation ago was being written off as doomed to desertification is recovering. David Niemeijer, an environmental geographer from Wageningen University in The Netherlands, has spent more than a decade studying the soils of eastern Burkina Faso. 'I went there expecting to find widespread land degradation, especially in the most densely populated areas,' he says. After all, the area had seen a decline in rainfall and a tripling of population over forty years. 'But there was no evidence of land degradation connected to human activities. Nor was there any decline in farm productivity. In fact, yields of many crops had risen sharply.' When he compared soil fertility today with data collected during a French survey in the late 1960s, he found no evidence of decline. No surprise, surely, when Burkina Faso produced 36 per cent more food at the end of the 1990s than at the start.

So, what are the farmers doing right? They are erecting low walls of stone and earth to keep soil from washing off sloping land in the occasional heavy downpours. They are spending more time weeding and thinning crops. They are adding manure. And they are managing the land better, forming gangs to tend each others' fields during busy times, and lending and borrowing land, livestock and farm equipment. 'Of course life remains hard,' says Niemeijer. 'These farmers are still never sure if they can feed their family, and they are not always in control of their destinies. But things are not going down the drain.'

Caution is clearly warranted. In 2001, I interviewed Boubacar Yamba of the University of Abdou Moumouni in Niger. He told me a similar story of revival from the Maradi district in southern Niger. Desertification had gone into reverse, he said. Well, maybe so. But in 2005, Maradi district was at the centre of famine in Niger. The desert margins remain perilous places; but they always have been. The question is whether they are doomed to deteriorate, and the evidence is that they are not.

Perhaps the best-researched example comes from Kenya. Sixty years ago, British colonial scientists wrote off the eroding, treeless hillsides of the drought-prone Machakos district of Kenya, east of Nairobi. Soil inspector Colin Mather called the bare hills 'an appalling example' of environmental degradation. The local Akamba people, he said, 'are rapidly drifting to a state of hopeless and miserable poverty and their land to a parched desert of rocks, stones and sand.' Similar reports came in the 1950s.

There have certainly been bad times. But, even though Machakos's population has risen fivefold since the 1930s, most years these hills are greener, less eroded and far more productive today than before. Farm output per hectare is ten times what it was in the 1930s and five times what it was in the 1960s. There are more trees. And with tens of thousands of kilometres of terraces dug on steep hillsides, erosion rates are probably at an all-time low.

According to Michael Mortimore, a British geographer who has written extensively about Machakos, the Akamba responded to the environmental crisis half a century ago by switching from herding cattle to settled farming. This gave them the incentive – and their rising population gave them the labour – to work the land properly, digging terraces, controlling weeds and collecting water in ponds for irrigation.

Every farmer seems to have his or her own story of innovation. On the road out of Machakos town, I dropped in on Jane Ngei, who had used an ox plough, spade and wheelbarrow to dig her own small dam to catch the rainwater that ran down the road past her farm. With bucket and perforated hose, she uses the water to irrigate a couple of hectares of vegetables, maize and fruit trees. The Akamba farmers are reaping the rewards of improvements like these, selling vegetables and milk to Nairobi, mangoes and oranges to the Middle East and avocados to France. The people of this area are also among those smallholders who are growing green beans for air-freighting to Britain, as we saw in Chapter 10 with no evident damage to their environment. Rather the contrary. The income is encouraging them to keep up maintenance of their terraces and irrigation channels.

Machakos is just a couple of hours from Nairobi, home of the UN Environment Programme, which still maps much of the district as on the verge of desertification. Yet when I asked, they said they had never sent anyone to research the reality. Other experts are starting to question the sweeping claims of environmental decline still being made by UNEP and other UN agencies.

Camilla Toulmin, head of the International Institute for Environment and Development in London, and a leading drafter of the Desertification Convention a decade ago, now admits that 'evidence for soil fertility decline stems from a few highly influential studies of land degradation in Africa, which have been quoted over and over again.' Much of the desertification story, she says, doesn't stand up to investigation on the ground.

Researchers tend to visit the desert margins so rarely that they have little history to back up their guesses about environmental processes, says Niemeijer. 'Every piece of degraded land has been seen as evidence of destructive human activity. But when we asked farmers about degraded land near their villages, they generally said it had been there a long time and was a natural feature.'

Deserts did advance in Africa during the droughts of the 1970s and 1980s. But if bad farming was to blame and the processes of 'desertification' were unstoppable, why does the Sahara retreat during years of higher rainfall? Mortimore says the image of desertification caused by human activity has become an 'institutional fact', too important for careers and reputations to be lightly dropped.

The truth is not that farmers never destroy soils, nor that deserts never advance, but that there is rarely anything inevitable or irreversible about the process – and that horror stories may misrepresent the reality. Even when soils have been in decline, as in Machakos, farmers have shown themselves capable of turning the tide. Moreover, it seems that even rapid growth of population can be a spur to change, rather than a curse.

*

The arid lands are only part of the story, of course. Even if poor people living in marginal environments can feed themselves, and maybe sell a few beans to Britain, it doesn't mean that the world as a whole can feed itself. Especially when half the world lives in cities. But there is good news here, too. Over the past four decades, worldwide food production has more than kept pace with the doubling of world population. There is currently an average of 2,800 calories of food available each day for every human on the planet – a quarter more per head than half a century ago. There is enough to feed everyone.

Moreover, there is potential slack in the system. It takes 2 kilos of grain to produce one kilo of chicken, 4 kilos for a kilo of pork or 7 kilos for a kilo of beef. So if only a third of the cereals fed to livestock were put instead on to human plates, the per-capita calories available daily would rise to 3,000. That is unlikely to happen; meat eating is growing fastest in developing countries. But it none the less shows the potential in the world's food supply system.

There are huge problems. The rich countries, with a quarter of the world's population, still take almost half of the world's agricultural products, largely because they convert more crops to meat. In Africa overall, agricultural productivity has actually gone down since the 1960s, while the population has continued to rise. Key crops like cassava and bananas are suffering ever more from diseases. The African bush is emptying of bushmeat, and the world's oceans are emptying of fish, both because of over-exploitation. A billion people are malnourished. The problem is now contributing to at least a third of child deaths round the world.

But all these problems have as much to do with the world trade system and bad government as with absolute shortages. Even when outright famines occur, there are usually stockpiles of food close to the starving. Even the food price rise of 2007 and 2008 does not change these basic facts. The issue is at root one of poverty rather than a global shortage of food. The starving are too poor to buy it or are cut off from it by conflict or persecution.

In some parts of the world, the critical problem is not a shortage of land but of labour. In parts of AIDS-torn Africa there is nobody to tend the land, and good fields are returning to bush. And in others, the problem is a shortage of water. But even here, there are often cheap technical solutions at hand that could allow farmers (the biggest users of water in most countries) to grow twice and sometimes four times as much food with the same amount of water in many places. The problems are not technical, and often not even economic. They are political and social – how to ensure that what needs to be done gets done. And to ensure that, where necessary, growing food has priority over growing resource-hungry but lucrative export and non-food crops like cotton and – potentially the biggest threat of all – biofuels.

But one thing gives me grounds for optimism. The sheer ingenuity of people. Farmers, in my experience, are among the most resourceful and inventive people in the world. I can see it on the fringes of the Sahara, where local farmers seem to know much more than the doom-mongers of the international community. And I see it too in the cities of the world. For people living in cities are growing huge amounts of food. By some estimates one meal in every five served round the world is grown within city limits. I begin to believe that, far from urbanization being a threat to food production, it is a spur to it. Large local populations, easily accessed at every roadside, mean that urban farmers have ready markets among people with the cash to buy. And they respond by meeting that demand.

In Kolkata, India, I have seen old waste dumps where 20,000 people farm the rich compost left behind by the city's garbage, and ponds full of sewage effluent where carp are raised in profusion. In Havana, there are market gardens growing organic produce on every patch of wasteland. In Lima, they raise guinea pigs for meat in squatter settlements. In Nairobi, chickens fatten in coops bolted to apartment walls. In Port-au-Prince, Haiti, people grow vegetables in old truck tyres, baskets and even kettles. In Moscow, scientists grow vegetables in their laboratory grounds as they wait for the pay cheque that never comes. Sheep graze the roadside verges of the Armenian capital Yerevan.

An estimated 800 million urbanites – a quarter of the urban population of the planet – spend some time each week tending to food plants. In some cities, farming is the biggest industry. Most of the poultry, pork and vegetables eaten in cities are grown within the city limits. In Bangkok, 60 per cent of the land is devoted to farming. In Greater London the figure is 8 per cent. In Bogotá, farming provides fifty jobs per hectare – more than a supermarket. Cairo has 80,000 livestock. Hong Kong produces two-thirds of its own poultry, a sixth of its pigs and half its vegetables. In Shanghai, about a third of the land within the city is used for agriculture, and almost a million inhabitants still work on the land. The city produces virtually all its own milk and eggs and most of its own vegetables, as well as much of its meat and 2 million tonnes of grain a year.

In Europe, urban agriculture is synonymous with allotments, where ageing city-dwellers grow their potatoes and onions on a strip of public land between the railway line and the gas works. But today there are long waiting lists to acquire a plot. Allotments are tended by over a million people in Britain alone, and many of them are young. For the rich world, growing your own is in part a luxury and a welcome change from supermarket shopping. For the poor in shanty towns, or in cities where services are breaking down, it is often done out of necessity. For others it is simply a good commercial opportunity. High demand means that urban farmers can make bigger profits than their country cousins. They often invest in novel systems for maximizing yields on tiny plots. Hydroponics, a system in which roots are suspended in a liquid growing medium, is popular in places as diverse as Singapore, Montreal and Bogotá. Because there is no need for soil, hydro-ponics is also great for rooftop gardens.

'Urban farming is often disparaged as being merely "kitchen gardening", or marginalized as a leftover of rural habits. But it goes far beyond gardening,' says Jac Smit, president of the Urban Agriculture Network run by the UN Development Programme. And it is, he says, an efficient use of resources. Typically, intensive production of vegetables in urban areas uses less than a fifth as much irrigation water and one-sixth as much land as mechanized rural cultivation.

City farmers even have free fertilizer in the form of human sewage. The distribution of night soil by bucket – once a fixture of urban life from Paris and London to Beijing – is rare now. However, some 10 per cent of the world's irrigated food crops are simultaneously watered and fertilized by the smelly stuff coming out of city sewer pipes.

Such methods can be dangerous, of course. Sewage carries disease-carrying pathogens. Leafy vegetables soak up air pollution, especially from car exhausts. Children may play in the back garden where pesticides have been sprayed. In Peru in 1992, sewage water used to irrigate urban crops helped spread cholera. And close contact with livestock such as pigs or poultry can bring diseases, including avian flu. For a long time city authorities discouraged or even banned farming in the city. But Smit says that view is changing. Recent studies in the Philippines and elsewhere have linked better child nutrition to the local production of food in urban areas. So a better approach would be to help make it safe, by educating farmers about the risks, and treating sewage to remove pathogens but leaving the nutrients, for instance.

But my point is this. Urban farming shows how people are resourceful and ingenious. In most places, and most of the time, we can and will feed the world. As B. B. Singh put it to me as we toured the farms of northern Nigeria, 'There is no reason why even Africa cannot feed itself.'

33

Beyond the Clockwork Orange: Why We *Can* Green Our Cities

A hundred years ago, the largest city in the world was London, with a population of 6.5 million. When I was born in 1951, the top dog was the world's first mega-city, New York, which had just topped 10 million people. Today there are at least twenty cities above that figure, including three each in India and China. Each of these mega-cities contains more people than the entire population of the planet at the end of the last ice age. The new world urban leader, Tokyo, has mushroomed to 34 million people. From mid-2007, for the first time in history, most people will live in cities. And most of the world's population growth is now happening in cities. There are 50 million more urbanites every year, 100 every minute.

Cities are the economic powerhouses of the world, consuming three-quarters of our resources and expelling their half-digested remains in clouds of greenhouse gases, billions of tonnes of solid waste and rivers of toxic effluent. Their environmental footprint is catastrophic. Returning the world's population to the countryside isn't an option. So if we are to protect what is left of nature, halt climate change, maintain the planet's life-support systems and improve life for the world's poor, we need a new form of city living. If the world is to save itself, the journey must start in the cities. Fortunately, the potential for green cities is huge. For cities are also the great innovators, the great investors and the great drivers of change. Better still, the sheer size and density of cities makes key tasks like recycling and banishing the car easier. Far from being polluting parasites, cities could hold the key to sustainable living.

There are no purpose-built eco-cities yet. But many cities have showcase eco-projects. For example, at the new £20-million home of Melbourne City Council in Australia, hanging gardens and water fountains cool the air, wind turbines and solar cells generate most of the electricity, and rooftop rainwater collectors supply most of the water. And Valencia on Spain's concreted Mediterranean coast has begun building a new green neighbourhood called Sociopolis, based on market gardens and ancient Moorish irrigation systems.

Other innovators are less exotic, but perhaps more important. In San Diego, refuse trucks run on methane extracted from the landfills they deliver to. Reykjavik is pioneering hydrogen-powered public transport. In Germany, they are greening the roofs of their tower blocks to grow food, encourage birdlife, collect rainfall and cool the streets below. Toronto air-conditions its buildings in summer with cold water from the depths of Lake Ontario. My city, London, has its congestion charge to end gridlock and reduce its carbon footprint. New York plans to copy it.

And the developing world isn't far behind. The southern Brazilian city of Curitiba pioneered bus-only roads, and then recruited the city's poor to recycle its garbage by offering groceries and bus passes in exchange. The air in two of south Asia's biggest and most polluted mega-cities, Delhi and Dhaka, has been transformed by switching tens of thousands of buses and motorized rickshaws to compressed natural gas. You can taste the difference.

All this is important, but tailpipe tinkering. A more fundamental think is needed. For the past century planners have designed cities as if resources like land, fuel, water and concrete were unlimited, and as if waste was something to be dumped as cheaply and as distantly as possible. Cities need a new metabolism, conserving their resources, cutting our carbon-based energy sources and mining their trash.

Let's start with the waste. The simple recycling bin should be a totem for the future city. Then, sewage needs rebranding as a feed-stock, returning plant nutrients to the land to grow more food. And liquid effluent, suitably cleaned up, needs a makeover as the new drinking water. We must 'close the loop', recycling metals, paper, glass, plastic and food leftovers.

It is common to think of rich countries as the recycling pioneers. But actually developing countries are generally better at it, because resources are expensive, while labour is cheap. Chinese street sweepers get paid a tenth of the salaries they could expect in Europe; yet every aluminium can they pick up and sell to a recycler has a cash recycling value the same as in Britain. Whole communities live on landfills from Manila to Mexico City, sorting through garbage for materials fit for resale. We may want to improve their circumstances, but we cannot afford to lose their services.

But the key, I think, is to maximize the virtues of cities through good urban design. Well-planned cities can boost recycling; divert waste heat from power stations to heat buildings; tap sewage to generate bio-gas; and replace cars with buses, trams and trains. The worst twentieth-century crime of urban planners was to design cities around cars. In the US, the architect Frank Lloyd Wright provided a blueprint for modern America in his 'Broadacre City', a suburban idyll of homesteads connected by an endless lattice of highways. It became a global template, stretching from Milton Keynes in the UK (once heralded as an urban 'autopia') to Brasilia, the modernist new capital that Brazil built in the bush in the 1950s.

The Frank Lloyd Wright generation 'worshipped at the altar of the automotive god, and idealised mobility and freedom', says

Peter Hall of University College London. He is a doyen among city planners, who did his own share of worshipping. Back then, the planners thought that people would in future have no desire to live in local neighbourhoods. They would revel in the freedom provided by the car to pick and choose their neighbours from across the city. Christopher Alexander, professor of architecture at the University of California, Berkeley, saw neighbourhoods not just as irrelevant, but as 'military encampments designed to create discipline and rigidity'. The subtext was clear: socialist neighbourhoods bad, capitalist freedom good.

But the result of this infatuation was not total freedom, but gridlock, suburban blight, the ghettoization of people without cars, and burgeoning crime and social dislocation in bleak nightmarish urban landscapes. More *Clockwork Orange* than Broadacre City. Milton Keynes is a British national joke, and Brasilia is surrounded by the favelas it was supposed to replace. As a non-driver, quite at home in London, I despair at the sheer impossibility of getting round many other modern cities without a car.

So, back to the drawing board. We must unclog the cities' arteries by fighting the car's hegemony. Not just reducing its pollution and beefing up public-transport systems, but transforming cityscapes to make the car as irrelevant as Alexander imagined the neighbourhood to be. 'Even if powered by biodiesel, hydrogen or sunbeams, the private automobiles still require massive networks of streets, freeways and parking structures to serve congested cities and far-flung suburbs,' says Richard Register, founder of the campaigning organization EcoCity Builders in Oakland, California.

Eco-cities need to be a lot denser than Broadacre City. Sprawling cities like Houston in Texas use cars ten times more than compact cities like Hong Kong. So some want a world of superdense Hong Kongs. Environmental futurologist Jesse Ausubel of Rockefeller University in New York envisages a twenty-first century of high-rise cities linked by underground magnetic levitation trains, and surrounded by expanses of restored country-side. But this eco-modernism sounds like a green nightmare – 'another ruinous ideological fashion', as David Nicholson-Lord of the New Economics Foundation puts it. People don't want to live in machines. They want neighbourhoods and access to green spaces and nature.

So is there a trade-off between eco-efficiency and pleasant living? Luckily the conflict may prove more theoretical than real. Super-compact cities may not be very eco-efficient after all. The densest cities in many parts of the world burn less petrol but run up huge air-conditioning bills to offset the heating effect from the closely packed forests of buildings. Stone, concrete and asphalt absorb more solar energy, and reflect less, than natural surfaces such as grass, water and trees. Air-conditioning systems themselves also give off heat, while tall buildings cut down the cooling winds. Super-dense cities cook. In summer, Hong Kong uses more energy to air-condition buildings than for anything else.

This urban 'heat-island effect' can be reduced by cutting direct sunlight through windows, increasing ventilation, cooling the air with water fountains and trees, even by painting buildings white. But the best solution is to get the urban density right: high enough for efficient public transportation, but low enough to minimize the heat island. Compact, low-rise cities such as London or Paris or Copenhagen seem to work best.

I hadn't realized that I have been living in an eco-city all along. And of course I have not. But London is a city better able to green itself than most. And now a group of architects dubbed the 'new urbanists' want to create green cities that people will want to live in, by building neighbourhoods with eco-efficient houses and low-rise apartment blocks, linked by wide boulevards with tramways down the middle and cycle lanes down the side, with roadside cafés and parks and Metro stations all within walking distance. A bit like the nicer parts of London, in fact. Or Paris, almost everybody's favourite city.

The eco-efficient city can also be a green and social place to live. Perhaps, says Hall, that is why rich people go green. He says once people have sufficient wealth and time, they go back to riding bikes and taking the train and sitting in cafés in pedestrianized city centres – and not having to drive everywhere. 'The shift backwards to neighbourhoods where the car is banished is happening most in the most affluent cities. You might say they can afford it. But it also shows that is what people want.'

But being green need not be a preserve of the rich. Another model of green living is, surprisingly enough, the shanty town. Remember Severina in Rio? Shanty towns are self-built by millions of people in the developing world, without a planner in sight. But they meet many of the ideals of eco-designers. They are high-density but low-rise; their lanes and alleys are largely pedestrianized; and many of their inhabitants recycle waste materials from the wider city. This is small-footprint living. And they have nooks and crannies that harbour wildlife. There may be sewage in the lanes, but there are few more diverse ecosystems than a ramshackle, chaotic favela. So perhaps something can be taken from the chaos and decentralized spontaneity of shanties, and combined with a designer eco-city. That would be my ideal city.

The rethink should go further. Twentieth-century planners saw no place in cities for growing food, or for untamed wildlife. Sure, they had 'green lungs', but these were sanitized parks and golf courses. Some blueprints for eco-cities today have similar failings. But in past centuries, cities kept large areas of land close at hand to supply fresh vegetables. In London it was the Lea Valley. And less formally, urban agriculture is still alive and well round the world, as we saw in the last chapter. If we are all urbanites now, maybe we are all destined to be part-time farmers, too. And why not? Sometimes it will be done out of pleasure, sometimes out of necessity, and sometimes for profit. Simple market forces ensure that farms in cities get good prices.

Cities can also be havens for wildlife. I live close to the River

Thames in London. All along the river, old industrial sites and their riverside wharfs have been abandoned. The derelict land is now being cleaned up and planted with upmarket apartment blocks. Greens love this. Friends of the Earth calls on the government 'to act to allow polluted land to be cleaned up for the benefit of future generations'. It demands that ministers set a target for 75 per cent of new housing to be on 'brownfield' sites. And the government is keen to deliver. One of the first promises from Gordon Brown after he became prime minister in 2007 was to build 'eco-cities' on brownfield sites across the country.

But hold on. Less than a mile from where I live, a small brownfield site is being redeveloped. It used to be called Gargoyle Wharf, an oil-storage depot close to Wandsworth Bridge. Greens regarded the site as a toxic wasteland. But the plants thought differently. And for a while after the depot was demolished, it was London's top site for flowers. 'We found more than three hundred species of flowering plants there,' says Nick Bertrand of the London Wildlife Trust. 'It was one of the most fantastic sites I've ever been to.' But no environmental campaigners came to its defence. In the end, everyone decided to ignore the evidence of their own eyes, and development has gone ahead. Such is the power of the drive to redevelop brownfield sites.

Ecologist John Box chaired a review of Britain's urban wildlife for the UN's Man and Biosphere Programme. He says that perhaps a sixth of all official Sites of Special Scientific Interest in Britain are on old urban, industrial and mining land. This is no accident. Industry often creates unique habitats. Some are irreplaceable because they are the result of industrial processes that are no longer used. At Nob End in Bolton, the nineteenth-century Leblanc process for manufacturing soda from common salt has created alkali waste heaps where vast swamps of orchids grow. And rare meadow grasses inhabit the limestone slag heaps left by early blast furnaces in the West Midlands.

And it is not just novel post-industrial habitats that attract wildlife to the cities. Britons' attachment to living in individual houses with their own gardens is a huge biological resource. Gardens, some ecologists say, have given Britain more biodiversity than it ever had in the past. But, thanks to the inanity of planners, back gardens are now classified as 'brownfield sites' and councils get Brownie points from the government for allowing developers to build on them.

Sheer madness, and born of the fact that we persist in believing that cities are environmental badlands, while the countryside is the exclusive home of wildlife. The truth is often the opposite. Many green fields that environmentalists want to protect are ecological deserts, says Peter Shirley of the Wildlife Trusts, whose members manage many of the nation's nature reserves. 'It is not true that building on greenfield sites is always bad and building on brownfield sites is always good.' But that is exactly what has been happening. This environmental philistinism has to stop. Cities need wild places as well as green places. The sanitizing of our environment can be an enemy to nature.

Cities are evolving in many ways. Often, say urban planners, they are ceasing to be conventional cities at all. They are merging into wider urban landscapes that the French geographer Jean Gottmann has dubbed 'megalopolis'. A big question is whether this development is good or bad for the greening of cities.

Megalopolis takes over when big cities become so unwieldy that they stop growing and instead spawn archipelagoes of urban centres around them. London has spread to create an urban region across south-east England that stretches west towards Reading and Oxford, north towards Cambridge, and now east along the Thames estuary. São Paulo is embracing a 'golden urban triangle' that includes Rio de Janeiro and Belo Horizonte. The people of Mexico City have fled their congested and polluted mega-city to surrounding cities like Toluca and Cuernavaca. Kolkata has dispersed across west Bengal. Tokyo is extending out to Japan's second mega-city, Osaka, creating a megalopolis of 70 million people, linked by bullet train. Shanghai is joining hands with Suzhou, Nanjing and Hangzhou, which will soon be just twenty-seven minutes away on a new maglev train with a top speed of more than 400 kilometres an hour.

Will megalopolis encourage or destroy the dream of eco-cities? It is easy to be gloomy. But, if properly designed, megalopolis could drive the creation of greener urban environments. The emergence of large urban zones with no single centre could reduce commuting, for instance, because employment will be more dispersed. Likewise, losing the big central hub could give people a greater sense of living in neighbourhoods. Tokyo has many intimate neighbourhoods. In urban Europe people talk without affectation about living in 'villages' within their cities. Some will see Megalopolis as a monster devouring the countryside. But maybe we need to rethink that distinction and bring wild things into the urban zone, which could embrace urban agriculture and green corridors more easily than conventional mega-cities.

Some say we can look back profitably for more ideas about how to create the cities of the future. To the walled medieval cities of Europe, such as Verona. Or Venice, the ultimate carless city that eco-planners can only dream of recreating. Or even the ancient cities of China. Suzhou, I noticed, is taking great pains to preserve its old walled gardens and waterways, even as it builds the brave new world beyond.

I pondered this as I spent an afternoon with Ma Cheng Liang, a man in charge of redeveloping Shanghai in a greener mould, including building a new purpose-built eco-city on an island in the Yangze delta. He outlined for me his many plans for 'ecological modernism' in the city. It sounded a little bleak and technocratic. More about eco-efficiency than building a place where people might want to live.

From Ma's office window, we could see below the huddled buildings of Shanghai's old town. As we talked, bulldozers were tearing down the buildings to make way for new office blocks. Ma saw this as progress. He wanted to do away with the past. Tear down the old towns and create a bright new, green, future. But to me, the old town was a dense, largely car-free enclave, mixing homes and workplaces and shops. It was a model of green design, the perfect embodiment of the dreams of the new urbanists. But he didn't see it. And still the bulldozers came.

34

Zero Carbon: Why We *Can* Halt Climate Change

The threat from global warming is greater than usually claimed. In my last book, *The Last Generation*, I explained why many scientists believe that the world faces a series of dangerous 'tipping points' that could make warming happen much faster and more violently than allowed for in reports from the Intergovernmental Panel on Climate Change, the IPCC. The threats include the runaway release of greenhouse gases from natural reservoirs like soils, forests and permafrost; the shutdown of the ocean currents and switch-off of the monsoon; and the rapid break-up of ice sheets, causing a sea-level rise of several metres within a century. All these could be unleashed as carbon dioxide levels in the atmosphere rise.

The IPCC is soft-pedalling on these doomsday scenarios in its most recent reports, because many of them are difficult to quantify and far from certain. But as one scientist put it to me, 'If you were about to board a plane and the pilot told you there was a one in ten chance of it crashing, would you still take your seat and buckle up for take-off? Yet we are doing that with the planet.' I don't know how close we might be to such tipping points. There are several decades of warming now 'in the pipeline' that are unavoidable, so we may already have passed one or more. In that sense, it could be too late. But I'll stick with the leading US climate scientist Jim Hansen, who thinks we may have a decade to turn round the supertanker. We could have longer, but you wouldn't want to bet on it.

Can we do it? Technically, absolutely. Can we do it without destroying our lifestyles? By and large, yes. As I hope the preceding chapter shows, we can have better, more fulfilling lives by adopting many green measures both personally and within the urban metabolism. And, as I will argue in the next chapter, this may be part of our coming of age as post-industrial people. There is a plethora of technologies that allow us to use energy much more efficiently and abandon generating that energy from carbon-based fuels: wind and nuclear, solar and biofuels, tidal and geothermal.

I am often asked 'What is the "greenest" form of fuel?' But I favour diversity. Biofuels are good – until we consume so much that we can no longer fill the boilers with rapeseed from Yorkshire and instead start plundering palm oil grown in the rainforests of Borneo. Wind power is good unless we cover every hilltop in the country with turbines. Tidal and wave power are good, but there would be an outcry about the pylons needed to bring serious megawatts from the best sites on the coasts of the north and west to the biggest markets in the south and east of the British Isles. All these energy sources are good, but in moderation.

What about nuclear? There is a conundrum here. If someone offered us the chance to use a tried and tested technology to produce up to half our electricity with very low carbon emissions, only a small impact on the environment, and with no requirement to rewire the National Grid, surely we would jump at the chance. But they did, and so far we haven't. It is nuclear power.

I have never liked nuclear power – less because of safety worries and more because I fear nuclear proliferation and the erosion of civil liberties needed to keep the technology safe. But in the face of the threat from climate change, I find it difficult to maintain my opposition. In general, I think the safety fears have been overblown by objectors to nuclear power. And it seems to me that, in the wake of 9/11, we have already lost many of those cherished civil liberties. I am quite certain that no more nuclear power stations should be built until the government has finally (after half a century of failure) come up with solutions to the big technical problems about what to do with nuclear waste. But I fear – and I do mean fear – that we may need this in our armoury as well.

Coal? It produces more carbon dioxide for a given amount of energy than any other major fuel. But maybe we need even that, if we can develop the technology to bury its emissions out of harm's way. Not otherwise, however. Coal should be banned otherwise. Everybody talks about hydrogen as the fuel that could solve all our problems. But it is not a source of energy in itself. It is just a way of storing and transporting energy. Before we can burn it we have to make it. And making hydrogen is a very energy-intensive activity. So tell me how you want to make your hydrogen and I'll tell you if I am in favour. But as a way of storing the intermittent energy from wind power and the like it could be a boon.

Maybe the future is not in centralized forms of energy generation at all. Some think that smart electricity grids of the future will allow us all to generate electricity in our backyards by any manner of means, and sell to the grid. Maybe a new generation of cheap solar cells will allow us to make our buildings out of them. Then our roofs and walls and windows could soak up the sun to give us power.

Most of these technologies are economic, with oil at its current $50-plus a barrel, or soon will be. Some are not yet quite as good as they seem, because they are themselves quite energy-intensive – think of the energy needed to make fertilizer to grow the biofuels, to build PV cells or refine the uranium fuel for nuclear power. That is one reason I would give priority to energy-efficiency measures. They are cheap, plentiful and often save money in the very short term. In many areas of life we can make huge improvements by simple and painless changes to the way we live our lives. The one area where there are no technical fixes at hand is air travel, which is the biggest source of emissions from many people with the biggest carbon footprints, including me. We simply have to give up flying as much as possible.

I don't have a magic formula for saving the world. The neatest idea I have heard is to combine burying CO_2 underground with biofuels. Biofuels soak up carbon dioxide from the air as they grow. So if you run a power station on biofuels and then bury the carbon emissions, you have built a system for sucking CO_2 out of the air and burying it back underground. That way we could even start lowering CO_2 levels in the air. And I think it makes a lot more sense than nutty schemes like shading the planet beneath a huge parasol put into space. Of course the biggest question with biofuels is whether we have the land and water to grow them as well as food. But it is an option.

Mao used to say: 'Let a hundred flowers bloom; let a hundred schools of thought contend.' Maybe that is right. There are almost too many options. Pick your own. One thing I am certain about. I just *hate* knowing that more of my electricity comes from Drax than anywhere else.

We may have to change things fast to avoid tipping points in the climate system. But maybe we will. For there could be tipping points in our political and economic and cultural systems, too. I do detect big changes afoot. Many large corporations, especially in Europe, are now actively asking for governments to set tougher targets on greenhouse gas emissions. They believe they are the quickest, smartest kids on the block, and that they can gain a market advantage over their slower rivals once the limits are in place. Not all corporations are like that, of course – and even the best will only act under strong public pressure. Yet I believe there is the potential for a 'race to the top' based in part on the profit motive. But if it is to happen, it will be because we, as customers and voters, demand it.

Some say that there is little point in the rich world getting its act together if developing countries like China, India and Brazil don't act too. They point out that China builds two new power stations every week and in 2007 became the world's biggest CO_2 emitter. Ultimately, that argument is correct. But remember this. China is the world's most populous country; you would expect it to have high emissions. Looked at per head of population, its emissions are much lower than ours. And it has been emitting them for much less time, so the amount of carbon dioxide in the atmosphere that came from China is much less than, say, from the US and will remain so for many years. If Westerners like me had carbon emissions like those of the average Chinese, there would be no climate-change problem right now.

Remember too that industrializing countries will want to manufacture energy-efficient goods to sell to the rich world. They will want to invest in the new energy technologies, not the old ones. And, increasingly, they see climate change as a threat to their own economic development. The Stern Report, published in 2006, on the economic implications of climate change made that abundantly clear. And by changing the language to recast climate as an economic, rather than a scientific or environmental issue, Stern has galvanized the world's political classes in a way that scientists and environmentalists failed to do.

My bet, at least on my more optimistic days, is that the whole world will soon be embracing a move to a low-carbon economy. It may happen with or without internationally agreed emissions targets, though I think that tough targets would make it happen faster, by increasing the economic incentives to cut emissions. The next generation may look back and wonder what the fuss was about. Maybe. I cannot guarantee it will happen. And it certainly won't happen if we sit back and assume that it will. Nor can I guarantee that it will happen before some speedy and violent tipping point in the natural world engulfs us.

Actually my greatest concerns are less about the applications of the technologies to fix climate change, which are there if we will only use them, and more about the winners and losers along the way. That is why I think the argument about Kenyan bean farmers is so important. If climate change becomes an excuse for environmental protectionism then, frankly, I hope we all fry. We have to cut our carbon emissions in ways that do not impoverish the poorest – those whose personal carbon emissions are the lowest. We need fairtraders, not green patriots. We need to maximize our positive social footprints as well as to minimize our negative ecological ones. But we can do it.

35

Defusing the Bomb: Why We *Can* Halt Population Growth – and Save the World

Some people see global population growth as the ultimate driver of our environmental predicament. There are, they say, just too many people with too many footprints. I don't want to be a people-hater, and I don't see people as 'pollution'. We are not born with original environmental sin. I am a humanist, and I think our problems today come not so much from too many footprints as from the much smaller number of large footprints. Like mine. Over-consumption rather than overpopulation is killing our planet. As Gandhi put it: there is enough for everyone's need, but not for everyone's greed. I also believe the human footprint can be good as well as bad, and we have to strive for that. But I grant you the strain of almost 7 billion footprints is profound.

Now for the good news. We can halt population growth. And we have a saviour. Her name is Isabella, or maybe Clara or Bianca – emancipated Italian women on childbirth strike. Thanks to them and a growing sisterhood round the world, the baby boom that the world has feared for half a century could be turning to a baby bust. The planet's population could be in long-term decline within another fifty years. Future generations may worry that their family tree is dying.

But let's start with Isabella and her friends. Isabella lives in Rome. She is in her thirties. She has a nice apartment, a nice job and a nice boyfriend, who still lives at home with his mother. So Isabella can see him when she likes. The last thing Isabella needs is children. She would probably have to give up the apartment. Her employers would swiftly find a younger model – and so might her boyfriend. Even if they did stay together, he would have to move in with her. He would leave a mess round the place, spend her money and be hopeless at changing nappies.

It is for such reasons that the women of Italy are making very few babies. With splendid irony, the home to the Catholic Church, with its fundamentalist opposition to artificial birth control, has the lowest fertility rate in the world. At 1.2 babies per woman, it is far below what is needed to maintain the current population.

And Italian women are not alone. In Spain, Greece, the Czech Republic and a veritable collective of former Soviet states such as Russia, Lithuania and Armenia, their sisters have fertility rates of 1.3. The average European woman has only 1.4 babies today. These are probably the lowest rates in non-suicidal populations in history. The only remotely comparable period in Europe was after the First World War, when a generation of young men were lost on the battlefields. A quarter of women went childless in the aftermath. But today there is no shortage of lusty men – only of broody women.

All this is quite a turnaround. For half a century, the world has been scared by forecasts of exponential population growth. One of the cornerstones of environmentalism has been that this demographic deluge will overwhelm the supply of resources such as food and water, while triggering rampant pollution and global warming. Such fears are not surprising. During the twentieth century, the world's population increased almost fourfold, from 1.6 billion to 6 billion. We passed 2 billion in 1927; 3 billion in 1961; 4 billion in 1974; 5 billion in 1987; and reached 6 billion in 1999. Every additional billion came faster than the last. The reason was simple:

falling death rates, especially among children, combined with continued high fertility.

The deluge is not over. Every year the world has 80 million more inhabitants. But we have now passed the point of maximum annual increase in numbers. It took twelve years to get from 5 to 6 billion; but it will take fourteen years to get to 7 billion, and perhaps three decades to reach 8 billion. This is no statistical blip. Almost since we started fearing the baby boom, women have been having fewer children. In 1950, worldwide the average woman had five children. Today she has just 2.6.

The rule of thumb among demographers is that a stable long-term population in the modern world requires each woman to have 2.1 children. The extra 0.1 is expected to compensate for girls who do not live long enough to have families. So global fertility is clearly fast falling to replacement levels. The sheer number of women of childbearing age means that cranking down population growth has a long way to go. But as the twentieth-century baby boomers age, the tide will turn. The population time bomb, the subject of a million millennial nightmares, is steadily being defused.

Looked at historically, our recent demographic surge is not so unexpected. Since the near-extinction of our species after the eruption of Toba all those tens of thousands of years ago, humanity's population has been increasing. But mostly the increase has been concentrated in a series of surges, generally following technological and cultural revolutions. The first revolution involved the complex developments post-Toba. The second revolution was the spread of agriculture and stable settlements after the end of the last ice age, 10,000 years ago. The third revolution was the Industrial Revolution, which is still working its way out round the world today. It has raised the world's population to 6.5 billion already. The key features of this revolution have been advances in food production, which have allowed the world to feed more people, and new methods of controlling diseases, which have allowed people to live longer.

The sheer scale of what has happened in the past century or so is without precedent. There seems little doubt that the twentieth century will stand out, perhaps for millennia to come, as a century of unique explosive growth in the human population. *Homo sapiens* – the naked ape with attitude and big ambitions – was at his most fecund. But demographers have long assumed that this great population surge will fizzle out during the twenty-first century, as most of the world's women settle down to a conventional Western family life with mother, father and two children.

They call this boom followed by stabilization the 'demographic transition'. It described well enough the progress until recently of the first countries to industrialize. In Europe the annual death rate declined from more than thirty deaths per thousand people in the seventeenth century to below ten today. With fertility rates initially remaining high, population growth rates in Europe at the start of the twentieth century reached a peak of around 1.5 per cent a year. Then they began to fall, as people responded to the greater survival rate among children by having fewer babies. In many developing countries, the transition has been telescoped into a few hectic decades, during which national population growth rates have often exceeded 3 per cent per year, and populations have doubled in less than twenty-five years. But the pattern remains the same.

All according to plan. Except that nobody told women about the demographers' endgame, in which fertility rates would settle down again at replacement levels. And there is a growing suspicion that Isabella and her sisters are leading the way to a different demographic future. On current trends, the world's population is primed to start diminishing for probably the first time since the Black Death in the fourteenth century. And not just in Europe. Already, more than sixty countries have fertility rates below replacement levels. The club now includes much of the Caribbean, Japan, South Korea, China, Thailand, Sri Lanka, Iran, Turkey, Vietnam, Brazil, Algeria, Kazakhstan and Tunisia. Other large developing countries, whose populations have soared in the past half-century, expect their own national fertility rates to fall below replacement levels within twenty years. They include India, Indonesia and Mexico.

A few of these countries have brought birth rates down through coercion. China's 'one child' policy is the most notorious. But that is not the situation generally. Often birth rates have plunged despite opposition from governments and religious leaders. Catholic influence has meant that the Brazilian government has been slow to develop state family planning. Even so, a third of married Brazilian women have been sterilized, and fertility has more than halved in twenty-five years, to 1.9 in 2005.

The case of Iran is even more remarkable. Despite a period of fundamentalist rule by the mullahs, fertility rates crashed from 5.5 in 1988 to just 1.8 in 2005. In late 2006, President Ahmadinejad reiterated the old mullahs' call for a home-grown baby boom, and for women to return to their 'main mission' of having babies. But he seemed out of line with both the clerics, who now back birth control, and his own administration, which runs a condom factory.

Some argue that countries stuck in poverty will buck the trend. But in practice, some of the world's poorest countries are emptying the maternity wards. Bangladeshi girls are among the least educated and most likely to marry while in their early teens. Yet they give birth to an average of just 3.1 children, half the number their mothers had. The garment workers in Dhaka and the poor women in the villages around Khulna told me without exception they were determined not to have more than two or three babies. Around half of them use contraception routinely. Provision is free, but there is no hint of compulsion.

Rich or poor, socialist or capitalist, Muslim or Catholic, secular or devout, with tough family-planning policies or none, most countries tell the same story: couples are engaged in a coital revolution. In Japan the condom is tops, in China the IUD is king, in Latin America it's sterilizing and in Europe the pill. Turkish men are reputed masters of coitus interruptus, while more trigger-happy

British males opt for vasectomies in record numbers. But however it is done, babies are out.

Why is this? Some point to urbanization. In poor rural societies, children are vital as labour in fields. But in cities, children cease to be economic assets and instead become economic liabilities – costly to educate, clothe and feed. People invest in material goods rather than children. Jack Caldwell of the Australian National University in Canberra, one of the doyens of demography, goes a step further. He argues that female emancipation is the natural social consequence of the shift from agricultural societies, built round the family unit, to the modern industrial world. 'Post-agricultural society does not need the traditional family,' he says. 'At the level of the individual, there is no necessity for either families or fertility. The individual has been freed.' In other words, the fertility crash is the logical, but previously unseen, conclusion of the demographic transition.

Perhaps so, but needs and wants can be different. Women may have children because they want them, not because they need them. The real answer may be simpler. Young women may no longer want to be wives and mothers. Tim Dyson, professor of population studies at the London School of Economics, says not having children has become a statement of modernity and emancipation. The spread of TV in particular has opened women's eyes to a whole new world, and modern birth-control methods are helping turn some of their aspirations into reality. In the modern world it is not so much literacy that leads to lower birth rates (though that certainly helps because it is a practical aid to getting on in the world), but more the flickering screen in the corner of the room that shows young women the world they could have if they could win a life away from rearing children.

Motherhood is an increasingly alien activity for many working women. As *Guardian* columnist Madeleine Bunting put it, for those who take the plunge 'motherhood hits most women like a car crash. Nothing in our culture recognises, let alone encourages, the characteristics you will need once a bawling infant has been tenderly placed in your arms.' And women have too much else to do. 'Go to rural India,' says Dyson, 'and you find that women are fed up with the men, who seem to be going nowhere. It is the women who are increasingly running the farms. It is the women who are getting jobs and taking charge. They don't have time to have children any more.' He exaggerates. But there is a new assertiveness in young women across the world that transcends the rural–urban divide.

We should not forget those parts of the world where fertility rates are not in freefall. The list is revealing. Of the thirty countries with the highest fertility rates, where five- and six-children families are still the norm, twenty-six are in Africa where death rates are often rising because of AIDS. Three of the others are Muslim states – Afghanistan, Yemen and Oman – where most women remain relatively ill-educated, in the home and cut off from outside influences. But these seem to be hold-outs. Fertility is falling fast now in Pakistan and Saudi Arabia.

Where is all this heading? Will the rest of the world's women follow the lead of Isabella and her friends in Italy? There is an alternative model. In Sweden, I met Astrid. She has two children and got a year's maternity leave when each of them was born. She works a flexible thirty-hour week and can use a crèche at the office when she needs. Her husband is a dab hand at changing nappies, and shares the 4 a.m. feeding rota.

Not surprisingly, Astrid and her friends feel more able to have a family than Isabella's crowd, who have little chance of getting part-time jobs or securing places in crèches for their children. In consequence, Sweden's fertility rate is 1.7 children per woman. That's not enough to maintain the country's population in the long term, but neither is it an Italian-style demographic meltdown. Most northern European countries have maintained higher fertility rates than countries around the Mediterranean. Norway's is 1.8; Britain and Finland notch up 1.7. The most fecund women in Europe today are the French at 1.9.

Meanwhile, in Eastern Europe fertility rates have plunged since the collapse of Communism wrecked state-funded support services for families. In Soviet times, Olga worked in a university laboratory in Moscow, where childcare was rudimentary but universal. Her family badly needed her money to make ends meet, but at least she could pursue a career. Now she says that the new private employers are not interested in providing childcare and her daughter will not be able to have children and a career.

So will the rest of the world follow northern, or southern and Eastern Europe? Isabella or Astrid? Brigitte or Olga? Caldwell thinks the signs are clear. 'Italy is the future. The Mediterranean patriarchal model is far more common in the world than the northern European model of more helpful husbands.' Conservative family values lie behind the ultra-low fertility rates among the office girls of Shanghai and Tokyo.

If Caldwell is right, then a demographic implosion is starting to unfold. If current trends persist, we will begin to see absolute falls in the indigenous populations of most industrialized countries. Italy and Hungary expect a 25 per cent drop in population, and Japan 30 per cent. Eastern Europe could lose between a third and a half of its populations by mid-century – a trend exacerbated by the 'vodka effect', which has cut male life expectancy in Russia to fifty-eight years. By 2050, Russia may have fewer people than Uganda. By 2100, Britain's indigenous population can be expected to halve, while Italy's population could crash from 58 million now to just 8 million. Germany could have fewer people than today's Berlin.

Without a sharp rise in fertility rates, only mass migration into Europe can halt this. Perhaps that is how it will play out. The new demography may create a planet of itinerants as labour becomes globalized along with capital. We already see Indian workers building Dubai, Poles in the fields of England, Chinese foresters in Siberia, Guatemalan grape-pickers and housemaids in California.

But where will the new migrants come from if global populations start to fall? Demographers are reworking their predictions for future world populations. If the world moves towards an average of 1.85 children per woman, then world population would peak at about 7.5 billion around 2050, and then fall. By 2150 there would be 5.3 billion people on the planet. But 1.85 children looks increasingly like a rather high estimate. Most countries are heading for much lower figures. If women settled for even a Swedish-style fertility level, we would be down to 3.2 billion by 2150 – roughly half today's population.

What's the big deal? A decline in the world's population sounds like a good thing. It would reduce the pressure on the planet's natural resources. The air would be cleaner, biodiversity richer, soils more fertile, climate more predictable and pollution less toxic. But a world with a falling population will be different in other ways that might be less agreeable. For one thing, the world's population will be very much older. The average age of a world citizen is around twenty-nine years today. By 2050, it will be over forty, with a fifth of the world's people over sixty. The average Japanese or Chinese will be over fifty.

A greyer world might be less innovative and more conservative. More boring, perhaps. It would be a world in which the richest countries compete for diminishing supplies of migrants. Eastern Europe, which is already suffering what the World Bank calls a 'transition from red to grey', may simply curl up and die.

So is demographic decline a 'bad thing'? When I first wrote suggesting this, I got a splendid letter from California historian Theodore Roszak. 'I can't recall an exercise in social analysis more wrongheaded,' he wrote of my article. 'On what grounds do you assume that something like our current human numbers are optimum?' I don't, as it happens, believe in any optimum number. But his main point was to sing the praises of the old. 'When there are more people above the age of fifty than below,' he wrote, 'the longevity revolution may at last offer industrial civilization the preconditions for sustainability.' We will be older, but wiser. That point I certainly take. And I concede it took an older man to point it out.

We are coming through the greatest surge in human population in our history – a change almost as profound as what happened after the eruption of Toba. And it has the potential to alter the psyche of our species as much as Toba did. Roszak's longevity revolution may be part of that. By the end of this century, *Homo sapiens* could well be more conservative, less innovative, more boring than he was in the twentieth century. But that may be no bad thing. A stable, sagacious society that has thrown off its current adolescent restlessness and settled into middle age sounds appealing. The tribal elders may take centre stage once more. We might look after our planet much as fastidious middle-aged couples look after their homes.

But we do need children, too. And there is something wrong with a society that doesn't want to produce them. There may be nothing wrong with a century or so during which fertility rates fall to 1.6. There would be a great deal wrong with a global fertility rate of 1.4 or below.

As countries seek to revive their childbearing resources, they may flirt with draconian measures, cutting women out of the workforce and keeping them at home, banning abortions, and restricting access to family-planning services. But that is unlikely to work. Women won't stand for it. Instead, Dyson says we need a continuation of the 'renegotiation' of gender roles under way across most of the world, and most advanced in northern Europe. Paradoxical as it may seem, the female emancipation that has reduced family size so dramatically in the past fifty years will need to be extended rather than dismantled if family sizes are to rise from the worst-case Italian model. It is the incompleteness of emancipation that is the problem.

As women grab their new freedoms, the most pressing need is to instil new responsibilities in men – and in the state. In most of the world today, fertility is plunging far below replacement levels because women have decided they want to become more like men. Right now that leaves little room for babies. To change that, men must take the plunge and start to become more like women: better housekeepers, better child-carers – and perhaps better custodians of the planet, too. The future of *Homo sapiens* could depend on it.

The twentieth century was tumultuous. It may go down in history as a 'golden era' of human inventiveness, but also of human folly. The party to end them all. But the twenty-first century is the century when, in the cold light of dawn, we discover if our species has the resources to live with the consequences, and put right the damage. We face the most almighty hangover, as the toxins unleashed by our century-long binge work their way through the Earth's system. We have to detoxify. We have to sober up. We have to come to grips with exactly how much damage we have done to the planet, its land and oceans and atmosphere, and figure out what it will cost to repair it. We have, in short, to grow up. Luckily, we will also be growing older. The typical world citizen will before long be in his or her forties. A time for responsibility, we can hope. So this is not elaborate metaphor, but more or less literal truth.

As we grow up, we have to feminize our society, green our society and become better custodians of the planet. There is no guarantee we will make it. We have no reason to believe that our luck will hold. We may already have done too much damage, and be doomed to see our civilizations wrecked by climate tipping points, and our numbers crashing through disease and hunger and war. But I do believe we still have the ability, and maybe the foresight, to mend our ways. Politicians talk, apparently seriously, about reducing greenhouse gas emissions by 80 per cent and more by mid-century. Global corporations are responding to real market pressures when they declare that they are going carbon-neutral and selling organic and fairly traded and environmentally certified produce. They have corporate social responsibility departments because they need them. There may be some cynicism involved, some greenwash. But I do believe that they increasingly recognize that these are jobs that have to be done.

There will be false dawns and dead ends. Maybe putting a tiny wind turbine on your roof is a silly idea. Maybe it makes more sense to incinerate your old newspaper and make some energy than to drive it across the country for recycling. Maybe mass-produced biofuels are a dumb idea. Maybe we are kidding ourselves sometimes when we buy fairtrade products and genuinely believe that they are fairly traded. But we should not make the perfect the enemy of the good. And if it doesn't happen everywhere, all the time – as it certainly won't – then we have to build on the occasions when it does. Buy the organically grown, fairly traded cotton socks and coffee. Call, like Paul von Vlissingen, for the wild, and for an end to light pollution so we can see the Milky Way again.

I think we need to remember the personal, as well as spending our time calculating carbon footprints. My journey for this book was about people as well as my environmental footprint. I cherish meeting the AIDS grannies keeping their families going in South Africa, and the one-man ethical jewellery business taking on the giant mining corporations, and the Milonge brothers recycling my old clothes, and Ranabhai who knew exactly how much better off he was growing organic cotton, and the Wonder Welders, and Ado with his sheep in Kano, and many others. I hope that some of the girls on the production line of Suzhou get to become 'queens of trash' like Cheung Yan. I hope Nellie, the flower girl, survives to see her children grow up and have a better life. I wonder whether Aisha and Miriam and Akhi will go back to their villages or stick it out in the city, whether George Tagarook will get his new fire engines and if Sammy Cheng will keep churning out mice for the world. These small pictures help make the big picture. Just as my footprint is part of the global footprint of humanity.

Humanity; our species. We are all the children of Toba. Some 70,000 years ago we almost foundered before we started. Then, our nemesis was a rogue volcano. Now it is ourselves. In every good story there is a moment of high drama. A moment when futures are sealed. When events turn on a twist of fortune or some trick of fate. When you are part of the story, it is probably hardest to know when that moment arrives. Probably most generations think that theirs is special. But we do seem to be close to the moment when the fate of *Homo sapiens* may be sealed. When we can choose to follow our good or our bad instincts. I cannot pray to a god, so perhaps I will pray to Toba that we make the right choice.

The oldest known human footprints are in the mud of Laetoli in Tanzania. They were left more than 3 million years ago by a species of humans long since extinct. We, *Homo sapiens*, have been clever enough to find and understand those footprints. No previous species on the planet could have done that. It would be a shame if our cleverness, forged in the long, dark night after Toba, were to be our undoing.

Sources and Acknowledgements

I have resisted the temptation to pepper this story with footnotes and references. Generally, like any journalist, I have indicated my sources in the text, whether they are personal observations, direct conversations or printed and online sources. Anybody, particularly students, left in doubt is welcome to contact me at Pearcefred@hotmail.com.

This was a long journey and many people provided me with personal help along the way. Some don't even know they helped; others would rather you didn't know; and still others I have, no doubt, failed to remember as I write this. But thanks anyway to the following:

At Goldfields, Willie Jacobsz was keen to get me underground, and Rob Chaplin and Melville Haupt kept me safe and informed while I was down there. Also in South Africa, HelpAge International organized my extraordinary journey among the country's AIDS grandmothers.

On Mount Kilimanjaro, John Weaver of Twin Trading was a most assiduous guide, while Simon Billing back in London swept up my later queries. Raymond Kimaro, general manager of KNCU, was welcoming and, at Cafédirect, thanks go to Katya Bobova. Harriet Lamb at the Fairtrade Foundation offered great advice and assistance at the start of my researches. Tim Morris at the Badger Brewery, Rachel Duffield at the Lighthouse Bakery and John Lister at Shipton Mill all gave their time and enthusiasm.

WWF took me to Mauritania, Alaska and Chengdu in China. In Mauritania, park ranger Antonio Araujo introduced me to desert fishers, while Pierre Campredon and Luc Hoffmann talked good sense. In Alaska, thanks especially to Denise Meredith and Pam Miller.

Iqbal Ahmed and Alec Dodgeon at Seamark may not be happy with my take on their industry, but I thank them none the less. Tutu, Dadu, Quazi Mukto and Abu Hasan Bakul all helped me in the heat of Khulna. In Dhaka, Khushi Kabir, Nazma Akter and, especially, Khorshed Alam helped me with both prawns and the rag trade. Thanks also to Bob Pokrant, Bill More and Juliette Williams.

Stefan Padulosi of the International Plant Genetic Resources Institute, now renamed Bioversity International, has been a fount of information on wild and orphan crops of all sorts. Emile Frison provided invaluable support for my researches into bananas, as did Rodomiro Ortiz on an earlier trip to his research station in the Niger delta, run by the International Institute for Tropical Agriculture. That trip, organized by Anne Moorhead of the IITA, also took me to Cameroon to explore cocoa farming in that country, where Stephan Weise was also a great help, and to Kano, where I heard B. B. Singh's views on feeding Africa.

In Kenya, Michael Mortimore, an independent-minded Africa hand in the best tradition, introduced me to Machakos. Dicky Evans and Richard Fox facilitated my visit to Homegrown in Kenya, and John Simeoni and Rod Evans took me round.

In Australia, Tom Burke and Rick Humphries of Rio Tinto gave me the run of Gladstone. And, during the same visit down under, Kelly Chapman and Dan Hickey took me out to the cotton farms during a break from the Brisbane River*symposium*, scene of 'dump, burn and offset'. Thanks also to Allan Williams.

At M&S, Graham Burden did his best to help me understand the cotton business, and Mike Barry was candid on corporate strategy for sustainable development. At Agrocel in India, Hasmukh Patel and Dilip Chhatrola were invaluable. And later, at Maral and Arvind, Amit Baid and Yash Baheti respectively could not have been more helpful. I visited Uzbekistan with a grant from the International Water Management Institute, whose Tashkent officer Iskandar Abdulaev accompanied me to Karakalpakstan.

The UN Population Fund and Don Hinrichsen took me to the Philippines to meet Nellie. Logitech's Ben Starkie fixed me up with Sammy Cheng and his friends in Suzhou. Xiufang Sun talked me through the Chinese timber trade, along with Greenpeace and Scott Poynton of the Tropical Forest Trust and his colleagues.

Michael Renner of the Worldwatch Institute helped with war and the 'resources curse', as did Arjen Hoekstra on the virtual water trade and Tricia Feeney on the coltan scandal. Thanks to Sten Nillson at the International Institute for Applied Systems Analysis in Austria, along with Siberian partners, for taking me to Noyabr'sk. But no thanks to Gazprom and its agents for curtailing my visit to Novy Urengoi.

Midwinter Productions fixed my journey on the Thames waste barge. Ray Georgeson and Doreen Fedrigo guided me through the recycling maze. Paul Llewellyn introduced me to the virtues of sewage on beaches. Lynne Wright introduced me to the Milonge brothers in Dar es Salaam. Thanks also to the people of Cookshop and the estimable Paul Joynson-Hicks for finding a new owner for Joe's phone in that same city.

I visited Chinese recyclers thanks to Robert Gibson and colleagues at Swire in Hong Kong and Xiamen. Priti Mahesh and Ravi Agarwal showed me the horrors of Mandoli, and Tony Roberts of Computer Aid International introduced me to Nairobi computer refurbishers. Mathis Wackernagel welcomed me to the Ecological Footprints conference in Siena.

The late Paul van Vlissingen, laird of Africa, berated me for an earlier article, before inviting me to his home near Utrecht to explain all. Peter Hall and Jesse Ausubel told me much about urban planning, green and otherwise. Thanks, as always, to the two Jims, Lovelock and Hansen, for their erudition on climate change and the science of our planet. Jack Caldwell was, similarly, a guru on demographics.

Parts of this journey, and much of my background knowledge, would not have been possible without the support of Jeremy Webb and the commissioning editors of *New Scientist* over many years. Some readers of that magazine will recognize snatches of material recycled here, particularly from my continuing blog, Fred's Footprint, to be found on its website at www.newscientist.com.

My editor Susanna Wadeson, and agent Jessica Woollard, latched on to my idea for this book with enthusiasm, and saw it through, latterly with help from Rochelle Venables, who weeded out many non-sequiturs and over-elaborations, and copy editor Brenda Updegraff.

And thanks finally to my family – the sometimes mysterious 'we' in the text – who sustained the household on which this narrative is based and cajoled me in a 'green' direction that I have often resisted, through laziness or a desire not to pollute this 'warts and all' investigation. Now, of course, I have no excuse.

Index

abortions, Manila 154
Abramovitch, Roman 222
Acer 160, 163, 165
Africa
  Darfur droughts 335
  desertification 108, 334–8
  fertility rates 366
  Homo sapiens evolution 328–9
  land management 334
  tourism 320–1
Agarwal, Ravi 291
Agnes 71–2
Agrocel 129, 131
AIDS
  clinics 73–4
  demographic effects 72–3, 366
  elderly carers 71–2, 73–4
  societal effects 72–3
air freighting
  organic food 102
  plant food imports 101, 111–12
air travel
  Buncefield fuel depot explosion 236
  CO2 emissions 233, 236–7
  Kyoto Protocol 236–7
  reducing 357
  short-haul flights 233
  total emissions 306–7
  UK airports 236–7
Akter, Nazma 143
Alaska
  caribou migration routes 217–20
  climate changes 218–19
  oil 214–20
  Prudhoe Bay 214–20
  racial issues 216–17

Albania, sage 57–8
Alexander, Christopher 347
allotments 342
aluminium
  environmental footprint 195–6
  properties 191–2
  recycling 199–200, 256, 285–6
  Rio Tinto Aluminium 192–4
  smelting 192, 194–7, 226
Ambrose, Stanley 327, 329–30
AMG Resources, steel recycling 256
Amnesty International 276
Anglo American, metal mining 203
antimony, China 205
apples, Kazakhstan 90–1
Aquaculture Certification Council 69
Aral Sea
  climate change 150
  drying up 146–7
  pollution 150
Archer Daniels Midland (ADM)
  cocoa 96
  palm oil 78
Asda 142
Associated British Foods 80
Association for Responsible Mining 246–7
Asustek 161–4
auctions
  coffee 31–2
  fish 49
Australia
  aluminium 192–8
  Brisbane 303–4
  coal 230

Australia (cont.)
  cotton 119–22
  droughts 120
  eco-projects 345
  Gladstone 192–7
  Kyoto Protocol 198
  Melbourne 345
  tea tree oil 59–60
Ausubel, Jesse 347–8
Awaj Foundation 141–2

Badger brewery see Hall and Woodhouse
bananas 84, 86–9
Banc d'Arguin marine national park 50–2
  fishing permits 51–2
  WWF 51, 54
Bangladesh
  Awaj Foundation 141–2
  banking system 68
  child labour 143
  corruption in 65
  deltas 62–3, 66, 70
  Dhaka 138–45, 345
  family sizes 364
  female emancipation 144–5
  garment workshops 138–44
  Khulna 63–4, 67–8
  King prawns 62–70
  land grabbing 64–5
  wages 142–3
Bangladesh Frozen Food Exporters
  Association 67
barley malts, beer 38–9
Barry Callebaut 96
Bazalgette, Joseph 254
beaches, over-cleansing 263
Beckton sewage treatment works 254
beer
  barley malts 38–9
  brewery closures 37
  Hall and Woodhouse 37–9
  herb 39
  ingredients 38–9
  local brews 36–7
  summer ales 39
  water for 38
  yeasts 39
Bertrand, Nick 350
BHP Billiton 203
Bihar 289
bio-capacities 317–18
biodiesel, European Union laws 77
Biodiversity (formerly International
  Plant Genetic Resources Institute) 84

biodiversity loss, and sugar 83
biofuels 82, 355
  burying CO2 with 357
  and palm oil 77
  threat of 341
bismuth 207
black tiger prawns see king prawns
books
  carbon footprint 312–13
  research for 313
Borneo, rainforest clearances 169, 172
Box, John 350
BP, targetneutral scheme 305
Brasilia 347
bread
  Lighthouse 42
  processes 42
  stoneground wholemeal flour 42–4
  yeasts 42
breweries, closures 37
Brisbane 303–4
British Airways, carbon offsets 304–5
British Trust for Ornithology 262
Broadacre City, Lloyd Wright 346–7
Brown, Gordon, eco-cities 350
brownfield sites
  development of 351
  wildlife 350–1
'built environment' emissions
  CO2 emissions 242
  domestic greenhouse gases 242–4
Buncefield fuel depot explosion 236
Bunting, Madeleine 365–6
Burden, Graham 122, 128

cabbages 89
Cafédirect
  coffee 27–30
  and fairtrade philosophy 35
  prices paid 31–2
CAI (Computer Aid International) 299–300
Caldwell, Jack 365
Cameron, David 45, 103, 359
Cameron, Ray 219–20
Cameroon
  cocoa 94–7
  cotton 136
  slash-and-burn agriculture 95
carbon footprint
  books 312–13
  calculating 371
  publishing 313

carbon offsets
    see also CO₂ emissions
    aircraft emissions 303–4, 306–8
    availability 304–5
    British Airways 304–5
    Climate Care 308, 310, 312
    costs 308
    definitions 305
    forest maintenance 308–9
    Kyoto Protocol 304, 311
    Orbost estate 305–6
    programme range 304–5
    Sky 305
Carbon Trust 241–2
CarbonNeutral Company 305–6,
    311
cardamom 58
Cargill
    cocoa 96
    cotton 123
    palm oil 78
    Sun Valley chickens 78–9
caribou, migration routes 217–20
cement 240
cereals, for meat production 340
CETC (China Electronics Technology
    Group Corporation) 272
Chang, Mage 165
charities, textile recycling 266–9
cheese 40–1
Chen, David 162, 163–4
Cheng, Sammy 159, 163–4, 165, 371
Cheng, Shengchan 280–2
Cheung, Yan 284–5, 371
chickens
    free-range organic 39–40, 41
    soya fed 79
child labour
    Bangladesh 143
    computer recycling 288–90
    cotton industry 124
    India 124, 288–91
    Ivory Coast 97
    Pakistan 124
China
    see also Shenzhen; Suzhou
    aluminium recycling 285–6
    antimony 205
    computer industry 160–1, 165, 167
    deforestation 171–2
    ginger 58
    mobile phones 271–2
    one-child policy 364
    paper recycling 280–2, 284–5

plastic bottle recycling 256–7,
    282–3
power stations 358
Qiaotou 179
recycling ethos 282–4
small commodities markets 177–80
tin 205
traditional medicines 181–3
Yiwu 177–80
Zhangjiagang 169, 171
zinc 205
China Electronics Technology Group
    Corporation (CETC) 272
Chinatext, cotton 123
Chococo 99
chocolate
    see also cocoa
    fairtrade 98
    gourmet 99
    UK introduction 93–4
    world-wide consumption 94
Christmas decorations 178
chromium, Kazakhstan 205
cinnamon 58
cities see London; mega-cities; urban
    farming
city metabolism 239–40
civil wars 208–10
Clean Air – Cool Planet 305
Climate Care 308, 310, 312
climate changes
    Alaska 218–19
    economic implications 358
    Mount Toba eruption 326–7
cloves 58
CO₂ emissions
    see also carbon offsets
    accumulation 316
    air travel 233, 236–7
    built environment' 242–4
    burying with biofuels 357
    cement 240
    coaches and buses 235
    coal-fired power stations 228–9, 356
    global reductions 370–1
    global warming 354–5
    Heathrow airport 235–6
    targets 357
    train travel 232–3
coaches and buses 235
coal-fired power stations 228, 356
    CO₂ emissions 228–9, 356
    Drax 228–30
    imports for 229–31

Coastal Development Partnership,
Kulna 63
Cockerill, Ian 19
cocoa
Archer Daniels Midland 96
Barry Callebaut 96
Cameroon 94–7
Cargill 96
fairtrade 98
history 93–4
Ivory Coast 97
middlemen 96–7
Nestlé 96
price crashes 96
processing 98
smallholdings 94–6
western discovery of 93
coffee
auctions 31–2
Cafédirect 27–30
cooperatives 28–30
fairtrade 32–4
global trading 31
Kilimanjaro 27–9
organic farming 30
prices 28–9, 31–3
roasting 33–4
shipments to London 33
Starbucks 30
coltan see tantalum
community projects
fairtrade coffee 32
fairtrade cotton 131, 133–4
Compal 165–6
Computer Aid International (CAI)
299–300
computer components 160–4, 161–4
metals for 205, 207–8
computer recycling 288–91
child labour 288–90
copper recovery process 288–90
illegal imports 291–2
computers, reuse 297–300
Computers for Schools Kenya
297–300
conferences, ecological footprints 318
congestion charge, London 345
Congo 276–7
conservation, herbs 56
consumption, globalized 7–10
contraception
Philippines 153–5
religious attitudes to 153–4, 364–5
cooking, energy expenditure 103

copper
production 203, 204
recovery 288–90
Cory, household waste management
251–3, 261
cotton
Australia 119–22, 124
Cameroon 136
Chinatext 123
Cragill 123
Dreyfus 123
Dunavant 123
fairtrade 128–30, 134
genetic modification 125, 132–3
India 124–5, 128–31, 133
Maral Overseas 133–4, 135–7
Marks & Spencer 122, 132
Pakistan 124
Plexus 123
Reinhart 123
social costs 126–7
spinning and knitting 136–7
USA 124–6
Uzbekistan 124, 147–8, 151
world production 123–4
Cotton Australia 120
Crossness sewage treatment works 254–5
Culham nuclear-fusion research
reactor 226
Cure, Lynne 251

Dairy Crest 40
dairy industry, depression of 40
Dar es Salaam
innovative enterprises 278–9
Milonge brothers 264–7
mitumba 264–7
Phones for Africa 278
textiles recycling 266–9
wildlife sculptures 278–9
debt slavery, Mauritania 186
deforestation consequences, China
171–2
Delhi
computer recycling 292
LNG transport 345
Mandoli 287–92
Dell computers 160, 163, 165, 166
demography
see also population growth
AIDS 72–3
and migration 367–8
desertification 334–5
reversals 108, 335–8

Dhaka
  garment workshops 138–45
  LNG transport 345
Dickens, Charles, *Our Mutual Friend*
  253–4
domestic environment
  greenhouse gases 242–4
  zero-carbon homes 244
domestic recycling 251
Drax coal-fired power station 228–30
Dreyfus, cotton 123
Driefontein goldmine 15–18
droughts
  Australia 120
  Darfur 335
Dubai
  electronic waste trading 291
  gold smuggling 21
  mitumba trading 266
dump, burn and offset 303–4
Dunavant, cotton 123
Duncan, Anne 194
Dyson, Tim 365

e–waste brokers, Environment Agency
  296
Earth, ecological statistics 315
eco-efficiency 316
  town planning 349
eco-projects
  mega-cities 345
  urban transport 345
ecological footprints
  see also CO₂ emissions
  conferences 318
  European 317
  global 317–18
  Homo sapiens 333
  urban 314–15
Edwards, Rob 305
elderly carers, South Africa 71–2,
  73–4
electricity
  see also power stations
  aluminium smelting 192, 196–7,
    199, 226
  cooking 103
  domestic use 242
  from incinerators 261
  'green tariffs' 311
  imported 227
  National Grid 226–7
  renewable sources 227–8
  world–wide consumption 315–16

electronic waste
  European Union directive 277,
    293–4, 296
  landfill 287
  metals recovery 288–92
  UK recycling 293–6
Ely 184–7
EMR (European Metal Recycling) 295
endangered species, traditional
  medicines 181–3
energy intensive production,
  agribusiness 102–3
Environment Agency, e-waste brokers
  296
Environment and Development,
  International Institute for 103, 339
environmental footprint
  mega-cities 344–5
  personal contributions 242–4
  public services 241–2
environmental impact
  aluminium smelting 195–6
  metal mining 203–4
  oil extraction 220–2
environmental protectionism 359
Essissima, Joseph 94–5
ethical trading, supermarkets 70
Europe
  fertility rates 366–7
  global footprint 317
European Metal Recycling (EMR) 295
European Union
  beaches directive 263
  biofuel additives 77
  electronic waste directive 277,
    293–4, 296
  fishing rights 53
  sugar beet 81–2
  waste export ban 258–9
Eurostar 232–3
Evans, Dicky 104
evolution, *Homo sapiens* 328–31
Excel Crop Care, G. C. Shroff 131–2
extremism, humanity 5

fairtrade 371
  brands 32
  chocolate 98
  coffee 34
  community projects 32
  cotton 128–30, 134–5
  jewellery 245–7
Fairtrade Foundation 32, 103–4
famines, inefficient dealing with 340

farming
  see also urban farming
  energy intensive production 102–3
  livestock 211
  Nigeria 335–6
  water usage 341
favelas
  Brasilia 347
  Rio 114–16, 349
  women's power in 114–16
female emancipation
  Bangladesh 144–5
  population growth 369–70
fertility rates
  Africa 366
  Bangladesh 364
  China 364
  Europe 366–7
  global decline 369
  Iran 364
  Muslim states 366
fertilizer, from sewage 255
fishing
  depletion of natural stocks 49, 50,
    51, 53
  fresh-fish auctions 49
  Mauritania 50–2, 53–4
  poaching 51–2
  preference for line 54
  Senegal 52–3, 54
  'sustainable' 53
  trawlers vs *pirogues* 52
  world-wide 49–50
flour
  stoneground wholemeal 42–4
  wheat for 43–4
Fonebak 277
food
  see also plant foods
  cooking 103
  imports 100–2
'food patriotism', David Cameron 45,
  103, 359
food production, and population
  growth 340
Forest Stewardship Council
  approved paper 312
  tropical hardwoods 175
Forest Trends 170, 175
forests
  as carbon offsets 309
  maintenance 308–9
Foundation for Adolescent
  Development 154

Fox, Richard, Homegrown 111
Foxconn, mobile phones 271–2
Friends of the Earth 101, 350
Frison, Emile 84
fruit pickers, immigrant 46–7
fuels, greenest 355–7

Gala, coffee roasting 33–4
Gandhi, Mahatma 360
Gap 141, 142
garlic 89
garment workshops
  Dhaka 138–44
  H&M 140
gas
  domestic use 242
  power stations 227
  Siberia 223–5
  storage projects 227
gas power, public transport 345
Gazprom 222–4
  UK takeovers by 224
gemstones, finance for corrupt regimes
  208–9
genetic modification
  bananas 88–9
  cotton 125, 132–3
genetic resources, plant foods 89–92
ginger, China 58
Girardet, Herbert 239–40
Gladstone
  aluminium smelting 193–7
  ecology 192–3
  power station 193, 196–7
glass, recycling 255–6
global footprints
  comparative 317–18
  world-wide 317
global warming
  CO_2 emissions 354–5
  threat of 354–5
globalization
  coffee trading 31
  consumption 7–10
gold
  certificates of origin 247
  ethically sourced 245–7
  extraction process 18
  in history 20–1
  hoarding 21–2, 134
  origins 15
  power of 21–2
  prices 19, 21
  smuggling 21

South Africa 14–22, 205
gold mining
  access shafts 14–15
  Fanakalo language 17
  quartz containing 22
  recruitment for 17–18
  safety 16–17
  smuggling 17
Gold Standard 21
Goodall, Chris, *How to Live a Low-Carbon Life* 244
Gottmann, Jean 351
gourmet chocolate 99
grain growing, water for 211
green beans
  food miles issue 111–12
  Homegrown 104–6, 108–11
  hygiene 107
  Machakos 104–13
  Marks & Spencer 105, 107, 109
  smallholdings 104–6, 109
  traceability 107, 112–13
Green Gold 246
greenhouse gases *see* CO_2 emissions; nitrogen oxides
Grimsby, fresh-fish auctions 49
Grosvenor, paper reprocessing 257–60
Gujarat
  Agrocel 129–31
  organic cotton 129–32
  water supplies 130–1

H&M 140, 142
hafnium 208
Hall, Peter 347, 349
Hall and Woodhouse brewery 37–9
Hammond, Geoff 317
Hanson, Jim 355
Harris, Frances 336
Haupt, Melville 19
heat-island effect 348
Heathrow airport
  CO_2 emissions 235–7
  fuel supplies 236
  land use efficiency 237–8
  noise issues 238
HelpAge International 72
herbs
  in beers 39
  conservation 56
  oregano 55–6
  sage 57–8
  thyme 56
Hewitt, Geoff 119–21

Hewlett-Packard 160, 163, 165
Hickey, Dan 120
Hindu philanthropy 133–4
'hobbits' (*Homo floresiensis*) 325, 328, 331
  extinction 332
Homegrown, green beans 104–6, 108–11
hominids *see Homo erectus*; *Homo floresiensis*; *Homo sapiens*; Neanderthals
Homo erectus 325, 327, 331
  extinction 332
Homo floresiensis ('hobbits') 325, 328, 331
  extinction 332
Homo sapiens
  African evolution 328–9
  artistic evolution 330–1
  common characteristics 5–6
  conspicuous consumption 333
  cultural evolution 329–30
  ecological footprint 333
  future of 372
  geographical spread 331–2
  ice age survival 332–3
  social evolution 330
  survival skills 332
  urbanization 344
  virtual extinction 325, 328–9
  volcanic winters 325, 328–30, 331
household waste
  see also sewage
  collections 251
  food growing on 341
  landfill sites 261
  Thames barge transport 252–3
  transfer stations 251–2
How to Live a Low-Carbon Life, Chris Goodall 244
human rights
  see also child labour
  Mauritania 184–5
  Uzbekistan 147, 151–2
humanity, extremism 5
Humphries, Rick 193–4, 197–8
Hurn airport 237–8
hydroponics 342

IBM 163, 165
ice ages, *Homo sapiens*' survival 332–3
immigrant fruit pickers
  conditions 46–7
  pay 47

imports
  air miles 101
  carbon footprints 101–2
  plant foods 100–2
incinerators
  electricity generation from 261
  pollution from 260–1
India
  Bihar 289
  cardamom 58
  child labour 124
  computer recycling 288–92
  cotton 124–5, 129–31, 133–5
  Delhi 287–92
  gold hoarding 134
  Hindu philanthropy 133–4
  Maral Overseas 133–4, 133–5,
    135–7
  Toxics Link 290–1
  water shortages 130–1, 133
indium, uses 207
Indonesia
  palm oil 76–7
  rainforest clearances 172–3
innovative enterprises, Tanzania 278–9
Intergovernmental Panel on Climate
  Change (IPCC) 354–5
International Crisis Group 151
International Institute for
  Environment and Development 103,
  339
International Institute for Tropical
  Agriculture 95, 335
Iqbal Ahmed
  see also king prawns
  business empire 61–2, 68–70
Iran, family sizes 364
iron
  see also steel
  extraction 205
Italy, rocket 56, 90
Ivory Coast, cocoa 97

JCPenney 141
jewellery, fairtrade 245–7
Joynson-Hicks, Paul, Phones for
  Africa 277–8
just-in-time
  assembly 166
  retailing 106

Kazakhstan
  apples 90–1
  chromium 205

Keen, David 209–10
Kenya
  coffee 27–34
  Computers for Schools 297–300
  desertification reversals 108, 338–9
  farm outputs 338–9
  German presence in 34–5
  green beans 104–13
Khosa, Veronica, AIDS clinics 73–4
Khulna, king prawn industry 63–4,
  67–8
Kilimanjaro coffee 27–30
Kilimanjaro Native Cooperative
  Union (KNCU) 30–3
king prawns
  certification scheme needed 69
  fry hatcheries 65–6
  introduction to UK 62
  landowner threats 64–5
  middlemen 66–8
  organic farming 64
  processing plants 67
  Seamark 62, 68
  sustainability 69–70
Kinyua, Patrick 106–7
Kirkham, Ruth 40
Klor, Babubhai 131
KNCU (Kilimanjaro Native
  Cooperative Union) 30–3
Kombe, Jackson 29–30
Kyoto Protocol
  air travel 236–7
  Australia 198
  carbon offsets 304, 311
  Ministry of Defence 242

Lagavulin, Islay single malt Scotch
  44–5
Lamb, Harriet 103–4
land, multiple functions for 316
landfill sites
  heavy metals 287
  household waste 261
Lea Valley 349
Leach, Matthew 260
Letterewe, Scotland 321–2
Lighthouse bakery 42
line-fishing 54
Lister, John 43–4
livestock farming 211
Lloyd Wright, Frank, Broadacre City
  346–7
local food 36–7, 45
Logitech 160–1

London
  congestion charge 345
  greenhouse gases 242
  household waste 251–3, 261
  Lea Valley 349
  materials recycling 255–6
  MI6 headquarters 241
  public services 241–2
  sewage 23–4, 254, 261–3
  Wandsworth Prison 241
  water ring-main 241
London Wildlife Trust 350

Ma, Cheng Liang 352–3
McDonald's 79, 102–3
Machakos
  desertification reversals 338–9
  green beans from 104–13
Macharia, John 108–9
Madagascar, vanilla 58–9
Mahesh, Priti 290–1
Makinga, Norman 297–9
Malaysia, palm oil 76–7
malnutrition 340
Mandela, Nelson 320
Mandoli, computer recycling 288–91
Manila
  abortions 154
  contraception 153–5
  Foundation for Adolescent
    Development 154
  prostitution 153, 155
manures, changes to natural 335–6
Marakele wildlife park 320
Maral Overseas, cotton 133–4, 135–7
margarine
  from palm oil 76
  from whale oil 75
marine national parks, Banc d'Arguin
  50–2
Marks & Spencer
  Blue Horizon jeans 145
  cotton 122, 132, 142, 145
  fairtrade coffee 32
  fairtrade cotton 128, 134–5
  green bean imports 105, 107, 109
  materials 'rucksacks' 204–5
Mauritania
  debt slavery 186
  fishing 50–4
  racial structure 185–6
  slavery 184–5
meat production 340
mega-cities 344

absorption of urban centres 351–3
eco-projects 345
environmental footprint 344–5
recycling mantra, necessity for
  346
wildlife in 349–50
Melbourne, eco-projects 345
Melgar, Junice 154–5
metals
  see also aluminium; gold
  antimony 205
  bismuth 207
  chromium 205
  copper 203, 204
  global corporations 203
  hafnium 208
  indium 207
  iron/steel 205
  materials 'rucksacks' 204–5
  mining footprint 203–4
  mobile phones 273–5
  palladium 207
  platinum 205, 207
  recycling 210, 256, 288, 290–1, 295
  rising demands 206
  ruthenium 207–8
  tantalum 273–6
  terbium 208
  tin 205, 276–7
  waste ores 204–5
  world demand for 202–3
  zinc 205
Mgase, Jacob Rumisha 28–9
middlemen traders
  cocoa 96–7
  king prawns 66–8
Milonge, Boniface 264
Milonge, Geoffrey
  market sales 266–7
  mitumba imports 264–5
  Urafiki market 267–8
Milton Keynes 347
Ministry of Defence, Kyoto Protocol 242
mitumba
  Dar es Salaam 264–7
  Dubai 266
mobile phones
  assembly 271–2
  Foxconn 271–2
  Nokia 271, 272
  Phones for Africa 277–8
  reuse 277–8
  toxic chemicals in 272–5
  world-wide usage 270–1

money laundering, International Crisis
  Group 151
Morocco, phosphates 206
Morris, Tim 37–9
Mortimore, Michael 338
Moshi
  coffee auctions 31–2
  curing plant 33
motherboards 161–4
motor cars
  catalytic converters 207
  and urban design 346–7
Motorola 276
Murray, Craig 147–8
Musili, Tom, Computers for Schools
  Kenya 297–300
Muslim states, fertility rates 366
Musyoki, Jacob 104–6, 113

National Grid 226–7
natural resources, consumption rates
  314–15
Neanderthals 325, 328
  extinction 332
  and Homo sapiens 329
Nellie, Flower-stall Girl 153, 155,
  371
Nestlé
  cocoa 96
  fairtrade coffee 32
New Guinea, tropical hardwoods 170,
  171
Nicholson-Lord, David 348
Niemeijer, David 337, 339
Niger, reversing desertification 337
Nigeria, crop/livestock integration
  335–6
Nine Dragons, paper recycling 284–5
nitrogen oxides, ozone production
  307
NKD 143
Nokia, mobile phones 271, 272, 276
Novelis, aluminium recycling
  199–200
Noyabr'sk, oilfields 221–2
nuclear power stations 227, 355–6
  waste from 356
nuclear-fusion research reactors,
  Culham 226

offices, ecological footprints 315
oil
  Alaska 215–20
  Siberia 220–2

Orbost, carbon offsets 305–6
oregano 55–6
organic farming
  bananas 87
  coffee 30
  crop/livestock integration 336
  king prawns 64
  Nigeria 335–6
organic food, air freighted 102
overconsumption 360

Padulosi, Stefano 56, 90–2
Pakistan, cotton 124
palladium, source 207
palm oil 75–8
  and biofuels 77
  rainforest clearances for 76–7
paper
  burning 260
  Chinese recycling 280–2, 284–5
  Forest Stewardship Council
    approved 312
  manufacture 260
  recycling 257–60
  sustainable sources 312
Papua New Guinea, rainforest
  clearances 169, 173–5
pathogen risks, urban farming
  343
Paul Reinhart 123
peanuts 89–90
Pendolinos 233
people smuggling, to Canary Islands
  55
personal footprints 4–5, 242–4,
  318
  city metabolism 240
pesticides
  banana diseases 87
  cotton 124–5, 130
  natural 87, 130
Pethick, John 262
Philippines see Manila
Phones for Africa, Tanzania 278
phosphates
  fertilizers 205–6
  Morocco 206
phthalates, mobile phones 273
pineapples 89
pistachios 91
plankton, carbon offsets 310
plant foods
  see also foods by name
  air-miles issues 111–12

ancient varieties 89–90
benefits of local 45
carbon footprint 101–2
energy intensive production 102–3
extinctions 84
genetic resources 89–92
mutations 85–6
seasonality 100, 105
UK imports 100–2, 111–12
wild 55–60, 89–90
plastic bottles (PET), recycling 256–7,
282–3
platinum
South Africa 205
uses for 207
Plexus, cotton 123
plywood
Chinese originated 175–6
from illegal logging 169, 174–5
poaching, fisheries 51–2
pollution
imprint of 333
incinerators 260–1
Siberia 221–2
pomegranates, Turkmenistan 91–2
population growth
average family size 361, 362
family-planning policies 364–5
female attitudes 365–6
female emancipation 369–70
fertility rates 366–7
and food production 340
limiting 360–1
longevity 362–3
mortality rates 366, 367
potential diminution 363–4
stabilization 368–9
twentieth century 361–2
power stations
China 358
coal-fired 228–31, 356
natural gas 227
nuclear 227, 355–6
tidal 355
wave 355
wind 355
Poynton, Scott 175, 176
prawns see king prawns
prostitution, Manila 153, 155
Prudhoe Bay 214–20
public services, environmental
footprint 241–2
public transport, gas powered 345
publishing, carbon footprint 313

Qiaotou 179

rainforest clearances
Borneo 172
consequences 77–8
illegal logging 170–1
Indonesia 172–3
logging concessions 173–4
for palm oil 76–7
Papua New Guinea 170, 173–5
slash-and-burn agriculture 95
for soya beans 78
'sustainability' audits 174
tropical hardwoods 169–70, 175
recycling 10
see also reuse
aluminium 199–201, 256, 285–6
centres 255
computers 288–91
domestic 251
economics 210
electronic waste 294–5
ethos 282–4
glass 255–6
metals 210, 256, 288, 290–1, 295
paper 257–60
plastic bottles 256–7
steel 210, 256
textiles 264–9
Rees, William 315
Register, Roger 347
Rehfish, Mark 262
Renner, Michael 209
retailing
just-in-time 106
traceability 107
reuse
computers 297–300
mobile phones 277–8
Rhine, damaged ecology 321
Rimbunan Hijau, logging concessions
173–4
Rio de Janiero
favelas 114–16, 349
Rosinha 114
Rio Tinto, metal mining 203
Rio Tinto Aluminium
environmental claims 198
Gladstone 192–4
Tasmania 197
rivers, wildlife in clean 262–3
Rivoli, Pietra 269
Roberts, Tony 299–300
rocket, Italian 56, 90

Rosinha, Women's Association of
    114–16
Roszak, Theodore 368
Royal Swaziland Sugar Corporation
    80–1
rubbish *see* household waste
Russia
    coal exports 229–30
    gas 224–5
    oil 220–2
    Siberia 220–1
ruthenium 207–8

S & A Produce, strawberry pickers
    46–8
sage, Albanian 57–8
Sahara, efforts to reverse spread 334
Sainsbury's 47
Salam, M. M. A., prawn processor 67
salep, Turkey 57
Scope, textile recycling 264–6
Scotch, Islay single malt 44–5
Scotland
    Letterewe 321–2
    Orbost carbon offsets 305–6
    wildlife reintroductions 321–2
Seamark, king prawns 62, 68
Sears 142
seasonality, plant foods 100, 105
Secret Intelligence Service,
    headquarters 241
Senegal, fishing 52–3, 54
servants, technological replacement of 3
Severina Euega, *favelas* 114–16
sewage
    Beckton treatment works 254
    Crossness treatment works 254–5
    Embankment sewers 254
    as fertilizer 255
    historical 23–4
    outfalls 262–3
Shenzhen
    Foxconn 271–2
    growth 271–2
    mobile phone assembly 271–2
Shipton Mill 42–4
Shirley, Peter 351
Siberia 220
    eviction from 224–5
    gas 223–5
    oil 220–2
    pollution 221–2
Silayan-Go, Aurora 154
Silver Spoon 80

Simeoni, John 107, 109
Singh, B. B. 335, 336, 343
Sites of Special Scientific Interest
    350–1
Sky 305
slavery
    Mauritania 184–5
    debt 186
Sloan, Sir Hans 93–4
small commodities markets
    specialist producers 179–80
    Yiwu 177–9
smuggling, gold 17, 21
social costs, cotton goods 126–7
Sociopolis, Valencia 345
Soil Association 102
soil contamination, metals recycling
    288, 290–1
South Africa
    AIDS 19, 71–4
    coal 230
    gold 14–22, 205
    platinum 205, 207
soya beans, rainforest clearances for
    76–7
Spain
    Sociopolis 345
    thyme 56
spices
    cardamom 58
    cinnamon 58
    cloves 58
    ginger 58
Sri Lanka, cinnamon 58
Starbucks coffee 30
steel, recycling 210, 256
Stern Report (2006) 358
strawberry pickers, S & A Produce
    46–8
sugar
    beet 80–2
    as biofuel 82
    cane 211–12
    and loss of biodiversity 83
    Swaziland 80–1
    Tate & Lyle 79–81
Sun Valley Foods 79
supermarkets, ethical trading 70
Sustain, food imports 101–2
'sustainability' audits, rainforest
    clearances 174
'sustainable' fishing 53
Suzhou City 159–60
    Asustek 161–4

Compal 165–6
  expansion 161, 164–5, 168, 352–3
  Logitech 160–1
Swaziland
  king's economic control of 81
  sugar 80–1
sweatshops *see* garment workshops
Sweden, family units 366
sweet potatoes 89

Tagarook, George 215–16, 371
Taiwan
  computer industry 160–1, 165
  mobile phone industry 271–2
tantalum
  mobile phones 273–5
  sources 274–6
  uses 274–5
Tanzania
  see also Dar es Salaam
  early *Homo sapiens* 329
Tasmania, Rio Tinto Aluminium
  197
Tate & Lyle 79–81
tea tree oil 59–60
terbium 208
Tesco 105
textile recycling 264–9
  Tanzania 266–9
  UK trade 265–6
textiles *see* cotton
Thames
  lightermen 253
  sewage in 254
thyme, Spain 56
tidal power stations 355
tin
  China 205
  Congo 276–7
Toba, Lake 326
Toba, Mount
  ash fallout 326–7
  climatic changes due to 327
  eruption 326–7
Tokyo 344
tomatoes 89
Toulmin, Camilla 339
tourism, Africa 320–1
town planning
  eco-cities 347–8
  eco-efficiency 349
  'heat island effects' 348
  and the motor car 346–7
toxic chemicals, mobile phones 272–5

Toxics Link, India 290–1
toys 178
traceability, green beans 107, 112–13
'trade not aid' 269
traditional medicines
  China 181–3
  endangered species 181–3
  Western attitudes to 182–3
train travel
  CO_2 emissions 232–3
  occupancy levels 233–4
  Pendolinos 233
  regenerative braking 234
  sleepers 234
Transparency International,
  Bangladesh 65
Trexler, Mark 305
Tropical Agriculture, International
  Institute for 95, 335
Tropical Forest Trust 170, 175
tropical hardwoods 169–70
  see also rainforest clearances
  certificates of origin 176
  Forest Stewardship Council 175
  UK embargo 175
Turkey
  oregano 55–6
  salep 57
Turkmenistan, pomegranates 91–2

UN Desertification Convention (1996)
  334
UN Environmental Programme
  (UNEP) 334
UN Food and Agriculture
  Organization 334
UN Man and Biosphere Programme
  350
Unilever 49, 75–6, 78
Urban Agriculture Network 343
urban design, and motor cars 346–7
urban farming
  allotments 342
  efficiency of 343
  history of 349
  hydroponics 342
  necessity for 342
  pathogen risks 343
  world-wide 341–2
urban transport, eco-projects 345
urbanization, *Homo sapiens* 344
USA
  see also Alaska
  cotton 124, 125–6

Uzbekistan
  see also Aral Sea
  cotton 124, 147–8, 151–2
  human rights 147, 151–2
  life expectancy 149–50
  population needs 150
  soil salinity 148–50

Valencia, Sociopolis 345
Valerio, Greg 245–7
vanilla
  cultivation 59
  Madagascar 58–9
  markets for 59
Virgin Trains 232–3
'virtual water' 212–13
Vlissingen, Paul van
  African tourism 320–1
  biography 319–22, 371
  Scottish wildlife reintroductions 321–2
  wildlife protection 321
volcanic winters
  hominids 327–9
  Homo sapiens' survival 325,
    328–30, 331
  Mount Toba eruption 326–7

Wackernagel, Mathis 315, 317
wages, Bangladesh 142
Wal-Mart 141, 142, 145, 165
Wandsworth Prison 241
washing temperatures 126–7
waste, EU export ban 258–9
Waste and Resources Action
  Programme (WRAP) 256
Wastesavers, textile recycling 265–6
water
  for agriculture 212–13, 341
  droughts 120, 335
  grain growing 211
  London ring-main 241
  personal usage 211, 213
  sugar cane 211–12
  'virtual' 212–13
watermelons 89, 91
wave power stations 355
Weaver, John 27–9
WEEE (EU Electronic Waste Directive)
  277, 293–4, 296
whaling

Alaskan traditional 215–16
ban on 75
wheat
  for breadflour 43–4
  water needed for 211
Wilcox, J. M. P. 265
wildlife
  African parks 321
  at sewage outfalls 262–3
  brownfield sites 350–1
  in mega-cities 349–50
  reintroductions 321–2
  river cleaning 262–3
wildlife sculptures, Tanzania 278–9
Williams, Allan 122–3
wind power 355
Wistron 165
women
  see also female emancipation
  cocoa smallholdings 95–6
  contraception 153–5
  green beans 109–10
Women's Association of Rosinha
  114–16
Wonder Welders 279, 371
Woodhouse, David, Hall and
  Woodhouse 38–9
working conditions, garment
  workshops 139–43
WWF (formerly World Wildlife Fund)
  51, 54, 182, 242
Worldwatch Institute 209
WRAP (Waste and Resources Action
  Programme) 256
Wright, Lynne 265–6

Xiamen, recycled paper 280–2

Yamba, Boubacar 337
yeasts
  baking 42
  beer 39
Yiwu, small commodities markets
  177–80

Zanzibar, cloves 58
zero-carbon homes 244
Zhangjiagang, tropical hardwood
  imports 169, 171
zinc, China 205